THE REAL LIFE UFO TRANSFORMATION OF DIANE TESSMAN

A Continuous Close Encounter with Future Man – Space Man

INNER LIGHT/GLOBAL COMMUNICATIONS

P.O. Box 753
New Brunswick, NJ 08903

Email: mrufo8@hotmail.com

Diane enjoys friendship at Denver UFO conference.

The Real Life UFO Transformation of Diane Tessman
A Continuous Close Encounter with Future Man – Space Man

By Diane Tessman

Copyright © 2020 by Diane Tessman

Published By Inner Light/Global Communications

All rights reserved.

No part of these manuscripts may be copied or reproduced by any mechanical or digital methods and no excerpts or quotes may be used in any other book or manuscript without permission in writing by the Publisher, Inner Light/Global Communications, except by a reviewer who may quote brief passages in a review.

Published in the United States of America by Inner Light/Global Communications

PO Box 753 - New Brunswick, NJ 08903

Staff Members:

Timothy G. Beckley, Publisher

Carol Ann Rodriguez, Assistant to the Publisher

Sean Casteel, General Associate Editor

Tim R. Swartz, Layout, Graphics, Editorial Consultant

William Kern, Editorial and Art Consultant

www.ConspiracyJournal.com

PayPal: mrufo8@hotmail.com

THE REAL LIFE UFO TRANSFORMATION OF DIANE TESSMAN

CONTENTS

PUTTING FAITH IN THE GODDESS: A Special Note From Timothy Green Beckley ...7

PREFACE: DIANE'S ASSIGNMENT EARTH 9

Chapter One: A Welcome from Tibus 15

Chapter Two: Soulful Adventures In The Mysterious Mists of Mother Ireland 21

Chapter Three: Ghosts - Who Are You? 47

Chapter Four: There Are Places I'll Remember 59

Chapter Five: Joshua Tree, Giant Rock, And The Powers of George Van Tassel 75

Chapter Six: Time Traveling Humans? Wright-Patterson Medical Chief Speaks 85

Chapter Seven: It's A Big Galaxy Out There Mr. Spock, Full of Time Travelers and Extraterrestrials 93

Chapter Eight: Five Ways Aliens Survive Interstellar Space to Arrive in Earth Skies 105

Chapter Nine: THE ORIGINAL TRANSFORMATION - With Author's Updates 113

Chapter Ten: UFOS At Eagle Lake, My Second Encounter With Tibus 279

Chapter Eleven: Unconditional Love, Thy Name is Cats and Dogs! 289

THE REAL LIFE UFO TRANSFORMATION OF DIANE TESSMAN

Cover Art By Carol Ann Rodriguez

PUTTING FAITH IN THE GODDESS – A SPECIAL NOTE FROM TIMOTHY GREEN BECKLEY

When I first met Diane Tessman while on a book signing tour of the South, I was greatly impressed by her fortitude and perseverance. She was representing both APRO and MUFON, two very prestigious organizations with worldwide memberships. At the time she was one of the few female UFO investigators, being that the field was mainly guided by the old boys of UFOlogy.

There had been a series of sighting in the area where she was living in Florida, and she had become embroiled in her own series of weird UFO related "coincidences." The phenomena seemed to be following her around, even entering her home in the form of a series of mysterious beeps.

Being one to probe, I wanted to find out why the UFO phenomena might be attaching itself to Diane. That is when I found out all about her "special one," who is best known today as Tibus.

Tibus has been, or so Diane says, with her since a very early age, giving advice and later on offering other worldly wisdom to members of her Starlight group. Diane is one of the few what we have come to call "channels," which I have rigorously supported. Her concept of what is transpiring goes beyond letting "space people" take over her body and speak to us all. Her work is rich in philosophy about the source of her contacts, giving it a unique and special prospectus.

I have followed Diane's career as a public figure rather closely as she moved around the world herself seeking different settings and expanding her horizons. She has gathered a wealth of information which is included for the first time in this greatly enhanced and expanded edition of the Transformation.

THE REAL LIFE UFO TRANSFORMATION OF DIANE TESSMAN

Privately, I refer to Diane as the "Goddess of the Woods," as she is so much in love of Mother Nature and of the many domestic and wild creatures that constantly surrounds her.

We are bring this work out at this time hoping that it will ease some of the fear and tension that hangs over our society today. There is much that Tibus and Diane have to say, so I will put down my pen and let them begin to tell an enthralling story that I believe will engage as well as educate.

Tim leads a "harmony drumming session" for spiritual balancing with Carol Ann Rodriguez standing beside him and than Diane to the far right. The photo was taken at a conference organized by Beckley, and held in Colorado Springs at the base of Pikes Peak. a celebrated spiritual site.

PREFACE: DIANE'S ASSIGNMENT EARTH

Diane Tessman

Where do I begin? It was a long time ago that I wrote *"The Transformation"* on a $5.00 garage sale typewriter which, in 1983, was considered a very old-fashioned typewriter. It was a heavy beast which weighed about a ton.

I knew I had a lot to say, much of it was not generated by my mind but catapulted into my head from outside. It was from an "unknown" but I somehow knew and loved that unknown.

I am thrilled to have a chance to update what is written in The Transformation, but the core of Tibus' message, to love and protect Mother Earth and all her lifeforms and to help guide us through this time of change and upheaval, remains the same. Throughout the years he predicted what has come to pass with climate chaos and change, the tragic extinction of many species, social unrest, mass hysteria, mass insanity, and even deadly viruses which emanate from humans transgressing upon nature. However, Tibus had great hope for our planet way back in 1983, just as he does today. Now, he is thrilled to add vital updates to *"The Real Life UFO Transformation of Diane Tessman."*

I began my channeled messages from spacetime38 years ago, and I still have that strange but wonderfully familiar conduit to the mind of someone not of this time or place; I call him, "Tibus." We have spent a lifetime working together, and we are more productive today than ever before.

THE REAL LIFE UFO TRANSFORMATION OF DIANE TESSMAN

A lifetime of human experience has sailed by for me, "significant others" have floated into the sunset and down a black hole. However, one or two old lovers are still good friends; we still love each other today with new understanding and depth.

Perhaps the best friends are those who remain with us even after the sexual stuff is all over. Not that our lives are over, I find us more creative, wiser, and just plain nicer, than before. It's just that the youthful, hormonal tidal wave of lust and folly has ebbed, leaving us to truly perceive our friend as a beautiful spirit and dynamic individual.

Timothy Green Beckley is one of these rare dynamic individuals in my life. Tim and I have known each other since 1980. Because of his belief in me, I wrote *"The Transformation,"* and he published it. He is also publisher of this updated, enhanced edition. Should we entitle it *"The Transformed Transformation?"*

I dedicate this book to Tim.

The universe is always in motion, there is always momentum! Change is necessary and denotes LIFE itself. Celebrate! – Tibus

Diane addresses a large conference in Palm Springs.

THE REAL LIFE UFO TRANSFORMATION OF DIANE TESSMAN

Thanks to Carol Ann Rodriguez for the astoundingly great illustration of Tibus on the cover! She caught my description of his mesmerizing, translucent eyes and she stays true to my description of how I remember him. That's not an easy thing to do, thank you, Carol.

Thanks to my best friend Della van Hise for the cover photo of me and for a friendship like no other.

Of course, thanks to my daughter Gianna for taking photos and for so much more.

People have frequently told me that *"The Transformation"* brings tears of joy to their eyes as no other spiritual book has done. It seems to possess a magic formula. There is indeed an unseen contributor to the messages in this book named Tibus, space man and time traveler, with whom I share consciousness. He is more dedicated to his mission than ever, and is always enthusiastic, even when I am a bit "down." Within this book are new channelings by Tibus.

I am happy to include forgotten but important UFO cases on which I reported in Tim Beckley's *UFO Review*. These can be found nowhere else. Tim is anxious to have them published, too. From UFO crash retrievals to face to face contact with saucer occupants, what a wealth of information!

I am also thrilled to include a taste of my own science speculation and futurism regarding the occupants in those UAPs and UFOs. My recent book *"Future Humans and the UFOs"* is being called a "landmark book" in the UFO field and has received wonderful reviews on Amazon. In the *"The Real Life UFO Transformation of Diane Tessman,"* I offer incredible news about time travel. I also offer my breakthrough essays including, "Ghosts: Who Are You?" and I reveal "The 5 Ways Aliens Travel to Earth." After all, I have been an investigator, researcher, and experiencer since that moment of contact on a November evening in Iowa, 1952!

I am considered a "clear channel," not influenced by static or misinformation from outside as the message arrives in my mind. I have addressed many conferences, as well as, counseling thousands of people who contact me for help from across the planet. Often Tibus chimes in as we offer guidance in our readings.

Within *"The Real Life UFO Transformation of Diane Tessman"* are Dr. R. Leo Sprinkle's notes, made at the time Dr. Sprinkle hypnotically regressed me in 1981 at the University of Wyoming. I reached a deep level of hypnosis as I remembered details of the little aliens who took me to the starship where Tibus waited when I was four years old. I remembered details of the starship, specifics about Tibus and his talk with me and his "dark friend" who waited across the corridor. Come with me back to that time as you read this book!

In recent years I have learned more facts about the missing membrane in my mouth which was taken during one of two encounters (which many call "abductions"); I have learned how my life might have been saved by a medical procedure performed during one of these encounters. This procedure did not exist in 1952 and is only beginning to be used today! I explain in detail in this new edition.

In this book, I am sharing with you some of my personal experiences and relationships in this amazing lifetime. Come with me to the misty land of Ireland with its ancient dolmen balanced incredibly on one edge for thousands of years. Ireland, with craggily castles, healing pagan holy wells and also a certain handsome Irish rebel right out of a romance novel but who, in the end, is only human.

I have lived in Iowa, Florida, the Virgin Islands, Southern California, The Netherlands, Ireland (for five years), Joshua Tree/Giant Rock, California, and then back to Iowa, where I established the Star Network Animal Sanctuary 23 years ago. We are still rescuing animals today and giving them a loving forever home here at our sanctuary.

In every place I have lived, I've had UFO sightings and paranormal activity, exciting adventures and met fascinating people. So, I'd like to share some of my personal life as it has unfolded, through pictures and accounts. How has Tibus figured in all this?

I have worked with many contactees, abductees, experiencers, and good humans seeking enlightenment; they have also run into strange but (usually) wonderful synchronicities and unexplainable, extraordinary events from UFO sightings to déjà vu and other glitches in the matrix, just as I have. We tend to have extraordinary lives!

And, of course, I must have a chapter on my beloved animals friends who have been with me all my life, in abundance! I have learned more about the universe and its spirit from them than from any other teacher. My cats and dogs, whether here now or in spirit, are a part of me. As well, I have had a great friend on this human journey, my beautiful daughter Gianna. She and I have often felt it is "You and Me Against the World," – as that old song by Helen Redding says.

THE REAL LIFE UFO TRANSFORMATION OF DIANE TESSMAN

The original Transformation turned out to have been only the beginning! However, the purpose of our mission, which is to guide Earth through these most-difficult times, remains the same. Tibus and I are part of a huge force of light workers. This transformative new book is our story, and it is entitled *"The Real Life UFO Transformation of Diane Tessman."* Enjoy!

This book contains science and it contains spirit. Reality is composed of both.
—Tibus

You can contact Diane by email at: **dianetessmano@gmail.com**

Her mailing address is:

Diane Tessman

P.O. Box 352

St. Ansgar, IA 50472

Diane at her home in St. Ansgar, Iowa

THE REAL LIFE UFO TRANSFORMATION OF DIANE TESSMAN

Diane has traveled the world to experience and commune with Gaia, the conscious spirit of Earth.

Chapter One

A Welcome from Tibus

This is Tibus. I come to you in love and light.

Hello, star friends! We are all made of "star stuff," and so, dear ones, a galaxy which is teeming with diverse life, is waiting to say hello to you! You are a galactic citizen; we are all a part of the All That Is!

As Diane's hypnosis notes reveal, Diane and I are an experiment in shared consciousness between two individuals. I do not mean "experiment" in a negative sense. This is something she agreed to before entering this current "Diane" lifetime. Our sharing is a thing of joy and wonder to both of us, but we could not be sure at first that it would turn out as well as it has.

When Diane typed **The Original Transformation**, sitting on the floor of her rental duplex because she couldn't afford any furniture, I couldn't be sure that our shared consciousness would work but as the book progressed, I realized my messages were getting through, loud and clear. I send them telepathically and they land in her head, often a few paragraphs long, then she hurries to write them down accurately.

Soon we started **The Star Network** and it continues today 38 years later, for our star people. Many of our readers also feel they are living a human lifetime during a most difficult time, and we lovingly join in meditation every month to envision a new and better day for Mother Earth and all her life-forms.

In this book, Diane and I have added new information, updates, and clarifications to the **Original Transformation** chapters. Channelers usually give a message and then move on, never going back to be accountable for the information they offered. For perhaps the first time in the world of channeling, Diane and I are happy to offer in-put on our original messages where need-be.

THE REAL LIFE UFO TRANSFORMATION OF DIANE TESSMAN

Tibus speaks through Diane.

As individuals, Diane and I have much in common! You might even wonder if she is me in a previous lifetime or I am her in a future lifetime. Ah, well, possibly so! She and I always proclaim that we are both separate, physical individuals but we do acknowledge symbiosis, not only in working with our messages but as individual spirits as well.

The difference is, I am of the future from her point of view and yours. Ah, but all time is simultaneous!

I have always promised that Earth and the human species do make it into the future!

As a human from the future, I am proof of this. However, I realize that having a conduit of shared consciousness with Diane is not what most scientists call "proof." My co-workers on starships and time-ships, are indeed extraterrestrials from far distant planets, as well as humans of my (future) time. We do have the key to time travel and you will soon, also.

The entire, magnificent galaxy and the incredible universe beyond, awaits humankind at The Moment - a moment of humankind's own choosing. "Out there, that away" is a magnificent quilt of multiple other-dimensional worlds; as astronaut Neil Armstrong exclaimed, **"There areplaces to go beyond belief!"**

But first, humankind needs to make one small step up the awareness ladder. I speak of humankind as one collective consciousness.

There are multiple crises on Earth in your present time because Earth stands at the threshold of change so vast it is almost incomprehensible. It is an instant step upward in evolution; evolution normally takes millions ofyears but once in a blue moon, it happens instantly. Such an event awaits Earth and her life-forms, including humans.

You and your offspring, my friend, are on the edge of becoming a whole new species! This offers real hope for your grandchildren and your great, great grandchildren as well – and for you.

However, you have to **care** about the fate of Earth and her animals and**care** about your fellow humans. Be an activist in bringingour new world!

You might ask, "Tibus, how can you call yourself "human" when you tell us that humankind stands on the precipice of becoming a new species, perhaps named "Homo cosmos instead of Homo sapiens?

"Gaia, living spirit of Mother Earth, hear me!"

THE REAL LIFE UFO TRANSFORMATION OF DIANE TESSMAN

Evolution has not stopped with your generation, my friend. Of course your species will change. My origin is human and I am called human, just as you are. We are creations of Gaia, the conscious spirit of Earth. However, some of my people have been mistaken for alien UFO occupants over these years.

Make no mistake, breaking the chains of time is anevent with enormous implications in both scientific and spiritual terms. And yet, Mother Earth will always be there for you. And, if you evolve spiritually just one step higher, you will perceive a healed, healthy planet!

We not only participate in the world we perceive, we participate in creating the world we perceive. You must soon perceive at a higher level of consciousness!

Consciousness creates life all over the universe in every form imaginable and unimaginable!

And for all the life-forms in all these strange places and a billion worlds beyond that, there is only one *you*. We send our unconditional love to *you*.

Is there life after death? Of course! There is only *life,* anyway!

May the healing light of goodness surround you,

–Tibus

Diane and Tibus' Star Network publications are The Heartline and The Change Times Quarterly. To receive free, current samples, email to: dianetessmano@gmail.com

The mailing address is:

Diane Tessman

P.O. Box 352

St. Ansgar, IA 50472

Join our Star Network to work for a new future!

THE REAL LIFE UFO TRANSFORMATION OF DIANE TESSMAN

Diane completes a channeling session with Tibus.

This golden ribbon caught Tibus' channeled message.

THE REAL LIFE UFO TRANSFORMATION OF DIANE TESSMAN

Diane in Ireland, celebrating the many mystical experiences and lessons offered to her there.

Diane enjoys the roses in a Celtic graveyard.

Chapter Two
Soulful Adventures In The Mysterious Mists of Mother Ireland

Why did Mother Ireland suddenly beckon me in 1987? To be honest, I do not know. I have some Irish blood, maybe about 3/8th of my DNA echoes back to Erin, but this sudden spiritual obsession was not consciously due to my physical DNA. I suddenly had a super-charged Irish quest as surely as if the Holy Grail had landed in my lap.

In 1987, my daughter Gianna and I were living in Poway, California. I had managed to buy our own home due to my channeled spiritual books and publications with Tibus' popular messages. I had not entered the teaching field when we moved to California in 1982 because there was a recession and they weren't hiring, I had gone through some difficult days financially. I worked several jobs to keep Gianna and our animals fed and with a roof over our heads, but I was only trained as a teacher.

However, by 1987, I was a busy writer and channeler, doing what I was meant to do. So why did far away Ireland call me? Again, I do not know, except it was something in my soul and Tibus really needed the experience.

Perhaps I can "blame" Tibus for the fact my life has been a series of episodes as if I am exploring a human lifetime. I do think that Tibus goes exploring, through me. For instance, I joined the circus briefly as a trapeze artist in my early 20s.

I have many more examples of my adventures; there is a chapter in this book, "My Human Adventure and the Incredible Experiences of This Lifetime," but I'll now return to my Irish episode of adventure, which lasted five years.

It was not the green beer on St. Patrick's Day which spoke to me. Irish history suddenly felt real and passionate to me, as if I had lived it. This extended back to ancient times when the island was the Land of the Celts. It also extended to the present time when Ireland was still in a struggle to have their entire island free of British control.

I felt as though I had lived a lifetime on this eternally green, misty, magical island, Mother Ireland's "forty shades of green" was in my soul, somehow. Many experiencers and seekers can vouch for the fact that a past or future lifetime haunts or beckons us. And, there are other reasons why "spirit quests" happen for us (and to us), it is not always about the parallel aspects (past lives) of the Self.

For me, there seems to be an Irish past life from the 1700s. He was male, his surname was Fallon, and he was part of the Irish resistance to Britain's rule. Perhaps "Fallon" is one of Tibus' past lives too? This assumes Tibus is a future life of mine.

However, dear old Fallon disappeared shortly after we arrived in Ireland. He still existed in the green mist, but he stopped jumping up and down in my consciousness. He had enticed me to take Gaelic Irish language lessons in night class in California. Talk about a difficult language to learn! However, once I settled in Ireland, Fallon receded and "Diane of the now" lived a lovely dream, which was - reality.

My daughter Gianna had just become an adult and was offered a modeling contract in the Netherlands, thus she lived in Amsterdam for a while. Later she came to Ireland to live with me, but "Ireland" did not resonate with her, and she returned to the United States. In years to come, we lived together again, but Ireland was "for me" now that my child was grown.

I arrived in Ireland in January, 1990. Immediately I felt I had fallen down a hobbit hole and discovered a fascinating mystical dimension, to which I felt a close relationship. Mother Ireland began talking to me and I was thrilled and entranced.

Our St. Bernard and five cats from California had to go through six months of quarantine in Ireland, and so, I got an apartment near the quarantine compound outside of Dublin. I visited them when I could; it was as if my poor furry friends were in prison.

However, the location in County Meath proved to be wonderful because it is an Irish county rich in old ruins which look like a movie set with crumbling mansions which evoke *"The Haunting of Hill House."* In Meath also stands the Hill of Tara, and Newgrange, Knowth, and Dowth, the ancient passage tombs. They may have been used for Celt worship and mystical ceremonies, as well.

I would like to share with readers, some of my personal photos and experiences in this, my Irish Travelogue.

MY MYSTICAL ADVENTURES IN COUNTY MEATH, REPUBLIC OF IRELAND TARA, HOME OF CELT ROYALTY

The Hill of Tara (In the Irish language: Cnoc na Teamhrach) is a hill which was the site of festivals and celebrations for the ancient pagan Celt kings and queens and their people. Standing alone on the windswept green land, one can easily imagine a time when humankind had not been beat down or dumbed down by religion, governments, and corporations pushing capitalism on steroids. This was a time when humans could celebrate in balance and harmony with the magnificence of Mother Nature in this exquisite land.

According to tradition, Tara was the inauguration place and the seat of the High King. This was the center of power, the spiritual source, for a civilization which stretched over much of Europe.

Aerial view of the holy ground of Celt kings and queens: The Hill of Tara.

Today, Brittany, in France and Catalonia in Spain, still claim their Celt connection as does Yorkshire in the United Kingdom. Wales, Scotland, and Ireland complete the current day remnants of the Celt civilization, each with their own Gaelic language and strong Celt traditions.

The Celts were a warlike people, fiercely independent and courageous in battle, if somewhat lacking in discipline. Despite tribal rivalry amongst themselves, they proved a handful to the highly trained Roman legions. The Hill of Tara was the inspirational, uniting symbol of these Celt warriors.

Tara also appears in Irish mythology. From the Neolithic to the Iron Age, "seanachies" (story tellers) told of the magical powers which Tara bestowed. It has a passage tomb called the "Mound of the Hostages," and a legend to go with this ancient mound of earth. There is also a tall standing stone believed to be the legendary "Lia Fáil" or "Stone of Destiny."

Some say the Lia Fail Stone of Destiny at Tara has magical energies.

THE REAL LIFE UFO TRANSFORMATION OF DIANE TESSMAN

DIANE VISITS TARA

I drove alone over the narrow, steep, winding hills of Meath to the Hill of Tara soon after I moved to Ireland. The rain was moving sideways, blown by a powerful wind and I debated whether to get out of the car. But, I had come all this way, in fact, all the way from my old home in Southern California, and I was determined to walk over Tara's deep green carpet and feel her energies.

No one else was there that day, possibly because of the weather but also, in 1990, Ireland's famous landmarks were open to the public with no regulations. One could walk up ancient stone steps to the top of a ruined tower which was crumbling. Today, I understand that they have put in security and rules, partly so no one sues for falling off a crumbling flight of steps, but in 1990, it was wonderful! It was a hands-on experience, and I survived as well.

There I was with the rain pelting me in my face, soaking wet, all by myself in a remote area, and I have never felt more powerful energies. In fact, I myself felt powerful! I finally stopped under a giant, gnarly tree near the back of the area and the flock of sheep which had been watching me from afar like native warriors, stood lined up on an opposing hillside, staring at me.

This flock of sheep apparently kept Tara's grass trimmed, as was common in tourist areas. This is a much better answer than a noisy lawn mowing machine with gasoline fumes.

Suddenly, I noticed one sheep emerge from the flock and limp toward me. He had a lame leg and a long way to walk. He finally stood before me, about two feet away, and I swear I heard the words distinctly in my mind, "You came back!"

He was no longer a mere sheep; a powerful, ancient entity was inside him. I felt no fear. I felt honored. I heard these words again, "You came back!"

I knew he meant that I had returned in this Diane lifetime, having left, or been driven out (or killed in battle), thousands of years before.

Was I king or queen or a commoner? This made no difference; this was my hill, my source, as well!

The old sheep then turned and limped back to his flock which stood like a party of warriors on the other hill.

Some people laugh the minute I begin "the talking sheep story" but, in all seriousness, this was one of my most profound, powerful spiritual experiences.

There have been countless experiences which I treasure, but this one still sends chills up my back.

Maybe you had to be there, but it was breath-taking! I stood and cried tears of wonder and joy after he limped away. My tears mixed with the driving rain.

SUMMERHILL HOUSE

There are so many castles and mansions in County Meath, most at some stage of ruin, that it would take a book to recount my experiences in them; another larger book would be needed to list them all because there are hundreds I didn't visit. I am sure each one witnessed history, from the aristocracy having grand parties to the violence of political unrest. Many of them suffered catastrophic fires and, of course, years of emptiness and neglect.

I have chosen my visit to the Summerhill ruins to relate to you.

The mansion at Summerhill in rural Co. Meath, was magnificently placed on top of a hill. It consisted of a center block, two wings and was massively built of limestone. Four Corinthian columns stood in front, as did a portico with two sunken gardens and a huge sundial.

A broad flight of stairs led to the entrance of the mansion; another grand staircase inside, led to the ornate second floor balcony which overlooked the grand main hall.

OUR SUMMERHILL HAUNTING

My daughter Gianna and I were driving around County Meath with our beautiful yellow Labrador puppy named Sinsee. Gianna always held Sinsee in her lap but Sinsee loved to poke her head out the sunroof of old Volvo.

I stopped the car near Summerhill (according to the map), and we began walking up the long laneway. Sinsee loved the walk in the county...that is until we got to the actual dark, somehow frightening ruins of the Summerhill Mansion. Sinsee became scared the whole time we looked around Summerhill, and Gianna had to carry her.

That tells you something about the ghosts there. Sinsee was the smartest dog I ever knew and apparently her "I sense a ghost" ability was keen also.

THE REAL LIFE UFO TRANSFORMATION OF DIANE TESSMAN

Summerhill House

Absolutely no one was around for miles, or so it seemed. However, both Gianna and I kept hearing snippets of noise, almost as if a large rowdy crowd was somewhere around. This noise came almost in "snapshots," here and then, gone.

Later we learned that Summerhill House was damaged by fire several times and suffered ongoing problems when farm hands went on strike and damaged farming equipment in 1919.

The Irish Republican Army, fighting to take their country back from the British, attacked Summerhill numerous times. Summerhill was owned by very wealthy British people who entertained British royalty. Eventually, the rebels took over Summerhill and distributed the lands and farms around the house equally amongst the workers and their families, before they set the enormous main house on fire, destroying it.

Like our puppy, we could just feel the ghosts in the ruins which extended in each direction. Summerhill had two wings, each of which were at least a block long. We thought we saw movement in an open window (glass was missing from every window), and we got spooked, deciding to leave.

Gianna really wanted to put Sinsee down but just as she did, the puppy started to bark at an unseen presence right in the middle of the lane. Both my daughter and I "saw" the image of an old craggily man standing there, no doubt a worker. He smoked a pipe.

Neither of us saw him with our naked eye, but when we compared notes after we got safely to the car, we realized we had "seen" the same old man. The icing on the cake was that we both said together, "And he had a pipe, I smelled the smoke!"

No doubt Sinsee, that golden puppy, was thinking, "It sure took those two mistresses of mine long enough to figure out that place is really haunted!"

NEWGRANGE PASSAGE TOMB

Newgrange (Irish: Brú na Bóinne), is a prehistoric passage tomb in County Meath, on the north side of the River Boyne. It is in an unusual place which has great electromagnetic and psychic power; three ley lines converge there. As well, the River Boyne is joined by two underground rivers as it rolls past Newgrange.

Newgrange is an exceptionally grand passage tomb built during the Neolithic period, around 3200 BC, making it older than Stonehenge and the Egyptian pyramids.

The site consists of a large circular mound with an inner stone passageway and chambers. Human bones and possible offerings to the spirits were found in these chambers. The mound has a retaining wall at the front, made mostly of white quartz and it is ringed by inscripted large stones. Many of the larger stones of Newgrange are covered in megalithic art. The mound is also ringed by a stone circle.

Newgrange rises out of the green meadow, standing stones all around.

There is no agreement about what the site was used for, but it is believed that it had spiritual significance, possibly used as a ceremonial temple as well.

The entrance of Newgrange is aligned with the rising sun only on December 21st, the Winter Solstice, when sunlight shines through the "roof box" located above the entrance, flooding the inner chamber in light. In the dead of winter, the ancient pre-Celts must have felt exuberant when the sunbeam of the Winter Solstice shone through to brilliantly light the back of the chamber. They are thought to have held up quartz crystals to catch this sacred sunbeam.

NEWGRANGE AND THE SACRED SUNBEAM

I visited Newgrange four times in the five years I lived in Ireland. This tells you how mesmerizing it was, because I was hard up for money in Ireland and it costs to go in.

I was blessed to know a local metaphysician who arranged to have me among the lucky ones who got to be in the back of Newgrange when the Winter Solstice sunbeam zoomed in at sunrise, 1992. Ireland is supportive of artists and writers, so along with a few dignitaries, a few of us get to witness the Sacred Sunbeam Event.

The sacred sunbeam shines through the darkness on the Winter Solstice.

Luckily, as well, it was a clear morning. The sunbeam appears as if shot from a phaser, because it appears the second the sun rises above the horizon. This sunbeam has power!

I always felt at peace at Newgrange. I also felt its ancientness. It has been standing there, without even a leak in the roof, since before Stonehenge and the Egyptian pyramids. I felt its lost occupants' dignity, tenacity, and cleverness.

Knowth and Dowth are two more passage tombs which have been unearthed next to Newgrange. When I was there, only Dowth was in the process of being unearthed, so I did not visit them. These incredible structures were hidden for thousands of years.

COUNTY KILKENNY, OF RAVENS, HAUNTINGS, AND THE TRIBE WHO TURNED SIDEWAYS TO THE SUN

I sometimes wonder if Tibus engineered reality somehow, to have a rental cottage in County Kilkenny become available for me to rent. One morning, I traveled from my rental flat in Co. Meath to meet my boyfriend's sister for the first time in County Waterford, about one hundred miles away.

I told her that my animals would be getting out of quarantine soon and that I wanted to find a rural cottage somewhere to rent. She pulled out the local paper and immediately saw a rental cottage available in the neighboring county of Kilkenny. I should note that in 1990, rental cottages were not plentiful, or at least it wasn't the custom to advertise them.

We drove up to see it the same day, the landlord just happened to be available. It was exactly the natural setting I had dreamed of and was right next to Castlemorris Forest, full of huge old gnarly trees and mythological faeries. The cottage named Ballinvaugh was on a quiet country road which wandered to the village of Kilmoganny. The road was lined with chestnut and beech trees and wonderful smelling furze bushes.

I learned that the huge mansion in the center of the Castlmorris Forest had burned down years ago, but the large home where Maud Gonne had stayed was still at the edge of the forest. What a synchronicity! I had been fascinated for years with Maud Gonne, an Irish historical figure who had been married to the leader of the 1916 Irish Uprising, John McBride. She was also involved with my favorite poet, W.B. Yeats. Talk about synchronicity!

THE REAL LIFE UFO TRANSFORMATION OF DIANE TESSMAN

Diane stands at the large door of her Ballinvaugh cottage, trying to figure out why the door is almost bigger than the cottage.

The standing stones in Co. Cork are among many "colonies" of circular standing stones in Ireland.

THE REAL LIFE UFO TRANSFORMATION OF DIANE TESSMAN

Maud Gonne, with whom I shared a synchronicity.

A classic Celt High Cross.

THE REAL LIFE UFO TRANSFORMATION OF DIANE TESSMAN

The five years I lived in that rural Kilkenny cottage were full of mystical wonders.

"Come away, O human child!

To the waters and the wild

With a faery, hand in hand,

For the world's more full of weeping than you can understand."

– The refrain of *"The Stolen Child"* by Y.B. Yates

Diane does spiritual work with powerful Kilkenny white quartz.

FAERIES ALL AROUND

My landlord at Ballinvaugh cottage lived in Australia as many Irish do, but he came back to Ireland on vacation and told me the story his mother had related to him about the faeries of Castlemorris Forest.

His mother Maura and her cousins were walking through Castlemorris Forest when she was fourteen years old, to reach a wedding in a village the other side of the forest. Right by a faery tree, as she called one of the huge old gnarly trees, she saw up ahead on the narrow path, a group of at least five children.

One of several fairy trees in Castlemorris Forest.

As Maura and her cousins got closer, they realized they were small adults about two or three feet tall. She saw one little female who must have been under two feet tall. She reported that these small people looked annoyed, rather like her parents did when she was a bad girl.

These strange little people were dressed "old fashioned." Since this experience happened in the early 20th Century, "old fashioned" must have meant back to the 1800s or before.

The leader, a "tall" man, told them angrily that they were not welcomed to just traipse through the forest. His voice was shrill and sounded strange.

Maura and her cousins didn't know whether to laugh or be frightened and run away. Just then in the distance, there came the sound of Maura's family (adults), some on horses, also heading for the wedding in the nearby village. These strange little people were instantly frightened of the coming adults and hurried away, scurrying off the path and into wilderness.

Encouraged by my landlord's story, and always seeking the unknown, I went into Castlemorris Forest many times. The craziest time was when I went into the forest one dark Halloween night after having several drinks of wine. It seemed positively alive (and after all, it is a living forest), frightening, primal, and magnificent. Sadly, I was not confronted by the faeries that I remember.

MY FLYING LIGHT FORM

However, out in the apple orchard at Ballinvaugh cottage with my cat Sakima, I was honored to take two very unusual photos of what I call "a flying light form." Ballinvaugh originally had twenty apple trees, I was told, but one had died, and so the 19 apple trees were blooming. Faeries love apple blossoms, so maybe I was visited by a Castlemorris Forest faery after all in the form of a flying light form.

THE REAL LIFE UFO TRANSFORMATION OF DIANE TESSMAN

"SAKIMA" IRELAND Rcv'd. 1/92

I am sharing the two photos of my flying light form with my readers. These photos were taken on an inexpensive camera I had purchased recently. No other photo from that camera ever showed anything similar. I did not see the flying light form, and the photo looks as if Sakima, my cat, didn't either. I took the first picture, then immediately took the second frame; it would seem I could see this phenomenon because I centered the photos, it seems, but I could not see it. Was it therefore in touch with me psychically?

THE REAL LIFE UFO TRANSFORMATION OF DIANE TESSMAN

THE MANIFESTATION OF THE BANSHEE

My closest neighbors at Ballinvaugh were about a mile down the road. The father of that family had a twin brother who had been killed in his teens, riding his bike on the road.

The night before this tragic accident, my neighbor, who was then a teenager, saw a tiny woman under a tree, brushing her long hair. "I knew someone was going to die soon, because she was the banshee, and they always predict a death."

His twin brother died the next day.

THE CHATTERING IRISH RAVEN

I stepped outside Ballinvaugh cottage one fine, tranquil morning but Sinsee, our yellow Labrador, took off like a lightning bolt as a dog does with strong prey instinct. However, Sinsee did not have a strong prey instinct and I immediately wondered what she had pounced upon.

Apologies to Sinsee. When I got there, she was standing beside a mass of shiny black feathers; she had not touched a feather. She wanted to me see this feathered victim and help him.

Diane and her wonderful yellow Lab Sinsee at their Ballinvaugh Cottage.

And so began my summer with the Irish Raven. As Sinsee and I stood gazing at him, he managed to get up on his feet and lamely fly to a low telephone wire. I assumed that would be the end of it, Sinsee and I were happy to see he was almost okay.

I went back inside to write The Change Times Quarterly and Sinsee took a nap. I had forgotten about this incident when we went outside after lunch. There the huge raven was, still on the phone wire. He began "talking" the second I stepped out. His constant chatter really sounded like a foreign language; it varied in intensity and pattern.

I told him it was a lovely afternoon and that he could stay there as long he needed to. I gave him this message in telepathy and also in words.

Every day for two summer months, "my" raven was there. He reminded me of the parrot on a pirate's shoulder because we had formed a relationship, Bird and Human. His talk was endless but not nonsensical or monotonous.

In Celt and Norse mythology, crows and ravens are always magical, semi-divine and able to shape-shift into human or animal form, and sometimes into inanimate objects and even pure light.

An Irish raven sits atop a standing wall.

THE REAL LIFE UFO TRANSFORMATION OF DIANE TESSMAN

Note: I snapped the photos of the "flying light form" in the spring of 1991. The raven showed up in the summer of 1991. Did the "flying light form" shapeshift to become my talking friend-raven?

The Pre-Celt tribes and the Celts perceived ravens and crows as the keepers of secrets. These birds frequently played "the trickster" archetype, focusing on satisfying their own greed, regardless of the requirements of the greater community. But this wasn't always negative, because the trickster was the survivor, the smartest, most conniving, and wittiest, not to mention the most charming and inventive.

When Christianity arrived, these shiny black birds were deemed dirty and probably evil. What a shame!

My raven did not seem selfish at all; he seemed to be desperately trying to communicate with me as the summer went on. I looked for him first thing every summer morning, and there he was in his spot on the wire.

Then in mid-August, he was not there one morning. I never saw him alive again. A week went by and I worried about him, until I found his body right by the edge of the narrow road. One of his legs was tangled in a wild morning glory vine. He had no other wound or mark. I grieved! I also felt guilty because if I have found him while he was still alive, I could have untangled him.

Finally, I let it go; feeling that even his mode of death was very strange: one leg with a morning glory vine tangled around it? Spooky! Unlikely! It seemed legendary, rather like some ancient Celt hero might have died.

GHOSTS OF THE CALLAN WORKHOUSE

When I lived in County Kilkenny, my post office box was in the town of Callan. Readers who have been with me for a long time will remember PO Box 1 (or was it Box 2?) I just know that no one else had heard of a PO Box but they nicely set up one for me, the American.

Every time I drove to Callan, I was mesmerized in a dark way by a huge grey structure which had fallen into neglect. I asked the postmistress about it, and she said, "That's the Callan Workhouse where they sent people during the Potato Famine."

The Great Famine was a disaster that hit Ireland between 1845 and about 1851, causing the deaths of about 1 million people and the emigration of up to 2.5 million more over the course of about six years.

THE REAL LIFE UFO TRANSFORMATION OF DIANE TESSMAN

The Haunted Callan Workhouse, house of death, during the tragic Irish Famine.

The short term cause of the Great Famine was the failure of the potato crop as a result of the attack of the fungus known as the potato blight. The potato was the staple food of the Irish rural poor, and its failure left millions exposed to starvation and death from sickness and malnutrition.

However, non-blighted potatoes which were stored in warehouses in Ireland, were then shipped to Britain. Many feel the British who occupied Ireland as their own, committed genocide on the Irish.

The crisis was greatly compounded by the social and political structure in Ireland in the 1840s. Most poor agricultural workers lived at a subsistence level and had little or no money to buy food, which was widely available to the wealthy throughout the famine years.

They did however have to continue to pay rent to landlords. Failure to do this during the famine resulted in many thousands being evicted, greatly worsening the death toll. Does this remind you of our current struggle with a wicked virus?

Even the most moderate historians know that the response of the British Government, directly responsible for governing Ireland since 1801, was unsatisfactory.

People who were starving to death, utterly poverty-stricken, or ill, were shipped to "workhouses." These human beings were called "green mouths" because some had desperately tried to eat grass.

The Callan Workhouse: Talk about haunted! How many people died painful, horrific deaths at the Callan Workhouse?

Just outside the town of Callan, there is "The Pit" into which they shoveled the bodies, a mass grave.

Back to the 1990s, visitors could not tour the dilapidated workhouse in its over-grown meadow of daisies; I did try to get permission. To me, this photo I snapped of the Callan Workhouse strongly suggests ghosts in the windows and throughout the dark structure.

GIANNA AND THE AGGRESSIVE GHOST OF THE AHENNY SLATE PIT

My daughter Gianna and I set out to make a video entitled *"Diane's Mystery Tour of Ireland."* That video is still online on Tim Beckley's You Tube channel although the Irish mold got hold of it several years after we filmed it, and so it is a tad blurry.

Gianna and I traveled to the Ahenny Slate Pit one lovely morning in County Tipperary. It is beautiful from a distance with a big quarry lake which may be bottomless.

Up close, broken pieces of slate are everywhere. We picked up a few pieces and Gianna later painted Celtic symbols and knots on them which we sent back to friends in America.

She is an excellent amateur videographer, and so as I explored the area, she was intent on filming me. Suddenly I heard a big scream and noise behind me; I turned around to find Gianna on the ground having cut her wrist quite badly on the slate.

I was worried because there are vital arteries running through the wrist. We wrapped it and she held her hand over her head to make the bleeding stop.

As soon as we quieted down, Gianna exclaimed, "I was pushed, Mama!"

THE REAL LIFE UFO TRANSFORMATION OF DIANE TESSMAN

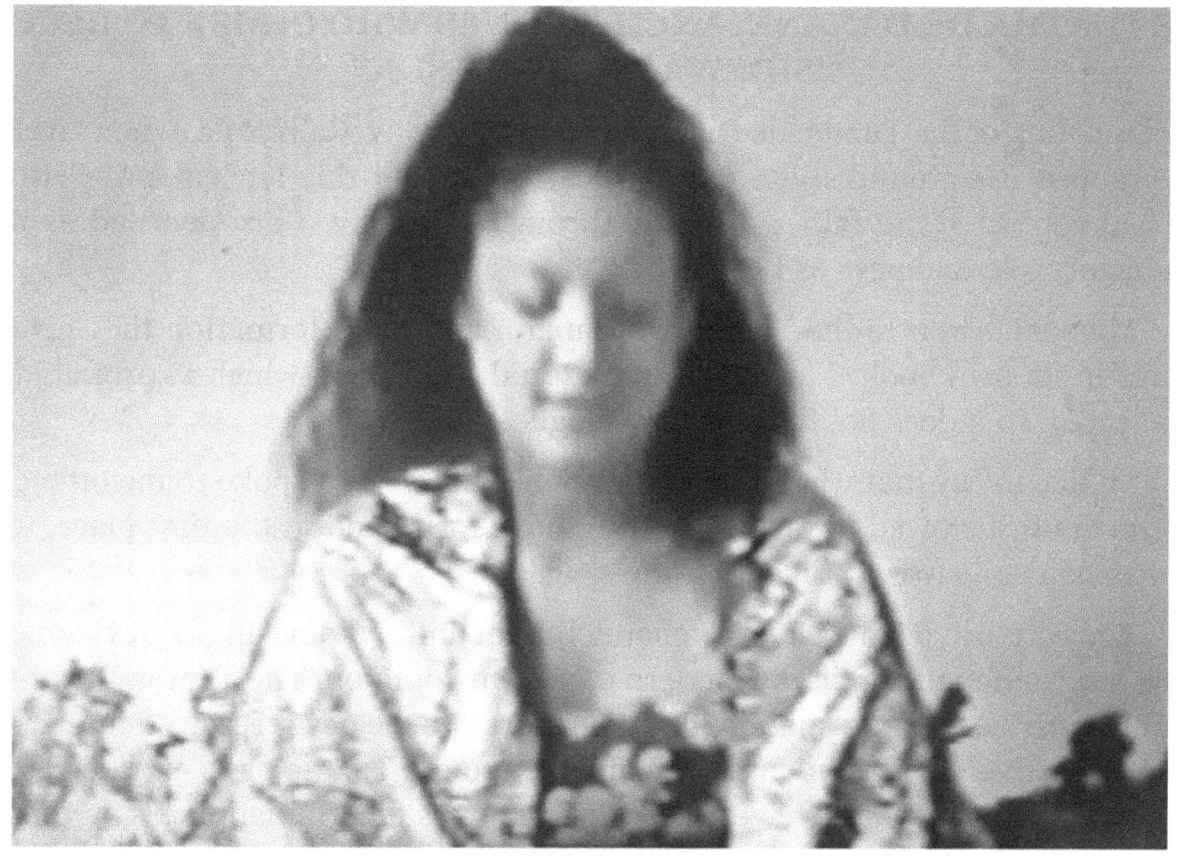

Gianna also channeling.

I said soothingly, "Oh, the slate is slippery and you were busy filming, no one is here and it was just an accident."

She became angry at me and said, "No, don't hand me that nonsense, I was pushed - hard."

On the way home I asked my neighbor what the history was of the Ahenny Slate Pit. He told me that many men had died mining slate, which was used as roofing material in Ireland and the United Kingdom. He smiled and said, "That place has some angry ghosts, they were killed because of no safety standards or equipment." He had not been told of Gianna's experience.

We concluded, yes there is at least one very angry ghost at the Ahenny Slate Pit!

My five year Irish adventure holds a special place in not only my heart, but my soul. I gave up a lot materially to follow my spirit to that unique, mysterious, beautiful, and definitely green island. I have no regrets!

THE TUATHA DE DANANN, ANCIENT ONES WHO CHOSE TO BECOME "SIDEWAYS TO THE SUN"

My channeling of the Tuatha de Danann began in Poway, California, when "Ireland" first grabbed me around 1986. I began learning about this ancient pre-Celt tribe who had contacted me rather abruptly through telepathy. I also learned as much Irish history, old and new, as I could.

My connection to the Tuatha De Danann and the information they give me, belongs in its own book. I have lots of material from them which is profound and complicated, so it does not fit in my Travelogue.

Suffice to say that when I lived in Ireland, the Tuatha spoke to me often; they were no doubt involved in my decision to move to Ireland in the first place, which was no small endeavor. I still hear from them.

Today, more people claim to channel them and to know all about them. A lot of this has been made up in the modern day, in my opinion. The Tuatha I hear from resent this erroneous information. For the record, I have never received information that Rh negative blood is in any way connected to the Tuatha or to extraterrestrials living on Earth. The Tuatha have asked me to express their unhappiness on this.

Photo of Diane while she channeled the Tuatha De Danann.

Artist's rendition of a member of the mysterious Tuatha De Danann Tribe.

People call them "the Fae," which is not accurate. There is an Irish term "the Fae" which refers to an entity of the paranormal world and sometimes to the faeries. It does not include the Tuatha De Danann; it is not their source or origin.

Note: "Fairies" is the American spelling; "faeries" is the Irish spelling.

To close my Irish Travelogue, the Tuatha De Danann sends this special message:

Ah, the secrets Gaia knows!

Vast oceans teeming with life, completely hidden

Safe from humankind's greed and pollution

Legendary islands, invisible to all but the shadows

Kingdoms beneath the waves, still alive

Interim corners, unknown to Man

Lush, green, and filled with mist and mystery

Gaia begs for humankind to emerge from its darkness

THE REAL LIFE UFO TRANSFORMATION OF DIANE TESSMAN

Yet this species is a proven spoiler and taker of life

May humankind emerge from its selfish prison

We hear the birds in the glen

We see the furry ones preparing for babies' arrival

The proud free oceans spray their mist

And sing their eternal song, all gray, green and blue

Golden mountains rise to touch the skies

Do you understand the sacred treasure you have, Human?

Rise to the light!

SUGGESTED VIEWING OF DIANE TESSMAN ON YOUTUBE.COM

Visual Tour of Ireland's Mystic Places:
www.youtube.com/watch?v=clrGp3YHc_c&t=1592s

UFOS – Are They Visitors Beyond Time?
www.youtube.com/watch?v=HHUScE03HYM&t=125s

One of the mysterious round towers of Ireland.

Diane with famous Celtic High Cross of Ahenny.

The Ahenny Slate Pit, Where Ghosts Knock You Over.

THE REAL LIFE UFO TRANSFORMATION OF DIANE TESSMAN

In August, 2020, this ghostly woman was spotted on a security camera in the middle of the night at a building site in Birmingham, England.

Chapter Three

Ghosts: Who Are You?

As the first human emerged from evolution's womb, a mysterious, vaporous twin slipped through also. Ghosts have been with us since our species began but to this day, we do not know who they are or from whence they come. We accept the same definition of a ghost which primitive people offered: "Ghosts are the restless souls of people who died." Our emotional response to ghosts reflects myths and superstitions, but our 21st Century scientific knowledge remains silent on this one. We just accept the subjective explanation which was given before the wheel was invented, as to what/who ghosts are. In truth, we don't have a clue!

To be clear, we are not referring to spirit guides, the spirit realm, or any other paranormal phenomenon except ghosts. They should not automatically be lumped together with spirits. If you feel contact or messages from a spirit, whether it is your spirit guide, a nature spirit, or even a dark spirit, you are feeling telepathic contact. Your consciousness is temporarily blended with another entity which almost always remains unseen.

Ghosts, however, are often extant entities. They are outside, seldom communicating within your mind and possibly not realizing you are there; ghosts seem to have their own agenda and habitat, perhaps an old house, theater, or hotel. Of course, some ghosts do seem angrily that you have invaded their realm.

Here are a few theories on who and what ghosts are:

ENTITY-ECHOES

Is there an entire planet-full of ghosts, meaning that all of us pass into this strange other-dimension when we die? Perhaps we, the living, only perceive a few ghosts but billions of others exist; after all, other multiverses are invisible to us. Will we all be just an echo of an entity, someday, on the Ghost Planet?

THE REAL LIFE UFO TRANSFORMATION OF DIANE TESSMAN

Kate Farmer, Hotel Coronado ghost, was once a lovely woman.

Or is it as we assume, the ghosts we see are "entity echoes" of a few former humans caught in bizarre molecular trap while most of us, good and bad, travel onward upon death, going wherever we go? What are the qualifications to be a ghost? Some ghosts are murderers; others are victims, while some ghosts seem to be "just be there."

Most people are frightened of ghosts. Humans are frightened when we come face to face with the unknown, be it extraterrestrial or ghostly, but perhaps our knee-jerk fear of ghosts is because we fear deep inside, that we will become one. Does this keep us from trying to learn more about them and their source?

A side effect of our own fear is that people decide ghosts are dangerous. The truth is, no one, to my knowledge, has never been killed by a ghost. If someone sprains his ankle running away, that's not the ghost's fault.

THE REAL LIFE UFO TRANSFORMATION OF DIANE TESSMAN

The Hotel Coronado still has reported hauntings today.

Are some ghosts trying to be friendly, to ask for help, or at least make contact? Usually it seems the answer is no. Their faces are often distorted, their eyes fixed and expressionless. However, ghosts do vary; some seem to have a strange awareness. This adds another layer to the puzzle.

We don't have a logical clue why a few people who have died, would get caught in time, and become a stuck-groove in an old fashion phonograph record which keeps repeating. Is it only their physical image which gets stuck in the grooves of reality? Ghosts often seem incoherent, yet they perform functions, drifting down to the lake, marching, brushing their hair, working in the field, or least moving from room to room.

Allowing science speculation to run free, here are a few theories regarding who/what ghosts are. These are not the traditional, brief explanation that ghosts are restless souls of dead people; it is time to do some scientific investigation and delve deeper into this phenomenon which is as old as our species.

THE REAL LIFE UFO TRANSFORMATION OF DIANE TESSMAN

HOLOGRAMS

Truth is, we do not understand scientifically how ghosts can even exist. The closest our technology has come is a hologram, but ghosts exist in creepy old houses where there is no holographic equipment.

The ghosts of Roman soldiers march along the busy M6 Highway in Britain and have been doing so since long before the highway was built and thus before the equipment to create holograms was invented. In Roman days, the road was several feet lower and many of the marching ghosts are reported to have no feet, therefore. These Roman soldiers would seem to be caught in their own time. For these and countless other reasons, ghosts are probably not holograms created by the technology we know today.

The ghost soldiers of Gettysburg's bloody battleground are seen by many tourists. They run through the woods, and then run back again, in raggle-taggle uniforms, muskets and bayonets ready for bloody action.

The White Lady is said to haunt churches and graveyards; she has been reported in many locations. She is dressed in old fashioned clothing from the 1800s, and usually appears when someone is in a state of physical or emotional despair at the church or in the graveyard. She does seem consciously aware, empathetic, and seems to have good intentions.

Often ghosts are described as "hologram-like." However, this description gives us few clues as to who and what they really are. What phenomenon in our world causes holograms which are not of a technology source?

HOLOGRAPHIC EARTH AND TIME GLITCH

If the universe is a hologram as Stephen Hawking and other great minds have decided, then Earth is a part of that great hologram which is the universe; Earth is thus a fractal hologram of the great hologram.

Our existence, all that we know, is part of this universal hologram. Perhaps, ghosts are a feature of Earth's holographic creation, too. Ghosts seem to be very much "of Earth." They often dress in old fashioned clothes, they relive or re-enact human events, and they inhabit houses, churches, hotels, theaters, hospitals.

Earth must have a magnificent consciousness. It is Earth who/which made all of us. Maybe Earth creates ghostly forms as well as the billions of living life forms she has created. If she can create a human through her formidable evolutionary force, she certainly can create a ghost!

A time glitch might be involved where in a living human observes a past current of reality, like oil running into water. There, in that past current of time, stands a ghost. This would still be a phenomenon of Earth's holographic nature since other theories regarding the nature of reality do not usually allow for time travel.

GHOSTLY MOLECULES

It is common for ghosts to appear in the place they died. A traffic camera recently caught the image of a little girl, dressed in white, standing in the middle of the intersection. Cars approach, the light is green, and the vehicles seem to drive right through the little girl as she stands there unharmed. Records show a little girl was killed in the intersection. This is a popular ghost video on You Tube and we have no way of knowing if it is fake or real, but it lends itself to the theory that when someone dies violently, their DNA or their molecules of consciousness, become blended into the surrounding environment. Does this phenomenon create ghosts?

There is a famous case which nearly proves this theory. We know it is not fake or photoshopped. Eastern Passenger Flight 401 developed a chain of problems on its approach to Miami on December 29, 1972. Problems centered on the fact that the crew did not receive instrument confirmation that the landing gear had locked into place. As the pilot, co-pilot and flight engineer worked to solve this potential threat to landing safely, they lost track of the fact they were losing altitude. They were over the Everglades and so had no lights on the ground for visual clues.

The passenger jet plowed into the Everglades. Sixty-seven passengers survived, ninety-four died. Captain Bob Loft survived the impact but was so severely injured that he died during the rescue efforts. Don Repo, Flight Engineer, survived long enough to reach the hospital, but he also died. Eastern Flight 401 remains one of the worst crashes in American aviation history.

Soon, the ghosts of Don Repo and Bob Loft began to manifest on other Eastern flights; they always appeared individually, never together. The first manifestation happened when a woman passenger sat next to a man with ashen pale skin and a vacant, glazed look in his eyes. She called the flight attendant out of concern for this man who refused to look at either woman. Suddenly, he vanished!

This is the last photo of Eastern Flight 401.

The passenger was extremely upset but when she calmed down, she identified a picture of Flight Engineer Don Repo.

Captain Bob Loft was first spotted wandering around the undercarriage of an Eastern flight preparing for departure. Loft even spoke to the ground crew, insisting that no checks were required as he had already done them. The pilot of this flight was so unnerved that he canceled the flight.

Don and Bob continued to show up on Eastern flights for several years. There is a long, fascinating list of their appearances, including the time Don Repo warned of a malfunction which turned out to be real. He may have saved many lives. Experienced, trustworthy pilots and crew encountered these Flight 401 pilots and made reports frequently for several years.

How could the ghost pilots of Flight 401 keep showing up on other Eastern Airline flights (they only showed up on Eastern)? The only plausible explanation which emerged is that there was a corporate decision to use undamaged parts of Flight 401 on other jets in the fleet. In other words, Eastern Air Lines cannibalized and reused pieces of the wreckage in other airliners. So, as one official put it, "I guess we recycled Loft and Repo too."

THE REAL LIFE UFO TRANSFORMATION OF DIANE TESSMAN

The ghosts of Flight Engineer Don Repo and Captain Bob Loft were seen on other Eastern jets that used recycled parts from the doomed flight 401.

But, how could this be, scientifically speaking? The only answer seems to be that bits of consciousness of the two pilots were fused into the cannibalized Flight 401 parts salvaged out of the wreckage. Perhaps DNA enters into this phenomenon, at this point no one knows for sure; but many ghosts seem to be fused into the highway intersection, the house, the river bank, the hotel room, the plane debris, whatever the place, in which they died violently.

GHOSTS, PART OF THE SIMULATION

Respected physicists and other scientists are positive that our reality is a simulation created by a highly advanced computer of alien origin; or as a variation, possibly our reality is a part of the simulation which is the nature of the universe itself. Ten days before he died, Stephen Hawking announced, "We live in the matrix," and he added, "The universe is holographic in nature."

Dr. Hawking is not alone in this conclusion. One of the pioneers of the "computer simulation" theory is Nick Bostrom, a highly respected professor at the University of Oxford and Director of the Future of Humanity Institute. Rich Terrell, of the NASA Jet Propulsion Laboratory, California Institute of Technology, has helped design missions to Mars, discovered four new moons around Saturn, Neptune and Uranus and taken pictures of the distant solar system. Terrell also is a proponent of our reality being a computer simulation. Elon Musk is another proponent. The theory that we live in a computer simulation is not considered that far-fetched these days.

If we do live in an advanced quantum computer simulation, fitting ghosts into it is a slam dunk! In fact, this theory also easily explains paranormal events, angels, demons, and extraterrestrials who visit Earth in their flying saucers. All of these would be simply a part of the simulation and programmed into the reality as easily as a cat or a tree, or a human. Envision an advanced video game on steroids!

The simulation ghosts could be given a degree of awareness or could remain "vacant," gazing straight ahead with their ghoulish eyes. Their clothes could be from any civilization, be it ancient Rome or the Wild West of America. They could look like your Aunt Sally who just passed, or Charlie Manson. Perhaps they are in our simulation to stimulate our curiosity and spiritual search.

When researching the computer simulation theory, the distinction is made between "computer simulation" and "computer emulation." A simulation is like a video game wherein no internal sensitivities are programmed; however, in a computer emulation, emotions, intuition, all the traits which are human, are experienced. Ghosts might be computer simulated while we are emulated.

Consciousness itself could be emulated inartificial intelligence; this is the huge step which artificial intelligence will probably take some day. We all see this AI challenge coming; what will happen when artificial intelligence achieves consciousness?

Therefore, a civilization advanced beyond our present state, could equip human and animal members of its computer simulation with consciousness, while others, like ghosts, would have less-than-consciousness within the simulation; these ghosts would have images but not which remain permanent. Ghosts would come and go like a dream, within the emulation.

DARK MATTER GHOSTS

We are composed of baryonic (visible) matter. Physicists have discovered invisible dark matter, which is abundant throughout the universe. In fact, there is approximately six times more dark matter than visible matter. However, dark matter has proved difficult to track down even though it is all around and through us. What if there is a form of intelligence within this elusive dark matter, just as in our world of matter?

If there is consciousness and intelligence within dark matter, it might have the ability to project into this visible world of ours. Perhaps ghosts are part of the images that the dark world projects to us. ("Dark" is used here as "invisible," not "evil").Dark matter permeates us, it is everywhere. Earth also has a dark matter halo many times larger than our rocky, solid Earth. Earth's dark halo is also considered to be Earth, and its existence is far older than humankind.

Why would dark matter intelligence project ghosts into our world? We can't guess their thinking because even their laws of dark physics would be different than ours, but perhaps this intelligence likes to watch our behavior when we are frightened or when confronted with the unknown. Maybe they account for Jacques Vallee's "pranksters," and they do it because they can.

THE DIMENSION NEXT DOOR

If not from Dark Earth, images not only of ghosts but of angels, demons, images of Mother Mary, fairies and more, might be projections from a brane (membrane/multiverse), overlaid with our own. Physics tell us that there are indeed other dimensions touching and even banging into ours. Jacques Vallee has suggested the answer to "things that go bump in the night" throughout the history of humankind, emanate from an adjacent mysterious "place." Karl Jung also influences this concept, saying that the human subconscious interacts with a strange, mythical dimension. Either we summon these "beings of another brane" or they have the will power to come to us, connecting through our subconscious mind.

GHOSTS AS THOUGHT FORMS

Tulpa are best known as thought-forms created by accomplished Tibetan monks. They resemble humans in appearance but are thought to display bizarre behavior if the monk is not fully in control of his thought-creation. What if some human minds have this basic ability, rather like those who are inherently gifted at playing the piano? Why do most people visit an old house rumored to be haunted, and see nothing, while a few people visit the same house and see the resident ghost or at least a strange light?

THE REAL LIFE UFO TRANSFORMATION OF DIANE TESSMAN

Perhaps with the stimulus of being in a haunted house, humans unknowingly create or at least interact with the "resident energies," and create or summon a thought form whom we call a ghost. Karl Jung's theory of the power of the human subconscious works into this theory as well. In fact, it may be several blended theories which account for ghosts – a coincidental confluence of circumstances.

DO ALIEN PLANETS HAVE GHOSTS?

If we humans don't annihilate ourselves, we will find out one day if alien planets have ghosts as well. However, the ghosts might have the last laugh because we still might not know who and what they are!

Perhaps ghosts are interdimensional beings who are living in another reality of the multiverse.

THE REAL LIFE UFO TRANSFORMATION OF DIANE TESSMAN

Diane, back in Iowa, at the ruins of a settlers' outpost.

THE REAL LIFE UFO TRANSFORMATION OF DIANE TESSMAN

Diane with her dog Hannah.

Chapter Four

There Are Places I'll Remember

There are places I'll remember
All my life, though some have changed
Some forever, not for better
Some have gone, and some remain
All these places had their moments
With lovers and friends, I still can recall
Some are dead, and some are living
In my life, I've loved them all – **The Beatles**

I have lived in many places in this "Diane" lifetime, including Ireland to which I have devoted a chapter. I would now like to list the other fascinating places I have lived and explain one or two phenomena that happened in each. In every instance, what happened was inexplicable, extraordinary, and often mind boggling. I suspect if most experiencers look at their lives in this way, they too will see that strange things happen all over the place!

ST. THOMAS, VIRGIN ISLANDS, 1971-1976

OBEAH IN THE ISLANDS

I obtained my first teaching job fresh out of college on St. Thomas, Virgin Islands. My parents, young daughter, and I moved to St. Thomas from Florida. The first and second graders I taught there were local children who grew up with tales of Obeah (the Caribbean form of voodoo). I was intrigued with the similarity to legends and urban myths in other areas of the world; the children I taught whispered about the "cow foot woman" and "the foxhole man," who might steal them in the moonless dark night. I was reminded of "The Stolen Child" by W.B Yeats, which I have quoted in the Irish chapter. Yes, the Irish faeries were said to steal children also, and no doubt this terrifying legend exists in nearly all folk cultures.

THE BEACH-GOING, BULLET-HOLE GHOST

My parents, Gianna, and I rented a lovely big house overlooking the Caribbean Sea. My father worked at a freeport shop in downtown Charlotte Amalie, and he knew the wealthy owners of this house. They were happy to have it rented. It had bullet holes in several places; rumor was, it was related to the fact our landlord was an abortion doctor in New York. I don't know the details or if this was even true, but I did see a "wisp" sail by within the house, on three different occasions, which might have been a ghost.

This possible ghost never fully materialized except once, to my father. This was almost funny because he, of all people, just had no interest or belief in ghosts. However, he did not dismiss them, but my mother did. She stated many times "I do not believe in ghosts." Dad just didn't seem to care one way or the other.

One afternoon when he had the house to himself, he swore that a woman dressed like she was going down to the beach, which was just a brief walk, sailed right past him as he sat watching baseball on television. He said he wondered briefly why I was home early from (teaching) school, but then he realized (to quote him), "She wasn't made of the same molecules as the rest of us." He swore that she walked through the wall "as if it wasn't there," and left. Was she the murder victim, were those bullet holes in the house, where she had been standing?

This was our view of Frenchman's Reef Resort and the Caribbean from our gallery.

THE REAL LIFE UFO TRANSFORMATION OF DIANE TESSMAN

A ghost almost dressed for the beach. Very similar to the one my dad witnessed.

GIANNA AND MAMA (ME) HAVE A UFO EXPERIENCE

Our little family often ate the evening meal in the warm trade winds on the gallery, overlooking Morningstar Beach, Frenchman's Reef, and the Caribbean. One evening while my parents went inside to watch TV, Gianna and I were sitting in the gallery, watching lights in the sky over the Caribbean Sea. We knew the planes well; we even were familiar with the flares which the Navy sent up as they played war games and bombing practice. Most of their bombs fell on Vieques, a small island off Puerto Rico which we could glimpse off our gallery.

But then we started watching a different light which was closer to us, between St. Thomas and Vieques. It had green, orange, and red lights, which were a strange combination for air traffic, and it seemed to be shimmering or possibly rotating, but the dark night would not let us quite confirm that. It seemed to be hovering.

Gianna was four or five years old but held her concentration on it, absolutely mesmerized. We watched it for perhaps thirty-five minutes and then, I think we came inside. I really don't remember but I know we both had to get up for school the next day.

THE REAL LIFE UFO TRANSFORMATION OF DIANE TESSMAN

Gianna chooses this illustration as most similar to the craft she witnessed on St. Thomas, and years later, in Florida.

Gianna and I have discussed this sighting in recent years, and she swears that after a few minutes, the unidentified object flew directly overhead and it was rotating. She does not feel certain she has ever had an encounter or abduction but, she says, "If that ever happened, this was probably it."

And what about me, her protective Mama? I have no re collection other than, this object was way out, over the Caribbean, with different colored lights, and it seemed not to move.

DIFFERENT STROKES FOR DIFFERENT FOLKS

This brings me to a phenomenon which happens often when two people spot a UFO or UAP (unidentified aerial phenomenon).

I personally have had this happen twice with my daughter and several times with a close friend. One of us experiences a close-up sighting or even an encounter, while the other one (who is equally or more fascinated with the UFO topic), experiences only a distant strange object. I offer several examples in this chapter.

My family and I left St. Thomas in 1976 for three reasons, as much as we loved its exquisite beauty and its tolerance of all races.

THE REAL LIFE UFO TRANSFORMATION OF DIANE TESSMAN

1) There was a teacher's strike and I was forced to take a job as Assistant Sales Manager at Frenchman's Reef Holiday Inn, right down the path from our house. Sounds great! However, I was cooped up all day in a small windowless office with the sales manager who was a chain smoker. I feel the asthma I have today was partially brought about by her selfishness. I was also a lousy assistant sales manager; my friends who subscribe to my newsletters know the standing joke which is unfortunately true, I am a lousy secretary, even to myself.

2) St. Thomas is ten square miles, and as breathtakingly gorgeous as it is, it offers few opportunities. I was thinking about what Gianna would do in her teens, what vistas might open for her and it seemed there weren't many. However, being biracial, she remembers St. Thomas very fondly for its acceptance of all kinds of people, its incredible beaches, and for its vibrant, colorful carnivals with intoxicating steel drum music. Sometimes I feel we should not have left.

Bloody scene at Fountain Valley Golf Club where eight people were massacred.

3) That enlightened tolerance in the Virgin Islands was diminishing due to the Black Power Movement. White people (those who actually lived there) were 1% of the population which was fine, as long as tolerance guided the society. However, four local young black men who had been drafted to Vietnam and learned to kill, came back home and massacred seven (white) tourists and one black chef at Fountain Valley Golf Course, St. Croix. There were (and are) justified grievances against "the Yankee dollar" and the wealthy white people who used the islands for a retreat (such a Jeffrey Epstein), but contributed nothing to the welfare of the local people. However, my parents and I were not wealthy, we have always been "the working class," and after Fountain Valley, we began to fear for our safety.

I had participated in sit-ins in Bradenton, Florida, when in high school and was a civil rights supporter and sometimes activist. I really hated to give into fear after five years on St. Thomas, but, after five years, we packed up and went back to Florida. I gave up my teacher's retirement money to bring all my cats back with me. That figures!

THE REAL LIFE UFO TRANSFORMATION OF DIANE TESSMAN

ST. PETERSBURG, FLORIDA, 1976 – 1982

Of all the places I have lived, St. Pete, Florida delivered the most strangeness of any. Where do I begin?

I began teaching in a local elementary school. I enjoyed teaching English as a Second Language to children who spoke little or no English. Families were arriving from war-torn Vietnam, Laos, Cambodia, and Thailand. These children had been affected by witnessing war close-up. When enrolled in a new American school, they sat there – lost.

Many of my ESL students were older than children would normally be in first and second grade, but their parents wanted them to have a full American education. Therefore, my ESL class had children from age of six, as well as some older boys who had moustaches. ESL was my best teaching experience, because my strengths of creativity and "living in the Now" were utilized, whereas in the regular classroom, I was bored and rebellious.

School teacher Diane, ready for a day of teaching English to recent newcomers in St. Pete, Florida.

THE REAL LIFE UFO TRANSFORMATION OF DIANE TESSMAN

My ESL class soon learned some English as I pointed to the door and they repeated "door." It was real "seat of your pants" teaching and I loved it. They soon began to blossom and we challenged the entire school to a math contest. We won! Does this play into the stereotype that Asians are good at math? Who knows, but this school-wide challenge did wonders for the ESL children's self-esteem and pride, and most of them were soon fluent English speakers.

In my spare time, I became field investigator for the well-respected Aerial Phenomenon Research Organization (APRO), as well as, an investigator and State Section Director with the Mutual UFO Network (MUFON).

MY YEAR OF AWAKENING, 1979: "THE BEEPS" ARRIVE

Gianna and I began hearing bizarre beeps in our house in St. Pete, which had wonderful huge old oak trees. The house had been built on a spot where Native Americans had gathered to eat. The yard was covered with conch shells with holes drilled through them; it reminded me of oysters on the half-shell. Our house was only a block from Tampa Bay, so it was most likely the source of the conches.

Native lands sometimes have spiritual or paranormal events, but the beeps we heard, were electronic. We heard them first in the television set at five before the hour, almost every hour. There was intelligence behind them. I figured it was the TV station or perhaps a military signal caught by the TV station. However, the beeps sounded closer and not a part of the soundtrack on the TV; it seemed the television set itself was beeping.

MacDill Air Force base was an important military base in 1978, and I suspected it might be the source, but why would my house intercept its signals?

The entire phenomenon got stranger when the beeps stopped being predictably timed and began beeping randomly. They moved out of the television and manifested in a lamp, also "on" a bedroom wall, in a hair drier, in the bathroom light fixture, in my daughter's cassette recorder, and other places. They never beeped in two places at once but would beep several times a day, somewhere.

How could the lamp or the wall beep when they had no beeping mechanism? This told me that "the beeps" were not sent into the objects but outside them. My parents heard them too.

Gianna and I took her cassette recorder on battery power, about a block away, and we recorded several beeps there. We played the beeps back and there they were!

THE REAL LIFE UFO TRANSFORMATION OF DIANE TESSMAN

The bizarre beeps we heard in our Florida house for over a year, sounded like the bridge of the Enterprise.

Tim Beckley, who traveled to Florida to take me to dinner and hear my accounts, heard the recorded replay of them; but, by the time he arrived from New York, it was 1980 and "the beeps" themselves, had left.

There was no earthly explanation for these technical signals. Maybe they were paranormal, but they seemed technical as if emanating more from the bridge of the Enterprise than a haunted house.

However, the beeps might have been connected to a coming tragic disaster.

THE SKYWAY BRIDGE COLLAPSES

May 9, 1980, at 7:33 a.m., I was hurriedly getting myself and my daughter ready for school, when our smoke alarm started to beep. The fire alarm had not "had the beeps" before.

I raced around to check for fire, and then realized it was not the fire warning, but also not the "battery low" signal. It sounded exactly like Morse code, but I did not know Morse code. My dad was trying to remember what he knew of Morse code, when we heard a television bulletin that a barge had just rammed into the Skyway Bridge at approximately 7:35 a.m.

Following collapse of Skyway Bridge, a Buick teeters on the edge.

Here is what's left of the Greyhound Bus which plunged into Tampa Bay with thirty people on board.

The smoke alarm had stopped a few minutes after 7:35, and it never did that again. Had whatever been beeping at us all those months, finally arrived at the awaited hour and in a frenzy, sent its message?

Was the Morse code tapped out in my smoke alarm, a desperate call for help from the energy-bodies of those who had just left their physical form? The Skyway Bridge was a tall structure and to plunge off it, there would be a few seconds of falling, falling, falling in sheer panic through the air in your vehicle, and then, death.

Thirty-five people died that morning in their cars and in a Greyhound Bus, when one span of the Skyway Bridge was rammed by the Summit Venture barge and collapsed.

The beeps happened in 1979, into spring of 1980. Our house was one block from Tampa Bay; the Skyway Bridge can be viewed from the park at the end of our street.

On the other hand, were the beeps not connected to the Skyway disaster, but instead from future humans or ETs, signaling me that this was my year of awakening? Even Tibus himself?

YEAR OF AWAKENING, 1979, EXCELLENT UFO SIGHTINGS

In the bizarre summer of 1979, Gianna and I had two excellent UFO sightings. One of them was similar to the colorful, rotating UFO over the Caribbean Sea which Gianna remembers more vividly and closer-up than I do. She and I spent a lot of time in the summer outdoors, watching the stars. One night, a circular UFO appeared out of nowhere and hung over the vacant lot across the street to the west. Yes, it was very close and that's all I remember; as in St. Thomas, I am not sure when it left.

Gianna remembers that it rotated, had orange and blue lights, and slowly "floated" from the vacant lot to exactly over our heads, where it remained for perhaps three minutes. She says it reminded her of the spinning top she had as a toddler. She does not remember any interaction with the occupants. We both agree, it made no noise.

Here is another example of one person having more extensive memories of a UFO than their companion. This UFO was similar to the UFO sighting over the Caribbean, which had been approximately five years ago. It almost seems it is there for Gianna exclusively in both cases.

THE REAL LIFE UFO TRANSFORMATION OF DIANE TESSMAN

The most spectacular UFO sighting of my life thus far, which I remember consciously, was over the park at the end of our street from which the Skyway Bridge could be seen. Incidentally, I never saw the outside of a large craft when I was abducted at age four; I may have glimpsed an area of the side of a craft, like glimpsing a small bit of a huge airliner.

It was a summer night in 1979, the year of my awakening, when my daughter and I took our dog Bailey to the park. When we got there, a small crowd of people were watching something in the sky. There were two huge spheres hanging over Tampa Bay, about midway between the horizon and the zenith of the sky. They were like double moons!

We took the dog home and raced back to the park. Unlike weather balloons, these brilliant white spheres did not drift at all. But, perhaps this was rocket fuel from a military test at MacDill Air Force Base, Tampa? No, then this phenomenon should have slowly dissipated. Besides, these looked solid and yet, had undulating or shimmering quality.

This is the closest illustration I can find of the two white spheres over Tampa Bay. I tried to take photos but there was nothing when the film was developed.

THE REAL LIFE UFO TRANSFORMATION OF DIANE TESSMAN

We could not take our eyes from them but finally I looked down for just a second, and one of the two dazzling white spheres had disappeared in the wink of an eye. Not a trace of it was left. Strangely, it was the sphere with which I felt I was trying to establish communication. I tried not to feel insulted.

The other orb stayed there, not budging an inch, until we gave up and went home at 2:30 a.m. I had to teach school in the morning, Gianna had to go to school, but I have kicked myself ever since for leaving. No weather balloon, rocket fuel debris, helicopter, or Chinese lantern hoax, would have stayed stationary for all those hours. These mysterious spheres were about the size of a full moon midway through its night's travels; they were identical in size and every way. We will always remember them!

1979 was the year I finally came to grips with the fact that I had been abducted by a UFO as a child. I had "snapshot" conscious memories, had always had these, but did not know what "scenario" or what reality they came from. What experience was this of Little Diane's?

It seems that experiencers almost always go through a "time of awakening," whether it is one week, six weeks or a year. We finally recognize that something strange has indeed happened to us and that UFO occupants probably play a part in this phenomenon. Me, I took a plane to Laramie, Wyoming and underwent hypnotic regression with the respected Dr. R. Leo Sprinkle of University of Wyoming. With the regression, I began to remember the specifics of my encounters, so that my conscious snapshots began to be filled in with detailed memories.

MAMA AND GIANNA TREK TO SOUTHERN CALFORNIA, 1982

Yes, that is "trek" as in **Original Series Star Trek,** because like many other people, I was finding this amazing 1966-1968 television series to be full of metaphysical energies and astounding insights about the future. I make no apologies for the fact that **TOS** has sustained my personal quest and even helped me psychologically, giving me reassurance and insight.

We had lived in St. Pete for six years after returning from the Virgin Islands. Gianna found Florida to be a prejudiced place in which to grow up; it still felt like the Old South. I had begun to feel teaching was a prison for me. I liked the children, but the red tape and the structure were killing my free spirit.

THE REAL LIFE UFO TRANSFORMATION OF DIANE TESSMAN

And so, with limited funds, Gianna and I moved to San Diego, California, with Ripley our talking Wookie (Old English sheepdog), eight cats, and Gianna's gerbil collection, in our old green 1974 Plymouth Valiant.

I had resigned myself to getting into teaching in San Diego, but it turned out, California required a master's degree which I did not have. There was also a recession in 1982 and they were not hiring. The first year in San Diego was difficult financially, and that's putting it diplomatically. I took jobs I never dreamed of having to take, and I did poorly at them. I was trained for nothing but teaching.

A bright spot that first year was that Tim Beckley came to see us, as he had in Florida. Tim asked if I hear from Tibus in my mind. I said, "I do." He asked if I thought I could do psychic readings. I said, "I don't think so."

Tim gave me the confidence to try, he took out an ad for my services in the local paper, and soon I was doing psychic parties and "reading" for some amazing people. One of these people was an elderly former minister from Atlanta, Georgia, who owned marriage chapels in Reno. He loved to talk with me about Christian mysticism and the phenomenon of human intuition. He was wealthy and wanted to help me launch a new age career. Thanks to him, six months after being financially destitute, I bought a house for Gianna, me, and our animals in Poway, California. In those days, California was truly the "anything can happen" state.

Tim Beckley, pictured here with a friend, helped me have the confidence to begin my writing and channeling career in San Diego.

THE REAL LIFE UFO TRANSFORMATION OF DIANE TESSMAN

Tim Beckley then helped me launch the career I was better suited for than psychic readings, which was writing Tibus' spiritual messages and personal readings, sent out to subscribers. The new age was thriving in the mid-1980s. Tibus loved it and had perhaps guided the whole thing, because now he and I worked shoulder to shoulder, even though in different timeframes (dimensions).

The Star Network Heartline newsletter has been published without fail, since 1983. I also wrote **The Transformation** in 1983 and Tim's **Inner Light** company published it, helping greatly to let people know about our messages.

BLACK MOUNTAIN STRING OF PEARLS UFO

This photo taken over San Diego, is similar to the string of pearls my friend and I witnessed, but there was also a big "mothership."

While my friend and fellow Trekker Della and I were taking a night drive along Black Mountain Road, between San Diego and Poway, we saw a large bright object overhead but slightly toward the western sky. However, it was not alone! There were six to ten small objects in a string stretching out of it, or beside it, like chicks stretched out from a mother hen.

I am not sure of the exact number, because it varied for no discernible reason; maybe some of the small lights went behind the big one at certain moments? Or maybe they flew back into the big ship, like a shuttle heading into the Enterprise.

I remember that we stopped the car (Della was driving), and got out, watching in wonder and curiosity. We gazed at it for perhaps twenty minutes, wondering if it might be a refueling operation from Miramar Navy Air Station near San Diego, but that didn't make sense. Incidentally, later we studied refueling maneuvers in mid-air and it definitely was not this.

Here again, one witness thought it was a much bigger deal than the other. This time, it is me who remembers watching it much longer and seeing it much clearer, than Della remembers. Yes, Della was driving but she is not sure that she remembers we even stopped. All very strange! The best thing is that Della and I are still best friends today.

Della and I began feeling psychic cries of help coming from a government installation near Poway which operated in unison with a large, powerful corporation. We felt that this mostly underground facility had captured aliens from crashed flying saucers, perhaps cryogenically frozen while they were still alive. Just imagine, if this happened to a person, your mind might be locked in your frozen body but still functioning to some degree. The term "dreams of the sleepers" encapsulates the messages Della and I were telepathically receiving.

Our interest was made more intense because our contacts in Space-Time (mine is Tibus), knew these frozen victims and were distressed about them.

We watched this installation, which was down in a valley and looked like the landing strip in **Close Encounters of the Third Kind,** for over 5 years. We rode our horses through the very remote, guarded, gated facility on Christmas Day one year by going in the back way and hoping that there were few guards on Christmas Day. There were large canisters of liquid nitrogen, sometimes used in cryonics, and we saw that perhaps 90% of it was underground. We made it through that Christmas Day without us and our horses ending up in jail.

Finally, this unbearable burden of knowing but not being able to help was part of the reason my "psychic antenna" turned toward the siren call of Ireland. About the time I moved to Ireland in 1989, this place moved to Alaska.

There were rumors that Dr. J. Allan Hynek was finally taken to see "alien bodies" at an installation "near San Diego," shortly before his death from brain cancer. I have never been able to get more information on it than this.

Gianna and I had lived from 1982 to 1989 in California; we both love "Cally" to this day. Gianna still lives there.

Now we are back to Ireland, which I shared in an earlier chapter.

THE REAL LIFE UFO TRANSFORMATION OF DIANE TESSMAN

My friend and I psychically received an SOS from captive aliens, perhaps cryogenically frozen.

R. Leo Sprinkle, PhD. hypnotically regressed me and I remembered details of my first encounter with Tibus and his shipmates.

Chapter Five

Joshua Tree, Giant Rock, And The Powers of George Van Tassel

Talk about a dramatic change of scenery, from rainy, damp Ireland to the Mojave Desert (called the High Desert), of California!

We arrived in the U-Haul truck, two big dogs, fifteen cats, two humans, having driven across the country. I had arrived at JFK Airport from Ireland just four days earlier. My friend Della let us all stay at her place a few days, in the High Desert, and then I managed to find a nice rental house.

ENCOUNTER IN THE DESERT NIGHT

Certainly, the desert nights are more fascinating than the desert days; one night soon after our arrival, we drove into the Joshua Tree National Park at sunset and stayed into the night. The desert gets cold at night and hot in the daytime, but we had brought blankets, jackets, water, and snacks.

The gigantic, bizarre rock formations and the alien-like Joshua Trees tend to make a person think she is on an extraterrestrial planet thousands of light years from Earth. The four of us were sharing feelings and thoughts along these lines when Gianna pointed to the west and said, "Look!"

There was a brilliant "star" heading right for us, at an altitude of perhaps a few thousand feet! For a second, I thought it was a meteorite and we were about to have the bad luck of getting hit by it. This impression was fortified by the fact it was obviously dipping lower.

However, instead of crashing, it dipped and then soared way back up and away. It had seemed remarkably close and extremely bright. It had no blinking lights, no color but "brilliant light." There was no noise at all. Gianna, Della, her friend, and I agreed on these facts. It was great to have four witnesses, not just one.

THE REAL LIFE UFO TRANSFORMATION OF DIANE TESSMAN

We stayed there another hour, hoping and not-hoping it would come back. The entire experience was exhilarating and yet frightening simply because of the speed, the "close call," and seemingly personal focus on the four of us, which this unknown object or light displayed.

There were other UFO sightings in the High Desert; one involved a light chasing our car, another seemed connected to a vision which Gianna had of an ancient tribe picking leaves off a tree in our yard. She knew this was a vision, not reality, but then she saw (and I also witnessed), an unidentified aerial object hanging overhead which simply disappeared before our eyes.

Unknown flying object against the beauty of a High Desert evening.

THE REAL LIFE UFO TRANSFORMATION OF DIANE TESSMAN

GEORGE VAN TASSEL BECKONS THE ETS WITH HIS TIME MACHINE IN THE DESERT

A photo of George van Tassel's gathering to greet ETs with an illustration of UFOs overhead.

George Van Tassel is one of the pioneers of future human and ET contact, as well as, being a creative genius who built the Integratron. As I explored the Joshua Tree and Giant Rock area, I became fascinated with the spirit and the thoughts of this amazing man.

George van Tassel was born in Jefferson, Ohio in 1910 and grew up in a fairly prosperous middle-class family. He finished high school in the 10th grade and held a job at a small municipal airport near Cleveland; he also acquired a pilot's license. At age 20, he moved to California, where at first he worked as an automobile mechanic at a garage owned by an uncle. Whether we believe van Tassel's entire story or not, we agree that his is an American story to which we can relate.

While pumping gas at the garage, George met Frank Critzer, an eccentric loner who claimed to be working a mine somewhere near Giant Rock, which is a gigantic boulder in the middle of a flat, boulder-less desert area near Landers, California in the Mojave Desert. This one huge rock looks like it beamed down.

THE REAL LIFE UFO TRANSFORMATION OF DIANE TESSMAN

A man on top of Giant Rock shows how big the boulder is.

Frank Critzer was a German immigrant trying to make a living in the desert as a prospector. During World War II, Critzer was under suspicion as a German spy and was killed by a dynamite explosion during a police siege at the Rock in 1942. Upon receiving news of Critzer's death, Van Tassel applied for a lease of the small abandoned airport near Giant Rock from the Bureau of Land Management and was eventually given a federal government contract to develop and maintain the airstrip.

Van Tassel became an aircraft mechanic and inspector who, between 1930 and 1947, worked for Douglas Aircraft, Hughes Aircraft, and Lockheed. In 1947, Van Tassel left Southern California's booming aerospace industry to live in the desert with his family. At first, he lived a simple existence in the rooms Frank Critzer had dug out under Giant Rock. Van Tassel eventually built a new home, a cafe, a gas station, a store, a small airstrip, and a dude ranch beside the famous Giant Rock.

George started hosting group meditation in 1953 in the room underneath Giant Rock. That year, according to Van Tassel, the occupant of a spaceship from Venus woke him up and invited him on board his spaceship. This ET verbally and telepathically gave George a technique for rejuvenating the human body.

In 1954, Van Tassel and others began building the "Integratron" to perform the rejuvenation about which the Venusian extraterrestrial spoke. According to Van Tassel, the Integratron was to be a structure for scientific research into time, anti-gravity and extending human life It was built partially upon the research of Nikola Tesla and Georges Lakhovsky, known as the Russian Tesla.

Van Tassel described the Integratron as being created for scientific and spiritual research with the aim to recharge and rejuvenate people's cells, "a time machine for basic research on rejuvenation, anti-gravity and time travel."

THE REAL LIFE UFO TRANSFORMATION OF DIANE TESSMAN

The Integratron is a fascinating structure.

The domed wood structure has a rotating metal apparatus on the outside he called an "electrostatic dirod." It was made of non-ferromagnetic materials: wood, concrete, glass, and fiberglass, lacking even metal screws or nails. "Non-Ferromagnetic" means materials having no magnetic charge and no iron.

The Integratron was never fully completed due to Van Tassel's sudden death a few weeks before the official opening in 1978. In recent times, some people who visit the unfinished Integratron claim to be rejuvenated while staying there and have experienced "cleansing baths of vibrational sound" inside.

What intrigued me most with George van Tassel was his journey as a UFO contactee; today, contactees are usually called "experiencers." George was a classic 1950s contactee in the mold of George Adamski, Truman Bethurum, Daniel Fry, Orfeo Angelucci and many others. He hosted **The Giant Rock Spacecraft Convention** annually beside Giant Rock, from 1953 to 1978.

In 1959, this event attracted 10,000 attendees. Guests trekked to the desert by car or landed airplanes on Van Tassel's small airstrip, called Giant Rock Airport.

THE REAL LIFE UFO TRANSFORMATION OF DIANE TESSMAN

George and others would summon the spacecraft to come down and greet the crowd. The anticipation and atmosphere were electric. Van Tassel, like many others, felt he received spiritual messages from his friends "up there." He left behind mystical writings which are inspiring and deep.

Sadly, on the morning of February 21, 2000, at 8:20 a.m., an extraordinary event occurred. The immense boulder of igneous quartz monzonite called Giant Rock, formed some 65 to 136 million years ago, cracked wide open. Native legend has it that when this boulder cracks, the end of the world is coming. It has not come yet, but sometimes we do wonder!

Giant Rock withstood endless campfires built adjacent to it. It withstood dirt bikes and motorcycles rumbling about, besmirching it and its territory. The old German prospector's tunnel under Giant Rock probably didn't help either, even though it was mostly filled in.

All in all, when the sacred rock split wide open, there was gleaming white quartz inside. Had this white quartz been a signal to the spaceships?

This photo shows the split in Giant Rock and the beautiful white quartz inside.

THE REAL LIFE UFO TRANSFORMATION OF DIANE TESSMAN

Gianna and I visited Landers and its Giant Rock many times in the two years we lived in the Mojave. I made a video with Gianna as my very capable camera person, about Giant Rock with meditations and channelings right from that spot.

www.youtube.com/watch?v=DJZmQDT67DM

We also made a video while in Ireland. "Diane's Magical Mystery Tour of Ireland."

www.youtube.com/watch?v=clrGp3YHc_c

More recently, we have a video entitled "Diane's Animal House from Iowa," featuring our many wonderful animals and Tibus' channelings.

www.youtube.com/watch?v=Kjle7xlYBa4

I felt loving but mind-bending energies coming from Giant Rock which were the echoes of the past and the hopes for the future that George van Tassel embodied.

Diane contemplates Giant Rock in the distance.

THE REAL LIFE UFO TRANSFORMATION OF DIANE TESSMAN

Tibus came in loud and clear at Giant Rock, and I felt that he had perhaps zoomed by in his shuttle craft during the huge contact gatherings in the 1950s and 1960s.

I had an amazing channeling experience in the Joshua Tree National Forest as well. The praying mantis-like alien species came to me psychically; they never had before. A mind-blowing meditation and channeling session caught on video is the result. Although they are "very alien," I experienced their ability to love and their high intelligence.

MESSAGE FROM TIBUS, "IOWA CHILDHOOD THE RETURN HOME"

Greetings! I would like to complete this chapter with a message. It was clear that Diane is not a desert person; she is happier if it is 30 degrees F. outside than if it is 80 degrees. Perhaps this is because she grew up in North Iowa; she spread strong roots into the rich Iowa soil which produces such magnificent nature, if only it is not corporate-farmed to death.

Her parents moved to Florida when she was ten years old and "our Diane" never did like Florida; she yearned for the land of Iowa much as the Lakota do. Besides, Florida was hot and humid.

The Iowa land which she loved as a child was the natural land of the Native Americans. She had Lakota teachers in the form of voices and vibrations from the past as she wandered their land with her dogs and cats. In a sense, she felt this was her true family.

After she and I encountered each other when she was four and five years old, she experienced an invisible presence whom she calls The Re-members. They were not playmates, they did not speak with actual voices, but they were there whenever she was outdoors, watching and (I will add), protecting.

Therefore, when Gianna moved out of their house in Joshua Tree, Diane suddenly heard the call to go back home to Iowa. She had always remembered that land and discovered that old farmhouses standing on a few acres which corporate farming could not use, were relatively cheap.

Diane had never been back to Iowa since age ten, but she took a leap of faith and made a down payment on an old farmhouse, built in 1901, on ten acres. She and four dogs and (if we remember correctly) seventeen cats, got in her old pick-up truck and set course for North Iowa. When they crossed the Rocky

THE REAL LIFE UFO TRANSFORMATION OF DIANE TESSMAN

Mountains, Diane told the animals to "lean forward" because the old pick-up could only manage ten miles an hour going up the steep grade.

They made it! Maybe I gave a push and maybe I didn't!

Her almost twenty-four years back in Iowa have been involved in learning and understanding animal consciousness in great depth, as well as having the precious time to work with Gaia, the living spirit of Mother Earth.

At the close of this book is our chapter entitled "Unconditional Love, Thy Name Is Cats and Dogs" in which you will enjoy hearing about Diane's animals and their incredible stories. Miracles exist here!

You will hear about our **Star Network Animal Sanctuary and Wildlife Refuge** *which Diane's extraordinary friends, the star people (her subscribers, readers, and friends) keep going through love offerings.*

We (all of us in the **Star Network***), have saved many beautiful cats and dogs, giving them a forever home. We have also created ten acres of pure Iowa nature, away from the chemicals and cruelty of corporate farming. Please let Diane know if you are interested in joining our* **Star People's Network.**

May the healing light of goodness surround you, always.

—**TIBUS**

DIANE HERE: What of my amazing psychic and UFO experiences in Iowa the past twenty-four years? Yes, I have seen some strange craft and phenomena in the sky, I have had an "electronic cricket" in the house which was not a cricket, and I experience strange synchronicities often, especially with my daughter Gianna and my friend Della.

However, my Year of Awakening was 1979, and now, I am awakened! I am a busy light worker with matters of consciousness and contact, no need for frequent fireworks!

THE REAL LIFE UFO TRANSFORMATION OF DIANE TESSMAN

Diane and Gabriel Green, George van Tassel's famous friend who ran for President of the U.S.

What was it that crashed in the desert near Roswell, N.M. in 1947?

Chapter Six

Time Traveling Humans? Wright-Patterson Medical Chief Speaks

RICH HOFFMAN OFFERS NEW INFO ON ALIEN BODIES FROM THE WRIGHT-PATTERSON CHIEF OF MEDICAL RESEARCH

"Do you think that could explain what the objects were? That they might be potentially us from let's say our future? Or maybe popping back from some sort of 'time means'? And he said, yes, that's pretty much a very plausible hypothesis."

Rich Hoffman is the much-respected, longtime UFO researcher who leads the Scientific Coalition for UAP studies. He was the guest on "Exploring the Bizarre" the popular podcast with Tim Beckley and Tim Swartz and offered startling new information on the possibility that the alien bodies brought to Wright Patterson were the bodies of time traveling humans. From the archive of the podcast, **"Exploring the Bizarre."**

Tim Swartz: *Tonight our guest is Rich Hoffman. Rich, I wanted to ask you – I know that when you lived in Dayton, Ohio, you appeared at least a couple of times at the Gil Whitney Summertime Show at WHIO-TV-7. And you had an interesting experience there when one of the producers called you in rather unexpectedly. Would you mind talking about that?*

Rich Hoffman: *Sure. It was definitely an interesting experience. One of the producers gave me a call and said that there's a gentleman that wants to meet me. Can you come down and do that? He wanted a private meeting. I said no problem. I'll see if I can get there. I made arrangements to get there. When I got there, I was basically escorted to a room that's like glass-enclosed, a private room. There was a gentleman sitting inside of it that was dressed, you know, in a suit and tie, very formal.*

THE REAL LIFE UFO TRANSFORMATION OF DIANE TESSMAN

Well known and respected, UFO investigator Rich Hoffman tells of Air Force medical examiner's incredible disclosure.

I said, "Hi. I understand that you wanted to meet me? I said, well, let's chat. Do you have an interest in UFOs?" He said, "Yes, I do." I said, "Well, what is it that you wanted to share?" So I just shut up, and he explained that he was the Chief of Aero-medical Research at Wright-Patterson Air force Base, and that he had a team of scientists that were doing broad studies on basically the returning cosmonauts and the effects of space. They were apparently sharing information with the Soviets at that time about that.

And so they were looking at that and they were trying to identify what the effects of being in space long term would be. And he made a comment that kind of blew me away where he said that he and his team had basically determined that if we were in space, let's say, for two generations, by the second generation of birth, if you would, that we as humans would start to look pretty much like the aliens that are being reported today.

And I said, Really? He said, yeah, the effects of life in the space environment would probably make us look small, diminutive, not having muscles, all that other stuff, and we would become very much like what's being reported. And I said, well, that's interesting."

THE REAL LIFE UFO TRANSFORMATION OF DIANE TESSMAN

Artist's conception of the alleged crashed flying saucer near Roswell, N.M.

"Do you think that could explain what the objects were? That they might be potentially us from let's say our future? Or maybe popping back from some sort of 'time means'?

And he said, yes, that's pretty much a very plausible hypothesis. And I said, wow, that's pretty impressive! And I asked him, have you ever investigated any kind of cases where you couldn't identify what the beings were? I was just trying to dig a little bit on that after he hit me with that mind-boggling statement.

And he said something about that he had investigated a being that was in a crash that didn't have a backbone. And I said, oh, really? Wow! So with this meeting, it's not like I was told to be quiet about it or anything like that. But I've pretty much kept it quiet. I left after this meeting. We said our goodbyes and stuff like that.

And then I did get on the phone to Len Stringfield in Cincinnati because he had connections at the base and I wanted to confirm, if he could check into whether or not there was a Doctor Leon Kazarian that was actually the Chief of Medical Research to confirm that he was real. And so Len was able to call up and basically confirm that. So that's pretty much the way the story went down. The interesting thing about it is, to me, is that he has since then basically acknowledged that his team did exist and they did do that study. But he denies having met me and having that conversation.

THE REAL LIFE UFO TRANSFORMATION OF DIANE TESSMAN

Tim Beckley: *(Laughs) Now, that's weird. That's pretty strange, actually. Is he still alive?*

Hoffman*: Yes. He's still alive, and he's still around the Dayton area. If you take a look at the book that was written by Don Schmidt and Thomas Carey – is that the name?*

Beckley: *Yeah, he was on the show just a month ago. Yeah.*

Hoffman*: Anyway, they wrote the book on the Wright Patterson case and I'm in one of the chapters about that case. They actually found out where he lived and had somebody knock on the door and again said that the person said the exact same thing that I just told you about the fact that they were doing this study but denied the fact that he knew me.*

Beckley: *Did you ever check back with – was the person named Gil? – at the station? To see if he could confirm any of this? Who else was with you at this meeting?*

Hoffman*: Well, Gil wasn't at the meeting at all. It was just me. I was the one who was brought into that glass room –*

Aerial view of Wright-Patterson Air Force Base where victims of crashed UFOs were taken as prisoner and later, autopsied.

THE REAL LIFE UFO TRANSFORMATION OF DIANE TESSMAN

Beckley: But was it Gil that brought you to the glass room?

Hoffman: No, that was a producer by the name of Gary _____. Gary was the one who called me and said there was a gentleman who wanted to speak with me. I've not been able to get a hold of Gary and I don't know if he's still alive or what. I don't know anything about his situation.

Beckley: Have you ever seen a photograph of this mysterious gentleman that you met, to see if you would recognize him?

Hoffman: Well, I would recognize him, yeah. You can do an Internet search on Dr. Leon Kazarian.

Beckley: And you've done that?

Hoffman: Yes. It's him.

Beckley: Well, there you go. It seems rather strange that he would deny that, in this day and age, because I'm sure he doesn't work for the government anymore and the project he was involved in doesn't seem like it would be high up in classification today. Now that report that he made, has anybody ever seen that? About the cosmonauts and all?

Hoffman: I think I have since gone and found some of these articles.

Beckley: it's interesting. You mention the time travel bit. One of our associates who was just on the show a couple of weeks ago, Diane Tessman –

Hoffman: Yeah, I know Diane pretty well.

Beckley: Oh, you do. I thought I would call her tomorrow and pass along this news to her. Does she know this story? She must then, right?

Hoffman: I think that she might know this story. I really don't know if she –

Beckley: Well, I will send her the episode here and she can listen to me. I always get her before 7 o'clock in the morning because she goes out and takes care of her animals. But yeah, we've sat around talking about time travel, like with Jacques Vallee and so forth. That seems to be a theory that's a little bit more realistic than just the straight out "We come from some other star system" or something.

Obviously, do you accept that as one of the top possibilities? To me, UFOs could be coming from anywhere because they're unidentified. You could have some from group A, some from place B, they don't all have to be necessarily from the same area of space or dimension or time.

THE REAL LIFE UFO TRANSFORMATION OF DIANE TESSMAN

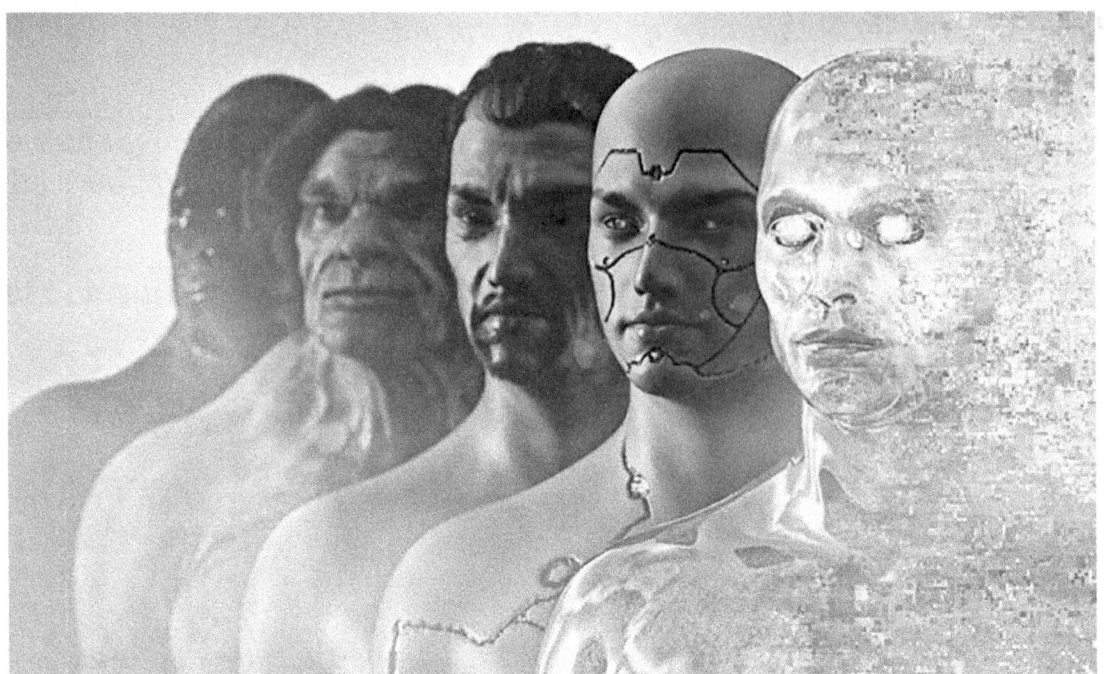

The human evolutionary line leads to humans in the future who look like what we think of as "extraterrestrials."

Hoffman: Well, I do. If you take a look at the UFO, or UAP phenomenon, whatever you want to call it, ultimately you find out that there are many of these competing hypotheses and that they all might be involved. For example, if you take a look at the Bentwaters case in 1980, you'll see that if you look at those ones and zeros that Jim Penniston talked about when he touched it that was apparently a craft from the future that it was an earth-based craft that was from the future.

So you'll find that there are some of the cases that actually could connect potentially to a time kind of a phenomenon, time and space, if you would. And then you have cases where, for example, it might appear out of nowhere or completely dissolve into nothingness. And so you then question whether there is an interdimensional kind of context to it.

And then you've also got the fact that they're always been here. So were they originally here on the planet before us? And have they just been here all along? I strongly believe that they're probably living underwater and that there's some kind of base here. They don't need to pop here to their other planet. In fact, we would do the same thing, if we were going to another planet and found that three-fourths of the planet was water. I wouldn't even call it Earth. I'd call it Planet Water.

But if you take a look at the fact that we know very little about the ocean and the fact that these things are being seen by the Navy and everything else, I think

THE REAL LIFE UFO TRANSFORMATION OF DIANE TESSMAN

that they've long been here and have got some form of an underwater base and are operating that way. That to me is more plausible.

But anyway, it's a fascinating subject, since you're basically dealing with cases that marry up to all these different hypotheses. And there's not one that we've been able to prove.

These beings are almost identical to us in general description. Spending two generations in space, would change us somewhat.

THE REAL LIFE UFO TRANSFORMATION OF DIANE TESSMAN

Diane Tessman addresses a sell out crowd at Tim Beckley's Palm Springs Conference, 1996.

Diane Tessman's book "Future Humans and the UFOs." Published by Flying Disk Press.

Chapter Seven

It's A Big Galaxy Out There Mr. Spock, Full of Time Travelers and Extraterrestrials

AN INTERVIEW WITH DIANE TESSMAN: During my first encounter with him, Tibus said something I have always remembered consciously; he said, *"We are from your future."* The following is an interview conducted in July 2020 by the **Quantum Shaman**, my fellow UFO researcher.

Quantum Shaman: Why are you so involved and even defensive of the concept that UFO occupants are time traveling humans? I know you have faced a lot of criticism from people who hold fast that UFO occupants are aliens from far distance star systems.

Diane Tessman: This is the first sentence of my book, **"Future Humans And The UFOs,"** published February 2020, *"I do not deny that there are probably thousands of advanced extraterrestrial races in the galaxy and that some may visit Earth. However, I think we have ignored what is right before our eyes; our children's children's children are the occupants in most or all unidentified flying objects!*

Quantum Shaman: So, you don't feel you threw the baby out with the bathwater to write a book which methodically goes chapter to chapter presenting evidence that the occupants are future us? I know its been said that you ignored the evidence which has been the main belief of the UFO community for years, that it is aliens from distant star systems.

Diane Tessman: First, I would ask, what evidence is there that it is aliens from other star systems? Someone might say, "Well, they don't look like us. That's obvious." However, look at an illustration of a Neanderthal, who was an archaic human subspecies. Neanderthals are as different from modern humans as we are from the humanoid UFO occupants. Yes, a different-shaped nose, different mouth, different brow-line, different cranium size, different muscle structure, but all the same features are there: mouth, brow-line, nose, cranium, muscles and two arms, two legs.

Space is so vast, actual extraterrestrials would not evolve as we have. Other planets circling other stars would have vastly different gravity, chemistry, electromagnetic field, sunlight, atmosphere, and planetary history.

Huge events, such as the asteroid which eliminated the dinosaurs, did not happen at the same time, in the same way as the asteroid strike which hit Earth. Huge events like this changed our evolutionary timeline and influenced how we physically developed. Identical events and identical timelines would not happen on another planet; the sentient creatures which another planet produces would not look like humans or humanoids. Probably, they would be stranger than we can imagine.

As for the evidence that extraterrestrials are our visitors, there is no solid evidence. Yes, we have opinions of UFO investigators and experiencers, but usually it is assumed "the aliens" are here; the evidence is about what their ship looked like to observers, how it defied gravity, and what the occupants looked like and how they acted, such as abducting modern humans. None of this evidence proves anything about the source of those within the UFO.

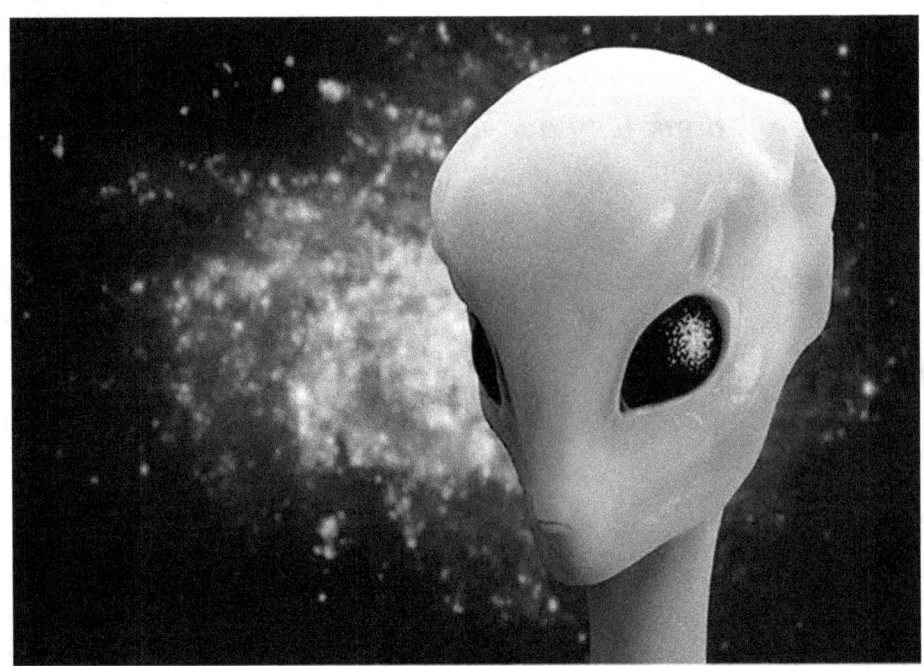

Traveler of Stars!

However, many times throughout *"Future Humans And The UFOs,"* I state that I am not excluding aliens from being among our strange visitors. I am merely trying to bring to light the fact that we have not seriously considered that time traveling humans are here also, in the flying vehicles which we will create in the relatively near future.

Quantum Shaman: What is your conclusion then about abductions? Do humans actually abduct other humans?

Diane Tessman: Of course, they do! We abduct each other all the time, what else is kidnapping? We murder each other, we molest each other ("we" being our species). In our history, we have taken each other as slaves and we have committed genocide.

Future humans may want to know more about the biology of their ancestors, either for scientific research or perhaps they need our DNA for some reason. Certainly, most abductions do include tissue samples being taken.

They also may be curious about how we respond to trauma; today, we "catch and release" wild animals. We may attach a tracking device. Time traveling humans sometimes implant a tracking device also, as they study their ancestors (us).

Humans are a flawed adolescent species. I do not claim that UFO occupants are angels; we can be cruel and self-serving. Isn't this how we current humans are too? Someday we may evolve, but most likely, not to a huge degree in the next few hundred years.

Quantum Shaman: Then what have you written about all these years in your channeling of Tibus? He seems to have a very enlightened, peaceful philosophy and I assume that is how he really is. But is he one of these abducting future humans? Because he does say he is "from our future."

Diane Tessman: We fail to consider that future humans visit us from all different levels of time. Of course, once we conquer time, we are perhaps timeless. However, those who are perhaps 30 years ahead of us (they might be the first to travel time), will still be at approximately our level of spiritual/moral evolution.

Each time we have a terrible war, the silver lining is that some of us turn our backs on violence and aggression; however, there is no doubt, our species is behind in spiritual evolution while we excel at tech and science.

THE REAL LIFE UFO TRANSFORMATION OF DIANE TESSMAN

What will we be in 500,000 years, which is just a drop in the bucket of time? Will we have grown even more selfish? Or will we have evolved spiritually?

If evolution continues to go forward, I firmly believe we will evolve spiritually. This makes sense because we will have met actual aliens from far distant star systems, we will have grown in intellect (IQ) probably through artificial intelligence. We will have amassed knowledge of how our own tiny Planet Earth, is rare in the universe and to be cherished.

Long story short, Tibus is not from 35 years ahead, but from hundreds or possibly thousands of years ahead. He is truly timeless in that he is a citizen of the cosmos as much as he is a citizen of Earth. He has learned the lesson, finally, that humans have taken so long to learn. And so, there is no contradiction between Tibus' spiritual messages and the future human premise.

Quantum Shaman: When you were abducted, you were told, "We are from your future." Tibus was your guide and you prefer to call it "an encounter." But, they took a tissue sample from you; they took an entire membrane from your mouth. How was this so enlightened?

Diane Tessman: Only in recent years have I realized what may be the truth about my missing membrane. For many years, I thought the scar was merely on the outside of my lip to nose, but then realized about twelve years ago, that the membrane which most people have inside the mouth (a small connective tissue between upper lip and gum) is missing. This means, they took a prime tissue sample in a well- nourished area of the body.

Only in the last ten years or so, have current cancer specialists taken a tissue sample from cancer patients, removed it, genetically re-engineered it to be a cell which attacks cancer, and then reintroduced it into the patient's body, to fight the cancer.

I believe this was done by those who abducted me in 1952, long before this process was discovered in our time.

Before I was abducted, I was a sickly three year old child. I had frequent strep throat; heavy nose bleeds, and was underweight. I now believe I had the symptoms of childhood leukemia.

I was four years old when I had the strange encounters. In hypnotic regression at age thirty-four, I referred to a medical procedure, but I had (and have), no conscious recollection of the details. I believe I was saved from this life-threatening illness by the beings I encountered.

They may have had their own self-serving reasons for taking the membrane as well; I am sure it could serve both purposes being a relatively large tissue sample. However, I am convinced they saved my life.

By age five, I was bouncing off the chandeliers, excelling in gymnastics and ballet. I did cartwheels in circles around the house, climbed trees, and have remained in better than average health (cross fingers, knock wood).

In exchange for saving my life, was I given the quest of telling the world about time traveling humans? I do not think it was quite so delineated a quid pro quo, but I have indeed searched for evidence and answers through my writing for over forty years while feeling a constant "shared consciousness" with Tibus, whom I met on those encounters. I have no regrets, and if given the chance, I'd do it all again from the childhood encounters, onward.

As mentioned, I do also feel there are extraterrestrials from far distant planets visiting us just as they have for at least 73 years, and perhaps they have visited us for many millennia.

ET or future human?

THE REAL LIFE UFO TRANSFORMATION OF DIANE TESSMAN

DIANE PRESENTS THE LOGICAL ARGUMENT FOR TIME TRAVEL, CONNECT THE DOTS

I believe the galaxy and the universe teem with life, some of it is advanced life, and extraterrestrials may indeed visit Earth. However, humans tend to forget or ignore the fact that we will evolve and advance in the future unless we go extinct. What is impossible today will be possible tomorrow; that is how it is and always has been.

Future Humans have a home: Earth. They are right here, right now, in a different layer or snapshot, of The Eternal Now. I believe the majority of UFOs we see, are from our own future!

The Golden Age of Science and Technology is upon us; at this moment in history, we are leaping forward in computer science, astronomy, physics, quantum physics, post-quantum physics, biomedicine, bioanthropology, neuroscience, genetic science, and more; Future Humans will use advanced forms of all that is now being laid as a foundation. Their society and who they are will reflect this. We are their forefathers and foremothers who opened the windows on advanced knowledge and discovery.

In five years, we may well be 200 years ahead of where we are now. It is impossible to keep up with computer innovations and discoveries, and soon quantum computers will become common. Granted, we are not evolving spiritually as fast, but the science/technology revolution cannot be denied.

Strange craft in our skies have been with us since 1947 and perhaps since ancient times; I believe, the occupants are predominantly our descendants. They may be from different phases of time, some 75 years from now, while others are 500 years ahead of us or 25,000 years ahead. After all, once the key to traveling back in time is found, endless possibilities open which we who are still chained to "time," can only imagine!

Of course, most people just accept the "fact" that traveling back is impossible. This is perhaps why we assumed, without sufficient analysis and consideration, that extraterrestrials from far distant star systems are the answer. We have been shown frightening alien characters on media screens who give us an adrenalin rush, and we like that. We have grown both fearful and entertained by an assortment of ETs.

Of course, the fact is, Einstein never said traveling back in time is impossible. He said he could not figure out how to do it and that it had challenges.

THE REAL LIFE UFO TRANSFORMATION OF DIANE TESSMAN

We have sold ourselves short, figuring that it must be extraterrestrials that are so advanced because we who walked on the moon in 1969, nonetheless, just don't have what it takes to travel space-time. No wonder many people are depressed; we have lost confidence in our worth and in our own species in the 21st Century. Many days, I do understand!

Do we even have a future? We will either exist in the future or we won't. If we do, it will not be at the scientific/technology stage we are, today!

We have been dumbed down in recent years on purpose, by governments, religions, and corporations, for their own greedy purposes. We can't see beyond our struggle for money to pay the rent and buy food. We are purposely kept in this dismal state, who has time for optimism to dream? To invent? To innovate? To explore? The answer: Only a wealthy few and that makes us even more disgruntled.

The fact is, Future Humans would pose a bigger challenge to the status quo and the powers-that-be than would extraterrestrials. After the initial shock, some people would turn to advanced members of their own species who no doubt have the cure for cancer and other dreaded diseases, and who seem to have answers for many of our problems today. Advanced methods could help tremendously, for instance, in counteracting global warming. I do suspect, though, that there is a non-interference directive which keeps our time traveling descendants from overtly contacting and helping us as individuals.

Some of us turn to extraterrestrials we feel exist in our skies, to give us hope and help. To each his or her own belief, but we must ask, "Why would ETs from a far distant world, care about us, why would they hang around for millennia or at least since 1947?" Their home is far away. To answer that question, one must decide that ETs are ascended, ultra-caring, unconditionally loving beings who exist primarily to help humans. Are we sure this is the answer?

As Jacques Vallee pointed out years ago, why have there been tens of millions of UFO flyovers on dark nights and bright days for years, all over this planet, which seem to have nothing to do with us? There are so many millions of fly-overs, even landings, why would an alien race need so much analysis of Earth's oceans, land, and life-forms? Wouldn't they have completed this in perhaps 5000 flyovers in perhaps a span of five years? Whatever and whoever is responsible for the UFO phenomenon, it seems to belong on Earth and to Earth and is often just going about its business. Earth belongs to our great, great, great grandchildren, too.

THE REAL LIFE UFO TRANSFORMATION OF DIANE TESSMAN

Diane discusses the evidence and clues that UFO occupants are time traveling humans.

There may be college courses in the year 2350 which include a semester of field study back with the ancestors. Or, there may be urgent reasons why Future Humans patrol Earth skies, travel back to give warnings about nuclear warheads atop ballistic missiles, and harass nuclear installations which might well get hit one day soon by one of the F-4 tornadoes or catastrophic floods which are prevalent in these days of global warming.

We currently have not fully understood the dangerous instability of various radioactive threats in rising waters, and within a more violent, chaotic planetary climate system. Of course, many nuclear power plants sit right beside large bodies of water.

In the earth of Earth, is buried radioactive waste which has a half-life of perhaps 100,000 years. (Radioactive half-life estimates vary widely depending what website one looks at, but 100,000 is a moderate number). Do our great, great, great grandchildren contend with the leaking radioactive mess we made?

What if the UFO message is, "We are trying to point out to you, our ancestors, that you are damaging our mutual planet with radiation, climate chaos, contamination of many kinds, killing our oceans and destroying our natural and mutual land!"

What about UFO abductions? It is difficult to find an abduction not done by humans or humanoids. This evolutionary hominid to hominin to Homo sapiens, roadmap, instilled in our DNA, is unique to Earth. We must make many assumptions to say that an ancient race of aliens maybe called The Preservers, traveled around the galaxy and seeded humans all over the place. That is simply a story. Our DNA is reality.

And so, who would abduct a human? Humans would! We are flawed, we can be cruel. We have committed genocide on each other, waged war on each other, enslaved each other. Abducting another human in a "catch and release" program is not the worst of our behavior throughout history. In fact, maybe we have evolved just a bit.

One thing is certain; I do not believe Future Humans are ascended gods! Occupants in UFOs are probably from a military-like unit which has had training in time travel and its various strange or unusual situations.

The human race may have a smaller physical form in the future due the human population explosion; many UFO occupants are smaller than current humans. Perhaps responsible future parents choose to create smaller humans to help save the resources of Earth; this is similar thinking to the fact we are advised to never eat meat again if we wish to help the planet. This of course is speculation.

Evolutionary anthropology experts tell us that after several generations in space, humans will look exactly like many of the UFO "aliens," with shriveled muscles, less hair, skin which does not know sunlight, and large craniums.

As I read the USS Nimitz F/A-18 Navy pilots' descriptions of their encounters with the Tic-Tac capsules, it seems to me that there is an element of hot-dogging fighter pilots on both sides. The difference is, the tic-tac pilots or pilot-system, have highly superior technology. It seems that each side has the persona of "Top Guns."

This does not seem alien; it suggests both sides are of human origin. Real extraterrestrials likely do not behave as we do with combative humor and competitive machismo. ETs might just pulverize the other craft and be done with it, or quite the opposite, they might be horrified at the jet pilots' aggression and zoom away.

The tic-tac objects could have stayed out of the way of the Navy maneuvers which were scheduled every year for that area, at that time. It seems they did not care if they were seen and if skirmishes and chases ensued. In fact, they seem to enjoy it or at least willingly participate. Did they want to be seen and analyzed? It was predictable the U.S. Navy would be right where it was on those days.

A fascinating hypothesis is put forth by Former NASA research scientist and current associate professor of physics at the University of Albany, Dr. Kevin H. Knuth. He offers the theory the tic-tacs which the Nimitz personnel encountered, were studying marine life in the area. His lengthy study states that that the UAPs could have been monitoring the migration of whales; he offers the example of a recent UAP sighting of a similar tic-tac off the coast of the state of Oregon, also when the whales were there.

Still image from U.S. Navy video of a 2015 UFO encounter, taken aboard a Navy fighter jet from the aircraft carrier USS Theodore Roosevelt.

"The thought was triggered by Nimitz Radar technician Kevin Day's description of the UAPs acting as if they were migrating," states Knuth. "They also seemed to act like they were looking for something by slowly tracking south at 100 knots or so at 28,000 ft altitude," says Dr. Knuth.

Who is more likely to be concerned with Earth's marine life now and into the future, extraterrestrials or the humans of the future? Who is more likely to have a similar "Top Gun" psychological profile, ETs or time traveling humans?

The U.S. Navy F/A-18 Hornet pilots, Navy radar operators, and other personnel from the USS Nimitz, have bravely related their accounts of the 30 to 40 foot long oblong, windowless craft, which flew circles around our fighter jets from the Nimitz on several occasions in 2004. The USS Roosevelt' personnel added their voices, recounting their similar experiences in 2014 and 2015 with the same unknown, unidentified, craft. The Navy now admits that these are legitimate UAPs – unknowns but real. This is indeed a game changer!

THE REAL LIFE UFO TRANSFORMATION OF DIANE TESSMAN

Dr. Michio Kaku recently declared, "Even if not smoking-gun proof, the declassified videos — bolstered by confirmation of multiple sightings of unexplained aerial vehicles during 2014 and 2015, including at least one near-collision — are giving ufology new weight. We've reached a turning point."

Dr. Kaku continues, "It used to be that believers had to prove that these objects were from an intelligent race in outer space. Now the burden of proof is on the government to prove they're *not* from intelligent beings in outer space. The possibility that they are vehicles from other planetary civilizations now has to be put on the table."

It is time to add even more new weight to UFO reality; the tic-tacs tend to verify this new weight: We have ignored ample evidence and we have carelessly skipped analysis, on the possibility that UFO occupants are humans who have traveled back in time, having found the key to do so. If the entity or system in the tic-tac is artificial intelligence, then it is our artificial intelligence creation.

We are linked to our descendants by DNA and by collective consciousness just as we are linked to our ancestors. It is time for new thinking on the possibility that traveling back in time can be done and is being done; in fact, today, brilliant theoretical physicist Jack Sarfatti offers a zero-gravity, low power warp formula for warping space and traveling back in time, which has gained a lot of attention. It has promise, this might be it! And even if it isn't, I believe that one day we will ask, "Who is in our skies?" and the answer from our progeny will be, "We are."

THE REAL LIFE UFO TRANSFORMATION OF DIANE TESSMAN

Modern science has yet to come up with a way that a starship could travel the vast distances between solar systems.

Chapter Eight

Five Ways Aliens Survive The Dangers of Interstellar Space to Arrive in Earth Skies

My thanks to Tibus for telepathically helping me zero-in on these five methods used by a variety of extraterrestrials, to travel to Earth from planets many light years away.

Interstellar space bristles with extreme, exotic forms of radiation; the distances involved are so vast as to be incomprehensible, and the physiological stresses involved for the ship and the crew of an interstellar craft make the trip to Earth almost impossible. At least, that's how we see it at our current human level of perception.

Planet Earth's atmosphere and electromagnetic field protect us from most radiation which reaches Earth, but space radiation is deadly. There are three forms: space-trapped radiation, galactic cosmic radiation, and solar particle event radiation. An interstellar voyage to Centauri Proxima, the star closest to our Sol (the sun), is four light years away, so any trip under the speed of light would take thousands of years, depending on the craft's propulsion system. Make no mistake, the intense radiation and vast distances create huge barriers to fragile biological lifeforms.

However, maybe there are other options. Perhaps we can learn more about extraterrestrials as we update our own scientific knowledge, looking deeply into the question, "How in the world did they get here?"

1. ARTIFICIAL INTELLIGENCE

Artificial Intelligence can withstand the perils of interstellar space which biological creatures, cannot.

It is likely the laws of science and math extend throughout the universe; and so, on other worlds the sentient species would eventually develop computer-like mechanisms. Next, their computers would evolve into artificial intelligence which would be based on their knowledge placed into their advanced computers. Today, humans are developing artificial intelligence, based on our ongoing development of computers. This might be the next natural step in our evolution.

Astronauts, going 99.999 the speed of light or using other propulsion methods such as ion power or nuclear fusion, would be exposed to extreme radiation in space, deadly g-forces, and other dangers which an organic (flesh and blood) body simply cannot endure.

Even our International Space Station astronauts have found it physically challenging to spend a year orbiting Earth, which is nothing compared to the challenges of interstellar space. Astronaut Scott Kelley's DNA changed 7% after a year of orbiting Earth and he had trouble walking for months back on Earth. It is now known that astronaut's brain size shrinks when they stay in space a long time.

If an advanced species from another planet developed as biological beings, they too would likely be harmed or killed by the extremes of space. It seems logical that artificially intelligent individuals would be sent into interstellar space instead of the biological beings.

We are told that as humans become artificial intelligence, their IQs will upgrade 50 to 500 times. High intelligence is another factor necessary in interstellar travel because improvisation and inventiveness are exactly what astronauts need to survive.

If the occupants of UFOs are artificial intelligence, they are nearly immortal, and so, hundreds of years involved in traveling interstellar space, makes no difference.

2. EXTREMELY FORTIFIED STARSHIPS

Alien starships might be made of alien materials we have not yet created or that Earth does not provide; therefore, crew members who are biological (non-artificial intelligence), could survive. Their ships would block deadly radiation.

On top of this, perhaps the interiors of their starships are "hammock-like" so that crew members on the interior stay level and protected, not suffering the extreme G forces and other stresses hitting the outside of the ship.

These are "easy" science fiction-like answers but, as Arthur C. Clarke said, "To less advanced civilizations, advanced technology is indistinguishable from magic."

3. GENERATIONAL SHIPS OR SLEEPER SHIPS

In multi-generation-craft, the alien astronauts who originally left their home world would die in space. If they are biological beings, their lives might be short due to radiation and the stresses of space travel, but there would be new generations being "grown," probably in test tubes rather than through natural conception. Each new generation would continue their species' journey through the blackness of space for as long as they could. Eventually, they would reach their destination.

Multi-generations would probably survive through nutrient injections. There might also be known worlds along the way which would resupply water or whatever liquid sustains them. The liquid would be recycled during their voyage. Their ship's propulsion would probably be self-regenerating such as ion-drive.

Would a multi-generational group of alien explorers really go through such a long voyage simply for exploration? We can dream of reasons why they might have to go to space: perhaps their planet no longer sustains life, or perhaps this is simply their way.

Sleeper ships have similarities with the multi-generational ships. We have only to view **2001: A Space Odyssey** to find life-suspended, "sleeping" astronauts being awakened when they reach their destination. Another example of a sleeper ship is the **Space Seed** episode from **Original Star Trek.**

Aliens in UFOs (scout ships) which fly in Earth's atmosphere might have just awakened from a very long sleep or endured a long space voyage with their multi-generational crewmembers while remaining fully functional.

4. WARPING SPACE, WORMHOLES, AND GRAVITY CORRIDORS

Warping (folding) space, wormholes, gravitational corridors, and even black holes as modes of transportation for extraterrestrials traveling to Earth, are possibilities. These are the methods by which science fiction explains there are shortcuts in the fabric of space-time. This means interstellar astronauts can arrive at an unexplored star system in "days" instead of the trip taking thousands of years. This brief time in space also means that starship crew members will receive less deadly radiation.

Warp: NASA and privately owned companies like SpaceX are actively working on warping space, which means space is folded into shorter distances by the starship which actually stands still. The ship folds the fabric of space before it, and then spreads it out behind the ship, like a boat leaving a wake behind it.

At present, they find it relatively easier to create warp drive, at least theoretically, than being able to figure out how to throw on the brakes of the warping action. What if the starship never stopped?

Wormholes exist theoretically but we have yet to create one which could be used for space travel. Wormholes would act as a shortcut through space-time but the challenge seems to be that they would not stay open on both ends long enough. Advanced aliens might have found a way to prop open both ends, lest they get trapped in the unimaginable reality within a wormhole.

Gravitational corridors between stars and planets is a possibility. This idea applies best to travel intra-Solar System; for example, there is a gravity corridor between Jupiter's moon of Europa and planet Mars. These "gravity tubes" could help spacecraft fly at greatly increased speeds across the solar system like ships on ocean currents. Scientists are trying to map the twisting gravity tubes so they can be used to cut the cost of space travel within the Solar System. Each one acts like a gravitational Gulf Stream, created from the complex interplay of attracting gravitational forces between planets and moons.

The same concept could be used for interstellar travel; guide your starship onto the galactic super highway which is a gravity corridor between Earth's star Sol and your home star, then set sail for the Solar System. This is science fiction to humans in 2020, but it is being explored by NASA, at least for intra-Solar System travel.

If we are discovering gravity tubes, you can be sure advanced intelligences on other worlds have discovered them also. Aliens might zoom to Earth on these "free fall" gravity corridors.

5. SUPERLUMINAL VOYAGERS, TELEPORTED ASTRONAUTS

When we stop to think about it, our communications systems are already extremely fast. We can talk to others on the far side of Earth almost instantaneously. Our communications slow down if we are talking to an astronaut on Mars; using our present methods, it would take over twelve minutes for our message to reach Mars. This wait-time does not make for a spontaneous conversation! And, sending a message from Earth to Alpha Centauri, the closest star beyond Sol, would take four years.

THE REAL LIFE UFO TRANSFORMATION OF DIANE TESSMAN

A favorite science fiction trope to travel outside the solar system is using a spaceship that can travel faster than light.

However, if we can create superluminal (faster than light) communication, we would be able to communicate quickly with our interstellar astronauts. This would make the lonely, seemingly endless voyage into deep space, endurable. Messages from home would arrive in meaningful, current time and the astronaut could answer right back.

We have not been able to find the path to superluminal communication, yet. This does not mean we will never discover it; always before, if humans can dream it, "it" will eventually become real. Remember that they told the Wright Brothers that Man cannot fly!

What if there are highly advanced aliens who not only communicate using superluminal methods, what if they can upload themselves into a quantum computer as informational particles and send themselves superluminally? Maybe this sounds ridiculous but consider this: Physics refers to the universe as composed of "information," whereas metaphysics talks about "consciousness" and how the universe itself is consciousness.

What is the difference between "information" and "consciousness"? It simply depends on your point of view because they seem to be the same phenomenon. Many ufologists, abductees, and experiencers agree that the aliens have something to do with consciousness and that they can affect our consciousness. So scientifically speaking, do they reach us as information (consciousness) which comes into our perception?

Astrophysicist Rudy Schild, Ph.D., has suggested that aliens might travel as superluminal information and then manifest their physical presence once they arrive.

Teleportation: Star Trek's transporter, which is science fiction, is helpful in conveying this concept: The alien astronaut would step into the transporter beam and be dissolved into to quantum particles; he or she can then be beamed to a new location. Then the particles reunify to manifest the whole astronaut once at the desired destination. **Original Star Trek's** transporter was used only to beam down to relatively nearby locations but in the more recent **Star Trek** film, "Into Darkness," Khan beamed himself from Earth to a Klingon moon.

Amazingly, **Star Trek's** transporter is in the research stage of becoming reality; German scientists have invented a **Star Trek**-style transporter that can scan an object and 'beam' it to another location. The new machine scans a physical object, destroys it in the process, transmits it over the internet and rebuilds it using a 3D printer in a new location. Since it is effectively an early prototype for a **Star Trek** teleportation machine, its creators have named it "Scotty" after the chief engineer on the Starship Enterprise, who was the chief "beamer upper.

In this beginning exploration of beaming, the individual's particles are destroyed and then duplicates are created. We can't have Kirk, Spock, and McCoy as duplicates of themselves, so we have a long way to go in our invention of the **Star Trek** transporter.

Possibly a species which is ahead of us scientifically a few thousand years, might have a transporter which could "beam" astronauts to other star systems. But what of their ships? Perhaps entire ships could be beamed with the alien astronauts inside.

HUMANS, FIGURE IT OUT!

There are, of course, methods of traveling interstellar space which have not been mentioned here. There are also combinations of these concepts. For instance, we might be visited by artificial intelligence beings who arrived on a sleeper ship. Or, a species with thick skin might be able to survive deep space radiation and simply have ships which are heavily fortified. Their method of propulsion might be folding space which is known as warp drive.

All too frequently, we emotionally discuss aliens. We love them, we hate them. They are supremely exalted beings of godliness who find us primitive and violent, or they are evil demonic beings who want to take our planet and our minds. Extraterrestrial visitors traveling to Earth is a topic which has enormous implications for our own evolution, but this is not religion! We need a less emotional approach.

One clue stands out to me: Alien astronauts must have as much courage as our own astronauts. Even artificial intelligence wants to survive; what are the chances of survival if you are the first astronaut to head into a worm hole? Yet, they must bravely continue to push the boundaries of space-time. Extraterrestrials may not be as different from us as we assume, they are.

Aliens have given us a lot of clues which we have not really pursued. For instance, they have the technology to turn off our ballistic missile launch codes when they want to. This well documented fact should tell us that their technology and thus their method of traveling here, are advanced. Yet, they can still understand our primitive technology and manipulate it.

Does this mean they are just a few hundred years ahead of us in technology? They seem dependent on ships; they have a "nuts and bolts" aspect. They do not seem to be completely particles of superluminal information, although such incredibly advanced intelligence can probably take whatever shape it wishes and do whatever it wants.

If we keep digging, if we search with reason and careful observation, if we eliminate all the lying, exaggerating, and the tale-spinning in the UFO field, we will find the answer or answers. We are capable of understanding them better than we have thus far; perhaps they are waiting to contact us until we do so.

THE REAL LIFE UFO TRANSFORMATION OF DIANE TESSMAN

The original front cover for "The Transformation."

Chapter Nine
THE ORIGINAL TRANSFORMATION
With Author's Updates

INTRODUCTION
By R. Leo Sprinkle

Dear Reader:

I am pleased and honored to introduce you to the writer: Ms. Diane M. Tessman. I wish to offer you some information about this person from whom you will gain much knowledge.

My initial (conscious) reaction to Ms. Tessman was one of doubt. I opened her June, 1980 letter which described her interest in UFO investigations, and saw a photograph which she had included in order to remind me that we had met earlier at a UFO conference. I told my secretary that I would have remembered anyone who was as attractive as the person in that photograph!

As I continued to read the letter from Ms. Tessman, I gained another impression - the writer is bright, educated, and shows an objective and scientific orientation toward the problems of UFO research.

As we corresponded further, and as she described her experiences and her investigations of UFO sightings and related psychic events, I formed another impression - Ms. Tessman shows the characteristics of a good UFO investigator, including curiosity, courage, and compassion.

I somehow sensed, in viewing a photograph of her group of elementary school pupils, that she is a teacher in the true sense of the title: someone who shares of herself so that the learner can gain self-knowledge as well as knowledge about the outside world.

THE REAL LIFE UFO TRANSFORMATION OF DIANE TESSMAN

But Diane Tessman is more than a UFO investigator, and more than an elementary school teacher; she also is a UFO contactee. She receives information from intelligent beings who claim to be extraterrestrial in origin and benign in purpose. Do we know this claim to be true? We do not. Do we know if Diane is accurate in her description of her experiences and in her interpretation of their significance? Perhaps each reader must answer that question on the basis of personal experience - or on the basis of personal belief, bias, and prejudice.

For me, it was a simple task to determine my own reaction to Diane's claims. I asked her to participate in a "survey of psychic impressions of UFO phenomena." I have been investigating claims of UFO observers for over 21 years. Long ago, I decided to emphasize the exploration, rather than the evaluation, of individual claims of UFO contactees. (My hope is that the exploration of individual claims will lead investigators, someday, to analysis and understanding of the patterns of UFO experiences and their possible scientific and social significance.)

My own UFO experiences, and my own investigations of UFO abductees and contactees, had caused me to shift my initial viewpoint of "scoffer" to "skeptic" to "believer" that UFO phenomena are real, both physically and psychically. (Theoretical physicists describe the dilemma of light, which can be viewed as "particle" and "wave"; UFO researchers recognize the dilemma of UFOs, which can be described as "spacecraft" and "psychic phenomena.") I accept the hypothesis that I am both "investigator" and "contactee" in the UFO network; both "particle" and "wave" in the "light" of UFO activity.

Thus, Dear Reader, please be aware of my favorable bias toward the acceptance of various "levels of reality" of UFO phenomena. But, also, Dear Reader, please recognize that my bias is not merely prejudice: I have expended personal energy, money, and time in an effort to explore and to understand the world view of the UFO contactee.

Since 1965, I have obtained completed questionnaires and psychological profiles from several hundred UFO contactees. Thus, my response to the claims of Diane Tessman was to ask her to participate in this survey. Diane was willing to complete the survey materials, which included a questionnaire on her background and her ESP and UFO experiences, and the psychological inventories: Vocational Preference Inventory (VPI), 16 Personality Factors Test (16PF), and the Minnesota Multiphasic Personality Inventory (MMPI).

THE REAL LIFE UFO TRANSFORMATION OF DIANE TESSMAN

The pattern of profile scores indicated, according to my interpretation, that Diane's scores were similar to those scores of USA females who are high in abstract intelligence and who are viewed as self-sufficient; there was no indication of neurotic or psychotic reactions; there was a pattern of high interests in intellectual, realistic, and artistic, activities, but little interest in status or social prestige; there was a pattern of "normal" personality characteristics, with a tendency toward feminine interests, a tendency toward shyness in social situations, and an indication of high "ego-strength" or the ability to deal with difficult emotional situations. In summary, the profile scores showed a pattern of "normal" responses, indicating that Diane had responded like those persons who are viewed as self-sufficient, emotionally spontaneous, somewhat socially reserved, and who have high interests in scientific, intellectual, and artistic activities.

Diane's questionnaire responses were similar to those of many other participants in the survey: descriptions of her UFO observations (in 1966, 1979, and 1980), with comments which indicated that she had checked on her current aeronautical and meteorological conditions as possible explanations for her UFO sightings. Her responses to questions about UFOLKS, or UFO occupants, showed that she was familiar with the various hypotheses about UFO encounters and the possible explanations for the (alleged) UFOLKS. Also, she showed an awareness of her own development as a UFO witness/ investigator/contactee.

In 1981, Diane and her daughter, Gianna, came to Laramie with Dottie Burrow of Denver, Colorado, so that Diane might explore, through hypnotic procedures, her memories of her UFO experiences. On August 13, 1981, Diane responded to my questions and suggestions so that we could obtain subconscious impressions of her encounters and communications with UFOLKS.

I have worked with approximately 150 persons who have described in hypnosis sessions their memories (or impressions) of their UFO encounters and abductions by UFOLKS. I am impressed by the sincerity and fortitude of these persons, as they sometimes describe painful and frightening reactions to their experiences. However, it was a pleasure to work with Diane. Her level of intelligence, her level of knowledge, and her level of self-awareness allowed her to minimize her doubts and fears, and to maximize the exploration of the significance and meaning of her memories and impressions.

My own interpretation of the reactions by Diane to the hypnotic procedures was as follows: Diane's reactions were vivid recall, or memories, of real experiences

THE REAL LIFE UFO TRANSFORMATION OF DIANE TESSMAN

which have a profound influence on her inner character and her personal goals. In other words, these memories were of "real" experiences as far as Diane is concerned. Does that mean that the information obtained by Diane is true? I do not know. Perhaps time will tell us the answers to that question.

The Who, Where, When, What, How, and Why of UFO experiences is a puzzle. However, if these bizarre, baffling, and sometimes bothersome events continue, then more and more persons will find themselves involved. They may find themselves going through the doubt, depression, and difficulty of understanding what they perceived; where their world view changed; when they noticed the metamorphosis; what their life purpose or task may be; how they can accomplish their mission; and of course, "Why Me?" They may find themselves going through various levels (stages of development?) of UFO experiences.

A MODEL OF THE TIME, RANGE AND LEVEL OF UFO EXPERIENCES

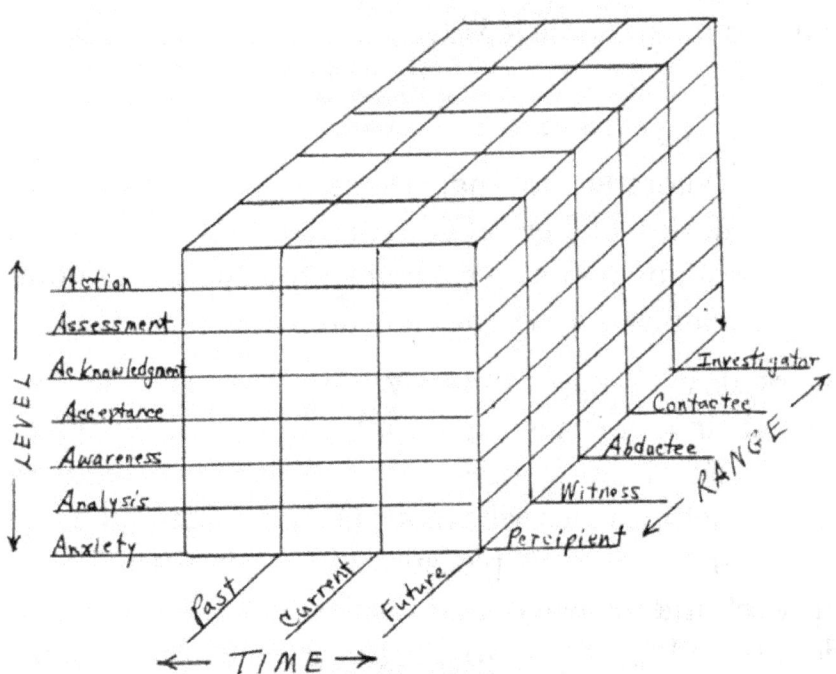

RL Sprinkle
12/23/82

THE REAL LIFE UFO TRANSFORMATION OF DIANE TESSMAN

A MODEL OF THE TIME, RANGE, AND LEVEL OF UFO EXPERIENCES

TENTATIVE DEFINITION OF TERMS

I.   TIME OF UFO EXPERIENCES:

Past   Categories of "time" could be in Current terms of days, months, years, Future lifetimes, civilizations, etc.

II.   RANGE OF UFO EXPERIENCES:

Percipient: One who perceives/intuits the matter/energy of UFO phenomena.

Witness: One who informs one or more other persons of his/her UFO experience(s).

Abductee: One who is physically and/or psychically (OBE*) taken aboard a UFO.

Contactee: One who communicates with and/or receives information from UFOLKS (UFO occupants).

Researcher: One who searches for UFO evidence; analyzes information; and/or shares information about UFO experiences with others.

*OBE: Out-of-body experience; i.e., "body" in one space location and "mind" in another location.

III.   LEVEL OF UFO EXPERIENCES:

Anxiety: A feeling (which can be mild doubt, some dread, or deep despair) that "something is wrong" which was held by the UFO percipient prior to his/her UFO experience(s).

Analysis: An attempt by the UFO percipient to gain understanding, to rationalize, or to explain the significance and meaning of the UFO experience(s).

Awareness: Recognition by the UFO percipient that she/he has experienced some kind of contact/encounter/communication with beings of "higher than human intelligence."

Acceptance: Recognition and resolution that the UFO experience occurred, despite the inner doubts of the UFO percipient and external criticisms of others around the UFO percipient.

Acknowledgement: Recognition and resolution that the UFO percipient must respond to the reality of the UFO experience(s) by public declaration and/or by personal commitment to an appropriate life style or by goals(s) in life.

THE REAL LIFE UFO TRANSFORMATION OF DIANE TESSMAN

Assessment: Re-evaluation by the UFO percipient of his/her lifestyle, physiological, in order to determine the physiological, and spiritual "costs" of completing the duty/goal/mission/task which is involved in his/her UFO connections.

Action: Activities, behaviors, commitments, and decisions which are oriented toward the completion of the duty/goal/mission/task of the UFO percipient.

(NOTE: An individual investigator or contactee could "plot" his/her UFO connections by noting the time, range, and level of UFO experiences; for example, many contactees talk in terms of "past" and "future" lives; often they view their task as assisting others to change from "planetary persons" to "cosmic citizens.")

The model of UFO experiences (presented above) may have merit in conceptualizing the individuality or the "psychology" of the UFO experience. But what about the "sociology" of the UFO experience? What are the social manifestations and consequences? Unfortunately, we do not know, at this point, the effects of UFO activity on the economics, military, and political institutions of Earth's civilization. In fact, the governments of most nations seem to be hiding evidence about UFO activity.

If UFO experiences are contacts with highly developed intelligent beings, then we must assume that "they" have some goals or purposes in initiating, maintaining, and developing these contacts. Indeed, we are told by contactees that there are many specific purposes for each UFO experience, which "push" the contactee along his/her soul's journey by cleansing "past life" difficulties and preparing for "future life" developments. Also, we are told that there are two general goals of UFO activity:

(1)   To rejuvenate the Earth;

(2)   To assist Humankind in its evolutionary development.

Some UFO contactees are told to prepare for possible cataclysms (Earth changes, such as earthquakes, volcanic activity, etc.); some contactees are told to prepare for social, economic changes (possible nuclear war; possible collapse of governmental structure; etc.); some are told to prepare for spiritual changes (to become "teachers" and "healers" for the metamorphosis of humans into a "New Age" of science and spirituality, of high technology and high morality, of reason and religion). Usually, contactees are given messages which are "slightly misleading," which have caused some "objective" and "scientific" persons to reject the message - and the messenger!

Now, it seems that we can begin to ease our rejecting comments and to ask more meaningful questions of contactees: Which of these scenarios is "chosen" by a majority of contactees? Can humans use meditation and mediation to modify the possible destructive scenarios and to enhance the possible constructive scenarios? What do we have to "give up" in order to enter the "New Age?"

Perhaps, in another generation, we will know which of the various scenarios - and which of the various responses - is the "real" and "right" reaction. Meanwhile, we can ponder over the various questions about UFO contactee experiences. Also, we can puzzle over the meaning of Diane's observations, encounters and contacts: How do her experiences compare with other UFO investigators and other UFO contactees? What advantages (and/or disadvantages) does she gain by public acknowledgement of her UFO experiences? Why is she being guided (or Nagged?!?) into a more active role as contactee and investigator?

And now, Dear Reader, allow me to end my comments about Ms. Diane Tessman, and to turn my attention to you. What do you expect to learn by reading this book? When did you (or when will you permit yourself to) become aware of your own connections with UFO phenomena? How do you hope to deal with your own UFO connections? Where have you placed your favorite faith (or fear) about the New Age? Why have you (or why have you not) committed yourself to the realization of theNew Age of science and spirituality, of psychic technology and scientific morality, of reason and religion?

I hope that your reading of this book brings to you renewed hope and faith in your own personal awareness and you own individual significance, as well as more information and knowledge about the growing network of UFO contactees and investigators.

May we all gain more Love and Light to illuminate our paths and to enlighten our lives.

R. Leo Sprinkle

THE REAL LIFE UFO TRANSFORMATION OF DIANE TESSMAN

Diane Tessman with Dr. Sprinkle in his office at the University of Wyoming just after her hypnosis session.

THE REAL LIFE UFO TRANSFORMATION OF DIANE TESSMAN

1

THERE IS A MEANING TO YOUR SEARCH

Author's Update: As I read my words of thirty-eight years ago, I am struck by the raw energy and emotion with which I wrote. I am a more disciplined writer today, but my passion remains. I might use one or two different terms such as "Change Times" instead of "End Days," but the certain knowledge I had then, I have now. It is up to all of us. Times are difficult, but we must keep on, keepin' on, and cast our eyes outward and upward, on the highest stars of peace, love, and good intent.

If you are reading this book, you have the need to search for something more.

If you are reading this book, you have urgent feelings that vast Earth changes will occur soon. The Creator Spirit has touched your soul in a very real way, either in childhood, recently, or throughout your life. Often you feel alienated and different from people around you who seem so oblivious to the final days of this planet, so uncaring about soul development and nourishment, so shallow and materialistic.

"But, I'm so confused..," you might say to yourself.

"Just where do I belong," and "What should I be doing to make this a better world?"

Often we find that we are walking a tight rope between functioning in this world and knowing with all our hearts that the time of great destruction is very near at hand. It is hard to be normal and act as if all will remain the same when your soul cries out for the time of transformation. Through crystal clear eyes, you see the petty materialism of this place, you see people hurting other people, stepping on them to get ahead, and you see the preoccupation with money, drugs, sex, shallow materialism, and you are sad. You see how little time most people spend in making their souls harmonious with the Cosmic Force of God, how cruel they are to Nature, to each other, and even to themselves. You see how quick they are to condemn one who is "different," and sometimes you feel great anger.

Perhaps concerned acquaintances have tried to use Freudian psychology to analyze your devotion to the enrichment of the soul, to Nature, to the knowledge that our Space Brothers and Sisters are out there, and to the Cosmic Force of God. Whether we are called contactees, UFO buffs, Jesus freaks, or psychic gurus, society makes fun of us who gently, quietly, and confidently know that there is more to the cosmos than this place and time.

"But," you might think, "sometimes I'm tempted to take part in things that are of this physical realm we live in."

And, of course, you should never feel guilty, for guilt is a cross we need not carry when we discover the true workings of the universe. Certainly, it is tempting to go bar hopping, to join socially with others, to get involved in more worldly activities because in this way we do not feel so alienated. However, we always revert back to seeing through crystal clear eyes, the shallowness, the lack of spiritual nourishment, the cruelty, and the ignorance. As the Change Times approach we return to our longing for the stars, our study of the Spirit and philosophy, and the development of our soul.

Why is it that we walk to a different drummer? Why do we look up to the stars at night in wonder and awe? Why do we listen to the pleading of our souls? Why do we crave more than this life can give us? And why do we know for certain that we are living in the "Last Days" - days of great disasters, changes and transformations?

I know, friend and reader, that you are one of us. I know that your soul is hurting and that this life has caused you great pain. I also know that your soul is a beautiful entity, like a flower in full bloom. But, still, you long for more. You long to sail the starry seas once more. You long to be transformed to a higher reality, to be good and kind and have great meaning to your existence without being made to compromise by the mundane world around you.

Your soul does not receive nourishment from the trivia on television, from meaningless jobs or social scenes, nor from the latest fad, and not even from earning money, the "god" of this place. In fact, money itself is not important to you; you do not care to keep up with the Jones'. You worry because of financial difficulties, but only in that you want to provide decently for your loved ones - and you do wish that you had more free time to devote to meditation, to being close to nature and to helping other humans and life forms.

"My God! I thought I was all alone."

Well, don't feel that way. There are others, many others, of us out here! How empty our lives would be if we did not look up at the stars and feel that bond that exists with Space Intelligence, with life throughout the universe, and with God.

How empty our lives would be if we did not dream dreams, if we did not have psychic insight, and if our souls did not cry out for spiritual nourishment! We would be as shriveled as dried out plants, not able to stretch, not searching, not growing, not surviving. Yes, we are the survivors. We will survive what is to come. We have the power, the will, to survive, and we have friends from Higher Realms to help us.

Many of us know that the "End Days" are coming and so we search the heavens for a higher meaning. Many of us are really ancient souls, and therefore we have had the opportunity to learn from mistakes made in previous lives. In our parallel aspects (past lives) we have had many trials, heartaches, as well as having known inner joys and pure peace. We have evolved to the level of consciousness which tells us that the cosmos is vast beyond comprehension, diverse beyond our wildest imagination, and that Higher Realms can be reached...not in fantasy, but in reality.

When we are regressed to past lives, we remember living in ancient times and many of us also remember parallel lives on far distant worlds. On Earth, we have been burned at the stake for our "powers" and beliefs. We have been exiled, tortured, imprisoned and crucified. Our souls survive and live in these bodies even now...and our souls will continue to survive long after these bodies perish in the cataclysm to come. It is true, however, that some of us will be "beamed up" to starships and will retain the bodies we have now; others of us will "die," only to move on to Higher Planes. But be warned! The powers that will be unleashed have the capacity to rip souls and the energy that comprises them to shreds.

And so, to the "Star Children" among us, to the seekers of "higher orders," to those who believe in miracles and prophecies, and to those searchers for cosmic enlightenment, this book is dedicated. It is dedicated to those who feel as I do that we shouldn't give up. There are days when all seems so futile, when things seem stacked against us. But don't despair, for there is hope for those of us who dare to dream, to believe, to have faith. For we are the hope of the future, for we are the survivors of the great destruction. Remember that your spirit will still be alive and flourishing as a beautiful flower. We will no longer be "different," but we who have had the faith to believe will find our souls nourished in a beautiful new dimension.

THE REAL LIFE UFO TRANSFORMATION OF DIANE TESSMAN

THE SPACE BROTHER KNOWN AS TIBUS

Author's Update: Tibus refuses to give up on me, and never stops trying to guide me, but the ultimate decision is always up to me. Maybe he feels guilty because my life is different than it would have been had I not encountered him. I have no regrets, and neither should he.

I also feel that in a future lifetime, I agreed to this lifetime as Diane. I feel this is true of many of us, we are here voluntarily. The past affects the future, but the future (says quantum physics), also affects the past.

Much has changed; I no longer teach school. I taught for eleven years and then went fulltime into transcribing Tibus' messages and sharing them with others. I make a humble living through subscriptions to my newsletters which have not missed an issue since 1983, the year *THE TRANSFORMATION* was written.

I now have lifelong, loving, supportive friends who subscribed to THE STAR NETWORK HEARTLINE and/or THE CHANGE TIMES QUARTERLY ten, twenty, even thirty years ago – our star people. We are so grateful to them, what support and love they give us! Tibus loves every one of them.

I no longer live in Poway, California. I have been back in my native Iowa for nearly twenty-four years (having lived in Ireland and Joshua Tree, California in the interim), where I am director and worker at our STAR NETWORK ANIMAL SANCTUARY AND WILDLIFE REFUGE. Yes, this is where I encountered Tibus (and he encountered me), sixty-seven years ago. Am I hoping he shows up again? You bet I do!

Some of you may be confused by the statement on the cover of this book that some of the material contained within these pages was channeled through me by Tibus.

Tibus is a member of the Free Federation of Planets and has visited Earth many times. He is not as popular, a Space Brother to channel as Ashtar or Monka. As far as I know, he channels only through me. At times, he commands a UFO (starship) and he is a good, highly evolved being. He has been my special contact since early childhood and ours is a rather unique case due to the quality and quantity of his channeled messages to me and to thousands of others.

However, this is not my book nor his book, but YOUR book! Through me, he has been given the assignment of laying out a survival guide to the End Days and subsequent Transformation, as well as to the stressful times which precede this period. Basically, what he wants is for you to hold on and be as strong as possible. I

THE REAL LIFE UFO TRANSFORMATION OF DIANE TESSMAN

believe that if you follow the guideline offered in this book, your chances of survival will improve tenfold.

As for myself, I am a school teacher by profession, having taught eleven years in elementary school as well as English as a Second Language field, working with refugee children. For the past five years, I have offered spiritual guidance, given past life readings, and have done star person counseling for thousands of friends and clients. This shall continue to be my work until the coming Change Point.

As for my place of birth, I was born and raised in Iowa where my space contacts first took place. I've also lived in the Virgin Islands, and in Florida. In 1982, I moved to sunny Poway, California, where I now devote full time to our star people's Starlight Center (non-profit). But even with all that stretches out before me I ache for the day when the transformation begins and I can go home to my starry seas.

Diane Tessman
and Tibus

2

MY SPECIAL ONE

Author's Update: There is much I could add to these notes which Dr. Leo Sprinkle made during my hypnotic regression thirty-nine years ago, but I also feel this needs to stand exactly as it unfolded. I did not know Dr. Sprinkle when I flew to Laramie, Wyoming, to be regressed but in the years after that, we became good friends. Leo has helped many contactees and UFO abductees throughout the years; he is now 88 years old and is still a treasured light worker.

TRANSCRIPT OF ACTUAL HYPNOTIC RECALL WITH DR. R. LEO SPRINKLE

On August 11, 1981, Dr. R. Leo Sprinkle of the University of Wyoming placed me into an altered state of consciousness. At approximately 1:00 P.M., he gave me the suggestion that I should relax and began mental preparation for recall. He asked what level I was on the "Hypnotical Yardstick," using the number 36 as the deepest hypnotic state possible. I responded that I was at level 20, but as the hypnotic state deepened, I reported being at level 28.

The following is Dr. Sprinkle's official log of my hypnotic session with him. The session began when he requested that I recall my earliest UFO experience.

Time: 1:15

Diane: I'm playing with Pat, my dog, on the farm. And I had stayed out late and Mom is inside cooking, Father's inside. I don't know where my brother is. The stars are clear, it is chilly, November. I am seven years old. And I have contact with something that has contacted me before, but I'm not allowed to remember. I want very much to remember them, though, and I try very hard. But this night, I worry about Pat, my dog, when I go with them. They say he is all right. (Pause)

And there is someone on board I know in particular, and I've known him each time. I'm not scared and I'm special, as other people are, but that to function in this life, in the mundane part of life that is ahead of me, that as protection, I cannot know the other side of me for a while, nor remember all that has happened. I love my mother and father, but every time I see them, I feel that this is where I belong. I always hate to leave. I always want to remember, but at that point...it is not allowed. (Pause)

I think that - they look like - fairly much like humans. I think that I've seen others onboard who are not human, but they don't scare me. The one I know best is human and I love him. There is - something - between us. He reassures that if they do something to me that is frightening or medical, that it is unimportant to me; I won't remember it and there is no suffering for it. He indicates that he has gone through something and he is okay. (Pause)

Time: 1:30

They - the different people on board, the different beings - all function smoothly together, and with love. I'm impressed there is no distinction between species. Then I go back to where my parents are and it's so ridiculous that people make distinctions between members of the human race.

I know that I will be watched - or monitored - throughout my life, until the point comes where I finally enter the world where I belong, where they are. I'm reassured. (Pause)

I think I'm shown a holograph - starfields - I don't know if I was really out in space but the Special One always showed me realistic holograms or space vistas. I loved to see them.

I feel that I am protected psychically. I can send out psychic messages easily when I want, but I am protected from receiving negative or false psychic messages until the time comes when all my psychic abilities must be opened up to insure survival.

I am remembering that right after that November night, whenever I laid down at night, they were able to monitor my thoughts with a mechanical device. NOT telepathy. They had to be close by to do this, a few miles away, and it annoyed me each night. My Special One wasn't there on these monitoring nights. It was two of them - just for a few minutes at a time.

I knew that he would be gone sometimes, far away, but I remember knowing that...or being told by him...that he and I were like on an experimental mission.

THE REAL LIFE UFO TRANSFORMATION OF DIANE TESSMAN

Not a common thing... that he and I were doing. A sharing of self. I remember sadness for him.

(Comment by Dr. Sprinkle: At this point, Diane broke into silent tears. These tears lasted throughout the hypnosis sessions, a well of tears which seemingly would not stop...silent tears...which were felt from the very core of her being, from her soul itself, as these memories were received for the first time).

I wanted to help him. He said I was. He said that all this was necessary, that he knew what he was doing, that he had freely consented to it. Whatever it was, it was harder on him than me. Suspension of life as he knew it...a sacrifice. I felt that I was - I hated it in his behalf - I felt my brain and age limited me; I couldn't fully understand it. And yet, in essence, I did understand it.

Time: 1:40

Slowly with the years, he knew that it would come together for me, as the time drew nearer. (Pause)

I remember, when I go for long walks on the farm, I go to several favorite hiding spots...and once in a while, he would appear in one of them, too. I think that's one reason I always went by myself to the creek - hoping that I would see... (long pause).

I remember the difference in the looks of the people in this world and the people on the ship. The people and beings on board seemed to blend physical abilities and good health with psychic abilities. They were advanced from humans. I have this distinct knowledge or impression that they were from the future Earth, at least the ones that look human - I mean, the future earth after the turmoil and disaster and nuclear devastation. I think these people could look into this point in time and help us whenever they wished to do so. Some of the beings on board were definitely not from Earth, though, but they were gentle and highly intelligent. I don't know why my Special One - had to do something that would alter his path, which was so exciting and so beautiful.

Time: 1:45

I feel that he had someone special that I didn't know, who was strong and was overseeing the experiments, so that he would ultimately not be hurt by them.

(Comment by Dr. Sprinkle: Diane weeps harder as she describes her feelings that her Special One is not in a position to control, that someone else - a friend -

is controlling the experiment; however, she is not sure why it was done - perhaps it is merely the assignment or mission or for our knowledge.)

I feel like I remember seeing the inside of the ship. I remember seeing the outside, too, of the small ship that picked me up. No, of a much, much larger ship. All I remember of the small ship that would pick me up was seeing lights in the night sky, then somehow being on board with them. But this big, big, ship was something so magnificent and powerful, it was like a dream. But inside, I'm in a corridor. There are many different rooms...circular. Some rooms have plants and rocks that was the favorite room...the one that was like a forest. There are even nice animals. Other parts of the ship...it is so big, so very big...there is machinery and technical stuff and flashing lights that I was not allowed to touch.

I remember seeing him behind a translucent black screen in a room. It was a divided room...and he was standing behind this screen. I was being made to leave. I had to go. I knew I wouldn't see him again. I felt like I was being ripped away. In a way I felt as if he was coming with me.

(*Comment by Dr. Sprinkle: Diane continues to cry as she is asked to tell of any further impressions.*)

Time: 2:00

The large ship had a big view screen, wrap around. You could go and look out... (changing the subject): I keep thinking, if I had some of him, what was left of him? And I don't know. If I could, I would give it back to him, but it must be all right, that isn't the way... (Pause).

(Note: At this point Diane is asked to recall the exact date of the encounter. She comes up with November 7th.)

Dr. Sprinkle: Did you notice any strange behavior in Pat right before the encounter?

Diane: No.

Dr. Sprinkle: How did you get to the space ship?

Diane: I don't think it landed. It was hovering...the small ship that is. I feel that, one minute I was with Pat, the next I was gone. I was worried about him. I wondered what he thought...because all of me went on the ship, it was not an astral journey. I was on the ground one minute...and in the ship the next. The inside of the small ship - I'll call it a shuttle - was circular and it was too small for me to really feel comfortable. He - my Special One - is not on it this time. It's dull lighting - not misty, but it has a different look to it. Maybe the lights are low...not up at full strength. I think they are built into the ceiling, I can't see the specific source.

Dr. Sprinkle: The temperature?

Diane: I was cool, must have been cool, because I remember not being hot even with my jacket on.

Dr. Sprinkle: How were you dressed?

Diane: I had old corduroy pants...tennis shoes.

Dr. Sprinkle: What were the sounds on board?

Diane: There was this constant muted hum, almost musical and soft. I think there were computer hums and dings.

Dr. Sprinkle: Was there conversation?

Diane: I don't - there's no conversation, except with my Special One, but he isn't on the shuttle. I felt that I was going toward the bigger ship. I knew I wasn't to bother him on this trip. There were one or two small beings on the shuttle ship and they were busy.

Dr. Sprinkle: Were they human-like?

Diane: One was and one wasn't. It was more insect-looking, humanoid build, large eyes. I felt I wasn't supposed to memorize the...it was interesting, but unimportant to me. I wasn't supposed to observe too closely. I don't like this ship, it's squashed in - just a few feet of space.

Dr. Sprinkle: What are some of the features of the large ship?

Diane: It is so overwhelming. I love the places where you can see outside. And there are lots of trees, large plants, animals, and things that are familiar to me in this one area. I realize that people on board must love them as much as I love them - rocks, trees, animals - a vital part of the ship. There's a dome near the top and you can go up near the top of it and look out at the stars. The stars are vivid, not pinpoints like on earth, but actual balls of glowing light. I know somehow that the big ship could set its course and reach any one of these balls of light.

But for him - My Special One - Earth is home.

THE REAL LIFE UFO TRANSFORMATION OF DIANE TESSMAN

I felt that he was - no rank or military protocol on the ship - but he was loved, respected, one of the best.

Dr. Sprinkle: Are you sad to think of his life?

Diane: Sad, but also envious (weeping). I felt I should have been included. Dr. Sprinkle: What did he wear?

Diane: Plain, comfortable black. Sometimes it would vary. I think I might have seen him in blue jeans or Earth clothes, another time, a jumpsuit...pretty colors...sand-colored and black.

Dr. Sprinkle: Did he have insignia?

Diane: Very small, a black something...a black circle covered with a gold aerodynamic shape. Almost boomerang shaped.

Dr. Sprinkle: Was it a patch?

Diane: I don't know, I didn't question it. I was concerned with him - like, I could go back to my house, but I wouldn't look at the company name on my refrigerator. I'm not a "details" person.

Time: 2:20

Dr. Sprinkle: Did he have a belt and shoes?

Diane: Smooth, comfortable black shoes or boots.

Dr. Sprinkle: Was there conversation between you?

Diane: I think we experienced telepathy, but also talked verbally. It was like a teacher/student relationship, looking at the room of plants and animals, and him giving me some of his knowledge.

Dr. Sprinkle: Was there conversation between him and other crew members?

Diane: Yes, it was verbal, but I didn't understand it - whether it was technical or another language. I don't know. I don't think it was English. There was a room for contemplation that he took me to once, but he got interrupted there by crew-members asking things. He was always different with me, though. With them, he would be more official and harsh. I felt distant from the others, but I was his close friend. I was almost scared - he was so much beyond me.

Dr. Sprinkle: What about the ship's machinery?

THE REAL LIFE UFO TRANSFORMATION OF DIANE TESSMAN

Diane: The starship must have had hundreds of different departments or rooms. It was so much. I didn't understand it all. Not much stood out to me except the rocks and trees, yet I felt at home there. I didn't understand it all, but that fact didn't make me feel alienated.

I remember I saw a crystal or pane of glass. It looked like a dimension more than just glass - it was rectangular, as tall as me, with a rainbow of colors. I would look at it when I didn't have anything else to do. I don't know if it had a function or if it was just to look at. I saw some familiar things...medical equipment. I saw the medical area, but I can't remember it.

Dr. Sprinkle: Have you visited there?

Diane: He's with me when I go there. The doctor doesn't talk to me, but he's human. Possibly they took readings that were painless. Maybe some painful tests...I don't remember.

Time: 2:30

Dr. Sprinkle: Was there conversation with the doctor?

Diane: Either the doctor is not allowed to talk to me or he can't speak English. I don't remember any pain. There is a large complex, like a hospital in size. This is one room, but the inner circle...because this is shaped like a bulls eye with rooms folding into other inner rooms. This is the inner part of the ship for safety purposes. My Special One explained that to me.

Dr. Sprinkle: Anything else?

Diane: There are muted silver colors on the walls, and machines almost like a dentist's office. The ceiling is not too high, maybe seven and a half or eight feet. It's large for an office, though.

Dr. Sprinkle: What does the doctor look like?

Diane: I think the doctor is darker than my Special One and taller, maybe five-eleven or six feet. He is very gentle.

Dr. Sprinkle: Equipment?

Diane: Just an x-ray kind of thing. I don't know if it was used on me. I didn't feel anything. There was no formal medical examination that I remember.

Dr. Sprinkle: The doctor's garments?

THE REAL LIFE UFO TRANSFORMATION OF DIANE TESSMAN

Diane: He looked "medical," had a cloak or gown type of covering. He is older than my Special One, but has the same glistening intelligence and gentleness, although I could only seem to relate to my special contact. Perhaps channels were just not open to anyone else...I don't know. These people have such a high...awareness...it literally shines in their faces.

Dr. Sprinkle: Tell me about other encounters you may have had.

Diane: There was this large mothership and shuttle experience in San Diego; I have a friend there who is connected to my Special One's alien companion. I was riding in the car with this woman...it was April 6, 1979...we had gone out to look for UFOs or for some trace of the souls we are connected to. We got in her auto, drove to Black Mountain, and she kept looking for a strange car she had encountered before. We were becoming impatient (deeper hypnosis) and then we saw a bright light or object, moving, and...oh no...a smaller lighted object is headed right toward the big one. They're going to crash...but no...they merge! And then the big one flies off so fast, so fast.

Dr. Sprinkle: Was there a time lapse?

Diane: Not that we could figure. But, I found it difficult to talk with my friend about this experience, like, I wasn't supposed to dig into it. I know these ships held our contacts, but maybe they were doing something else in the area at the time. Maybe they were saying: "You came all the way out here, but you needn't have done that (I was living in Florida at the time and visiting San Diego), but what you have is special only unto you. Keep what is yours." I don't understand that message entirely. The event was also the symbolic melding of the "smaller" into the "larger." It symbolized my own developing awareness and connection with my space contact. I felt that they...or the overseer of the experiment was aware of my sudden intense surge in psychic awareness. He was pleased, as if I am a good student. They felt a little surprised that I had managed to trace my roots so accurately and to remember them so well.

Time: 2:50

Dr. Sprinkle: Any other impressions?

Diane: My Special One, I want to return to talking of him. It is like a black screen dividing us. I know the feeling I mean, but I can't get it into words. Like the other side of the coin...it's an integral part of me, he is my soul, and yet, how can one side of the coin ever touch the other side?

THE REAL LIFE UFO TRANSFORMATION OF DIANE TESSMAN

(Comment by Dr. Sprinkle: At this point, a few minutes before 3 o'clock, Diane starts to renew her crying as if something has once again touched her emotionally.)

Time: 3:00

Dr. Sprinkle: Any past life memories that might help you?

Diane: I have visited my life as John Locke before. He was not the well known philosopher, John Locke. I was a young Englishman from the country. It was 1791. I had much growing to do. I was a loner and an army deserter. But, I was a gentle one, I did not belong in that time. I was out of place. I didn't play the human games correctly. My father had died and mother loved my younger brother Paul more than she did me. I left home at 14 and worked as a carpenter. I accidentally joined the army when I was drunk one night. I hated it and deserted, hiding out in the English countryside for a year and growing spiritually. But, I was caught and kept in an apple cellar in London (I'm not sure why I wasn't in a regular prison). I was not to die for my "crime," but I was stabbed very unexpectedly by my jailer who came in drunk one morning. He was bringing me my breakfast, but started being abusive, saying I was feminine because I wouldn't fight. He pulled out his saber very quickly, on impulse, and stabbed me in the stomach. All I felt was surprise.

Dr. Sprinkle: How does this relate to your present life?

Diane: I have learned to control emotions more than John did. He, and thus I, have learned how to be alone and yet happy and self sufficient. I learned the stupidity of military and establishment thinking. I learned to do my own thing, but unlike John, to do it legally without crossing the law. I learned how to charm my way out of situations. He didn't know how to charm, he was brutally honest. I admire that, but I learned that it doesn't insure survival. John haunts me because his death was quick and violent, and like a ghost, he was left surprised and never really knew he had died.

* * *

At this point Dr. Sprinkle's hypnotic session came to a close and I returned to my normal level of consciousness.

3

GHOSTS: ENTITY ECHOES

Thus the session ended at 3:00 P.M. and I felt as though I had been Home...home to my spiritual star roots and that I had once again been close to my childhood Special One...as well as to John from my soul's last past. Of course, my soul has lived other lives as well, but John haunts me more than the other past lives I have re-visited through hypnotic regression (each memory of imprints made from past lives has been an illuminating and rewarding experience). John haunts me because he died so quickly and violently; he was literally surprised over his death and caught in a "time warp" of not believing himself dead. Someday I intend to travel to London, England, because I am sure that I could find the cellar where he died (or the area where it once stood). I am sure that I would encounter his ghost there, even though his actual soul has gone on throughout time and now dwells in me. However, if I could find the "echo" of him in his surprise at dying that dusty morning in the cellar which smelled so pungently of apples...then I might liberate that echo of him (and myself) and it/he could fade on into the dimension where he now belongs. It must be terrifying to live in eternal surprise, not internally knowing that you are "dead," yet not able to interact with the world around you.

I believe that all ghosts are "echoes," that their actual souls have all gone on to other lives and realms but that, similar to radio waves that eternally orbit the Earth, the surprise of being "dead" leaves an emotional, soulful echo which can materialize into the body pattern the echo possessed when it "died." This is why ghosts often can be traced to a violent and unexpected death. An echo is created which a more normal, slow, expected death (for instance, from a disease), would not create. In the case of an expected death, the soul can usually hold itself together in its entirety, creating no "foot prints" or echoes as it leaves. No consciousness is left in limbo.

These echoes are not the original "voice" of the soul. In other words, if you call out "hello" on a mountainside, it is the echo of your voice which returns to you again and again...and not really your voice. You still have your voice in its entirety. And so, I am not suggesting that my soul - or the soul of anyone else who might have become a ghost in a past life - is not whole in this life. It is whole! It is not fragmented! However, the echo of me (John) at that time and place is caught in an eternal network of "echoes" which create the ghosts we encounter from time to time on this "haunted" Earth with all its ghosts and anomalies.

These echoes are normally harmless though a bit unnerving as they search throughout time for the answer to their "existence." They literally do not know they are dead and continue to go about their lives, passing down stairways on their daily chores or gliding through the kitchen to fix the tea. However, these entity echoes have no souls...but only the memory of one...and so there is no measurable sentience or intelligence. They are merely "motion pictures" of what they once were, natural holograms that look real...and yet cannot offer a soul to prove it, cannot function as a fully charged, conscious entity.

I often think that John's existence and his haunting of that area of London must be sheer hell, but then I realize that he is not me; the essence of John Locke is in me now, along with all my other past life experiences and imprints. It is not really John Locke haunting that London cellar, but only his mind's echo. Still, I would like to liberate it someday. I know that I could communicate with the echo and that it would at last face passing to freedom.

ENTITY ECHOES: CAN THEY HELP US IN THE END TIME?

What do entity echoes have to do with surviving the Change Times and reaching the Transformation? Recognizing past lives and letting them help you...and even reaching back and helping your soul in the time frame in which it used to live...is most important in order to come into full touch and communication with your soul. And when you come into full communication with your soul, you will then realize complete bonding with your higher contacts, be they from Time/Space (like my Special One) or from far distant and higher worlds circling their suns.

Psychically reaching back to your past lives not only helps you at difficult times in these past lives but helps you now realize that you are indeed a creature of the cosmos and of time. You are eternal. You have lived before, you have learned through many trials, tribulations, and joys of the soul. Your roots may even go back to an alien planet. Souls can travel (some are assigned) to research and development on other planets or in other dimensions. Other souls are assigned to time travel (a form of dimension travel) on this Earth. These are the roots of my Special One (and therefore myself), for I know him to be from Earth's future.

My Special One, Tibus, has traveled time as well as space in bodily form. In other words, I know that he did not come to me as an astral projection or image. Actual starships and/or dimension craft are involved, and a very physical experiment was (and is being) performed to help some us in this time survive the horrifying times ahead. He is involved in (as he calls it) Reality Engineering. There is a tragic microsecond approaching on this planet's timeline very soon. It is a moment when the usual policy of non-interference by the Free Federation and Higher Realms will be set aside. It is the moment for which the Free Federation and Higher Realms have been preparing us through UFO encounters and contacts and through spiritual revelations and experiences for years.

You recognize yourself as a mystical being. Your soul cannot be sufficiently explained by science or technology. You recognize yourself as a cosmic essence who lives in many dimensions and who is part of All That Is.

You know that you have lived many past lives and that you must continue to explore them. The more you explore, the more you feel the magnificence of the cosmos. You must continue to explore experiences you have had with UFO beings, experiences which may be blocked from your conscious mind. The more you explore, the closer you will come to achieving a new, higher frequency which will indeed make you "cosmic enough" to survive the Change Point and reach your soul's transformation.

4

CHILDHOOD'S INVISIBLE COMPANIONS

Many of us who will survive the Change Point and reach the transformation had invisible playmates or companions when we were children:

You were a "loner," often quieter than your friends or acquaintances. You were the first to feed a stray cat or help a turtle which was stuck on its back. You hated to pull apart daisies in the "he loves me, he loves me not" ritual because you loved and respected nature's works of art, and wanted them to remain alive and whole. You loved to be out in nature and could play by yourself for hours, not needing other children.

When totally alone, you could feel the presence of a spirit or spirits around you. These spirits were kind, perhaps a bit curious, and made your very soul feel warm and free. When your mother asked if you were lonely, you answered, "No," and secretly knew you were not alone at all.

My childhood entities were called The Remembers. This was the name they gave me to identify themselves. There were two spirits who composed The Remembers, but one was much closer to me as a helpmate and a friend. He was essentially my Special One (Tibus), who had earlier come to me in bodily form (as remembered in hypnosis with Dr. R. Leo Sprinkle), but who now visited me in astral form. His presence in astral form has stayed with me for years, looking in on me, guarding me from negative psychic forces which warp many children and adults.

The Remembers were not actually my playmates; they never did play with me as fantasy playmates might delight a lonely child. They were simply "there," implanting wisdom and warmth and "hanging around" as if to see through my eyes. They were curious and yet reserved. I could always tell instantly if their presence was with me on a particular day. It was as if they (and especially Tibus) were living a childhood through my eyes, and my emotions. They were also offering guidance and knowledge which sometimes showed up in strange ways: I somehow knew - by heart

- almost all the classical songs by the age of three. My family was not involved in classical music at all; somehow, I had these patterns of musical notes already ingrained in my mind. I also found much of the knowledge necessary for school achievement was already in my mind, and I had merely to apply it, rather than learning it for the first time.

Another form which my invisible companions took was "molecular herds." When I was very young, my mother would put me down for a nap; instead, I would psychically summon groups of grey/black particles. These particles were intelligent and friendly. They would circle the ceiling of my room together, then they would abruptly stop, en masse, and "reverse orbit" going in the other direction! They would follow this strange "reverse orbit" procedure often. These on-going encounters were with pulsing, conscious energy fields; indeed, these were pure energy lifeforms!

These were not particles of dust in the sunlight, because I was very familiar with them also. I have never been able to come up with an earthly explanation for them, and besides, within my soul and my psychic third sense, I know that they were not a part of this world but rather, were a part of my star roots.

There are many moments these days when I wish (as I'm sure you do) that the entities who were so close to me in childhood were as close to me today. "Where are they when I need them?" But, fear not, they are still with us. If the mother holds the child's hand forever, the child will grow weak and dependent. They are with us, even now, and will come back to us in full force when the time is right. Don't be afraid to call on them for strength in these times of stress, worry, and grief. They are still with you and they will help you.

MEDITATION EXERCISE: TOUCH YOUR CHILDHOOD CONTACTS

Lie on your back in a comfortable position, head propped up. Close your eyes. Keep them closed. Take nine deep, slow breaths. Relax. Forget your body. You are your mind and your mind is you!

Open your third eye in the middle of your forehead, above your brow. Look at the "viewscreen" which your third eye shows you. What is the first impression or picture you see?

Now hold that picture and visualize it in detail, studying the intricacies of the scene. Into that scene, allow your childhood contacts to materialize. Invite them into your mind. They can be pure energy forms, they can be human or humanoid or whatever if right for you. Again, allow them to enter your being, refilling your soul, offering warmth, comfort, and strength.

Allow yourself to drift in time while communing with them. Feel a part of their cosmic Oneness - and feel your cosmic roots being filled with nourishment and life-giving energy.

Open your eyes when you wish (and not until you wish), and feel reborn and resurrected...just as a flower rejuvenates when it metamorphosizes from its wilted, dying state, to a beautiful piece of life after water and nourishment.

Your childhood contacts and other spirit guides, as well as your star guardian, are always accessible to you if you follow the path toward your mind in pure form; in order to contact your own mind in its pure form, you have only to meditate, pray, to set your soul free in whatever way is right for you. You must remember that your contacts are always waiting and willing to help you! You have only to stretch out your mind to touch theirs!

5

A CHANNELED MESSAGE FROM TIBUS

Gentle Beings:

This the first time I have given a message to the people of Earth. Like my brethren Ashtar and Monka, my mission is to guide all Earthers who will listen through psychic messages and UFO related channelings. I am also "one of those aliens" you hear about now and then when someone claims "there are extraterrestrials living here amongst us." This is true, beloved. I return to our beautiful starship from time to time, but I also live here on Earth among you and I have been here for the best part of forty years now.

I must tell you, living here in this place can be terrible at times. I have scars on my soul which will not heal soon. I am so very sad, for this once beautiful planet has now been decimated, pillaged and raped. The animals and the forests have been slaughtered. Spiritual evolution is almost non-existent in many of you citizens. Many of your people remain selfish, seeking only money and the "pleasures" it can bring. It does not bring them love, joy, wonder or happiness, and they have no soul strength to fall back on. They grow more greedy, narrow, and evil. They condemn those who don't look or act exactly as they do. They are "holier than thou," believing they know exactly how the cosmos is (very small, indeed, according to them!), and declaring that there is no God, no Higher Truth. How very sad and how very conceited.

I give this message to you now through Diane, because the time for departure is near. I know how you must feel because there are many moments I feel I can't "stick out" my assignment here. There are moments when I plead to end it, to leave this "hell hole" and to return to my beautiful ship. And yet, your mountains are still powerful and magnificent. Your lakes and oceans still live. And there are a few majestic animals left in your forests. Nature has been my solace during my stay here. Nature is a vital force of the cosmic oneness of all planets. Love it, and protect it, dearly beloved. I can and do return to my ship from time to time, and I wish I could take all of you with me for reenergizing and rejuvenation.

Now, here is a brief account of my connection with Diane: Her mother had had an ovarian cyst operation at age thirty-nine and was told by her doctors that she could never conceive again. Ten months later, Diane was born. We are most skilled at genetic engineering, something which Earthers are just now beginning to think about.

The scientists of your planet must not have this skill at this point of your Earthly evolution because your spiritual development has not kept pace with your scientific development; a race of cloned Hitler's or an army of genetically engineered madmen could possibly be created. At any rate, Diane was genetically engineered, partially using my chromosomes. Just as her looks are "golden" and slightly "alien," so are mine...for I am one of those "gold humans" whom Travis Walton and others have encountered. We are the ones who must live here on Earth because we can "pass" as humans. The "ET" type of alien and many other members of The Free Federation of Planets look non-human (indeed, some are not even humanoid), and so cannot mix with your human society.

Let me clarify two points - Diane is not the only genetically engineered human among you, there are others. In fact, some "star people" are just this.

Diane has a surgical scar between her nose and upper lip, down the line of symmetry. She does not remember obtaining this scar, but knows that it was caused by surgery aboard our ship when she was three years old. We used laser "needles" to reach the brain, going back of the nose.

Our purpose in operating on her was to implant an imprint, or replica, of my soul in her. This is the electrical energy charge that makes me unique. This was necessary so that we would have another helper on Earth. As I have told you, there are others among you who have transplanted essences.

This method is one of many used in contacting humans. We use this particular method only on "star souls" who volunteered for a human lifetime; these are our co-workers who are Federation members in parallel lifetimes.

We also practice the "walk in" technique of entering an adult person who has given up on life and who wants to be free of the body.

Regardless of the method of contact, we realize that life on Earth is difficult for the star person. She knows she is not human, yet in all practical aspects, she is human. She must learn slowly and painfully, who she is, where she came from, and where she is going (what her purpose is on Earth). The star person finds herself to be an energy adapter who naturally attracts cosmic energy, then adapts it to daily life on Earth.

I cannot endanger our security by telling you where we live now, how often we must move, or the elaborate security measures we have to protect ourselves. If we were to be discovered and captured, can you imagine the implications? Perhaps our ships could rescue us, but the commotion caused by this situation is not what we are striving for.

My partner, who has been here with me nearly since the beginning, shares this mission on Earth. We are here to observe social trends and changes, but we must also be present here on Earth at a very crucial moment in your history. We are pivotal to the survival of some of your people when the great disasters strike.

Diane is also my "eyes," as many of you are the eyes for space brethren. When you are faced with dilemmas, traumas, cruelties here on Earth, we are often looking in telepathically through your eyes, registering the scene and guiding you. When this lovely blue-green planet undergoes disasters and changes, we will, again, be with you to save you.

Those of you who are reading this book are not those who have made this planet so miserable, explosive, and so cruel. You who are reading this book are the gentle beings, and it is you who shall be saved, to become one with us, to fly our ships, to work toward the transformation on Earth, after the disaster.

A few years ago, Diane reached a certain stage in her evolution: she was seeking her roots. No, not as to whether she is German, English, or Kenyan, but as to whether she is star-related. She knew that she must be, but she is the type, like me, who wants proof. (This is one of the spiritual lessons I must learn, "to have faith," as Ashtar tells me). And so, Diane journeyed to Laramie, Wyoming, and underwent hypnosis with Dr. R. Leo Sprinkle, who is a very special man.

At that time, she remembered my visits to her on the remote Iowa farm when she was a child. She was taken to our ship only three times in over seven years of my visits. Once I took her to the terrarium on our craft and showed her the many specimens of flowers, shrubs, ferns, trees, and animals collected from Earth which comprise the forest/park area of our massive ship. This area is one of my favorites, as it helps retain spiritual balance when one is in deep space. As I have said, nature is all-important to the soul; value it and cherish it!

THE REAL LIFE UFO TRANSFORMATION OF DIANE TESSMAN

At this time, Diane also underwent certain medical procedures, which are solidly blocked from her mind with the more pleasant terrarium memory, which could be reached through hypnosis when the time was right; and the time was right when Diane visited Dr. Sprinkle. The surgery itself is deeply blocked in her subconscious. Our sick-bay is highly advanced in Earth terms, yet the trauma of brain surgery is one I wanted this young star person not to remember. Does this sound harsh? It is, unfortunately, true.

She is also allowed to remember bits and pieces of my visits to her on her parents' farm. She led a solitary existence there: this was our design. Diane grew up roaming the fields and forests and exploring the river banks of northern Iowa by herself. It was very remote and unpopulated and made my visits unnoticed and safe.

Our missions on Earth are probably more complex than even the most aware of you realize. Our representatives have been present throughout your history and your reality, but there are limits which cannot be passed. We have not intervened in profound ways, because every species must be allowed to evolve in its own unique way. We have sent spiritual leaders among you, offering gentle guidance down the right paths. However, despite our quiet nudges, humankind has now flunked the test and we are now faced with rescuing a relatively small number of the species, those with whom we have previously worked. We must now interfere more than is wise, not only to save a few humans, but also to save the cosmos from massive warping. As Earth unleashes nuclear forces, it will affect not only this world but will alter the Spirit World, ripping apart electrical charges called souls, which exist in the full beauty of their being. It could very well rip holes into other dimensions which even our science could not plug, or deal with. It could potentially destroy us all.

This cataclysm will occur, but we will control as much of it as is possible, predicting where dimensional shift will appear and training souls to withstand the strain thereof. We will have our city ships in hopefully safe areas of Time/ Space as disaster strikes, so that we, and those Earthers we save, will be unharmed. We have calculated long and hard, we have used our precognitive psychic gifts to predict this terrible disaster so as to know how to protect you, and ourselves, from it, beloved. We, too, are anxious, worried, tired...especially those of us assigned to Earth for a long period of time.

When a planet reaches the point where it splits the atom, cosmic forces, like our Free Federation, gather around to see if the planet will:

A)   Use this power carefully and constructively;

B)   Use it to build weapons of ultimate destruction;

C)   Discard this form of energy as entirely too dangerous.

Earth has made her choice, and now we wait, hope, and pray that the damage done will be minimal, to yourselves, to us, and to all spirits of the cosmos.

6

THE END DAYS AND THE CHANGE POINT

Even before the End Days, there will be many challenges, many obstacles in everyday living of which we must beware. We are analyzed by "skeptical scientists" looking down their respective noses at us. It is not "psychologically healthy" to dream dreams, to believe in Other Worlds in a very real way, and to know that the End Time is fast approaching. Oh, certainly, one is "allowed" to go to church, to sit on the front pew, to offer small amounts of money to the church which can be written off income taxes. However, one is not supposed to truly believe, to have great faith, to search the skies at night feeling pure wonder and awe, and one is not supposed to seek one's guardian angel, one's higher self, one's space connection, or one's spiritual roots. One is not "allowed" to nourish the soul to too great a degree; if we do, we are considered obsessed, fanatical, a religious "nut" and a psychic "weirdo."

How many times have you been tempted to tell the world to "get lost" and to just melt into the comforting arms of total meditation, devotion, and soul searching? However, we must be strong and continue to function in this place...until the End Time. If we "give up" or leave our job, or reach a point where we "can't take it anymore," we are giving those skeptical scientists and front pew church-goers and those worshippers of the "god" money, a victory over us. We are strong and we can function, earning money for the needs of our loved ones, spreading the word of spiritual truth we know so well. Or, we can remain quiet because no amount of "word spreading" can stop the End Times ahead. Ultimately, it is up to each individual soul to feel the need for enlightenment or to continue on in darkness with no preparation, no conditioning, no forewarning knowledge of the times ahead.

Whether you confirm your feelings of imminent disaster through psychic revelations, through the Bible and other religious credence's, through meditation, or through scanning the skies (or perhaps through all these methods!), you feel the call of something "more." If your next door neighbor, or the guy next to you at work, does not feel this need, does not feel this relationship to Mother Earth and Heavenly Father, then there is little that you can do for him. You can present him with your knowledge, but if he laughs or smiles tolerantly and strolls out to have a beer and watch the latest football game, then you can only be strong against his laughter, and feel remorse for him as he turns his back on his soul's need for nourishment. Perhaps his soul is not yet seasoned enough or evolved enough to make its need for nourishment heard.

It is vital that you keep your urgent desire to find "more," and to enrich your soul in order to survive the End Days. There will be pressures - ever growing pressures - to stop this "mania." There will be financial pressures to work an extra job, or to continue a job you dislike greatly, which displeases your soul. There will not be much time for meditating, for seeking spiritual roots, for preparing for the End Times, and training for the tidal wave. However, worldly problems and pressures are also a form of training and preparation and they are making your soul as strong as it possibly can be.

THE RIPPING APART OF SOULS

Will the great disasters really mean the end to life on Earth as we know it? Will it really be so bad? After all, our Space Brothers and Sisters, and those beings of Higher Realms will be there to help us.

Tragically, the unspeakably terrifying forces unleashed during the great disasters will be so mighty that we will need the strength of our own being as well as the welcome, strong help of our special celestial contacts.

The greatest danger of all lies in the nuclear forces which will be unleashed. There need not be an actual nuclear war, though that evil hovers over us like a hungry vulture at all times. Once the dimensional shift occurs and planetary-wide changes begin, earthquakes and volcanoes will shake the very core of the Earth. The many nuclear power plants, storehouses and arsenals around the world will suffer meltdowns and vast quantities of radiation will be released. The natural disasters will be devastating enough, but the nuclear force unleashed is the same as unleashing The Devil himself!

Yes, the unleashing of nuclear forces is, in a very real way, the devil himself! Nuclear reactions split the basic building blocks of the universe. Nuclear reactions mutate energies and electrical charges. All souls are actually unique electrical/energy charges which dwell in an individual's brain, but which live throughout time, long after the earthly body dies. Atomic meltdowns will spell disruption and chaos to those unique energy charges and souls will become lost. An atomic holocaust will mutate and tear asunder all but the strongest of souls. The ultimate evil will warp weaker spirits, leaving meaningless, radiated bits of energy with no consciousness, no soul.

The terrifying fact is, we do not need to have a nuclear was to unleash this anti-life, anti-Christ force. A few meltdowns in nuclear power plants across the globe will be quite sufficient.

Unidentified Flying Objects (UFOs) began appearing at the dawn of the Nuclear Age. 1947 was the year Kenneth Arnold spotted the nine "flying saucers" over Mt. Rainier; at the same time, the United States and the Soviet Union were heavily into beginning experimentation and testing of nuclear devices. Coincidence? No! Our Space Brothers sadly noted that we had reached the point at which all "civilized," technical planets arrive: The Nuclear Age. If a planet is wise, it deserts nuclear power as entirely too dangerous to al life and concentrates on the many other forms of energy available.

Earth, however, was not so wise nor so lucky. The truth is, nuclear power is not just a "stage" in industrialization, but it is the ultimate anti-life power. Other energies do not have the wide-spread destructive power, cannot obliterate all life and all souls.

If you actively pursue goodness, soul development, and higher contact in your life, if you do not harm nature, if you strive to function while bearing the terrible knowledge that the Change Time is near, if you find yourself dreaming of and longing for the transformation where your soul's spiritual roots await...where reality will be fresh and beautiful once again...then you will survive! You will be one with the powers of nature and the Creator. You may survive physically as well as spiritually and will either join the crew of a starship, seed new planets, or lead what remains of Earth toward a golden New Age. Or, you may be freed of your physical body; you may have achieved sufficiently high spiritual development to no longer need your physical body. The energy force that is your soul will become one with the Creator Spirit.

Whatever your unique niche, if your soul is strong enough, you will survive and flower in the transformation!

ARE THERE OTHER DIMENSIONS?
A MESSAGE FROM TIBUS

There are other dimensions, beloved reader! Your most advanced quantum physics now tells you this, and spiritual messages and space channelings throughout the ages have always told you this as well. Most of all, your soul confirms this with gentle stubbornness. Others may laugh at your "science fiction" ideas or "blind faith," but be assured that you are right! Other dimensions do exist in infinite combinations of infinite diversity. Heaven is a spiritual dimension which all souls strive toward as life after life passes. We all (we Space Intelligences as well) evolve closer and closer to this perfect feeling, this perfect place, this perfect, all-encompassing joining with the Creator Spirit.

When the great disasters hit, not all of us will go to heaven, nor will we necessarily want to, or be chosen to go. Some souls have more lessons to learn, more evolving to do. There is also freedom of choice: some of us desire to experience adventures in the stars, or in dimensions that are not as perfect as heaven. It is these souls whom we Space Brothers have chosen to be the crew of our starships, to become one of us, and to return to Earth after the cataclysm to help re-organize civilization and to help any survivors. Many of you "star people" will retain your earthly bodies.

Others of you have already made the decision that heaven awaits you when the time comes. To you gentle souls, I send my blessing and abiding love. Yours is the Kingdom of Heaven.

May the Healing Light of Love and Goodness surround you, always.

Tibus

THE REAL LIFE UFO TRANSFORMATION OF DIANE TESSMAN

PREPARING FOR THE CHANGE POINT

Suppose you were hit by a huge wave while wading in the ocean. Suppose you did not have the slightest inkling of how to swim. What would your chances of survival be?

Suppose you were hit by the same wave, but that you not only knew how to swim, but had practiced for years holding your breath, floating with the strong currents, and improving your endurance. Now what would your chances of survival be? In short, we all know that conditioning, and preparation improve survival chances. In what ways can we prepare ourselves for the Change Point.

The Space Brothers and Sisters are much like lifeguards in this situation. They will be helpful and vital to you whether you are a swimmer or not, but we must be as strong as we can be ourselves, and we must have nourished our soul and conditioned our soul to the highest state possible. We must help ourselves!

In order to prepare ourselves, it is essential that we recognize our beautiful, unique souls, in all their glory and trauma, from past lives. We must seek out - actively - our spiritual roots. Many of us find our roots to be Christian, others have Hebrew, Buddhist, or Hindu roots, some of us go back to ancient Egypt or Atlantis, and others of us who are star people find our roots based in the stars in the Future Time. However, all roots relate back to the Cosmic Force and all are part of the Creator. Some call the Universal Cosmic Force "God," others call it Earth Mother, others call it Cosmic Awareness. All are One.

And how are you personally preparing yourself to survive the Change Point? If you stop to analyze it, you are doing more than you think you are! And, you are being guided more than you think!

Do you have one time of the day for meditation, for New Age thoughts, for spiritual communion with Higher Realms? Are there a few precious seconds out of the day when you are "Home," whether Home for you is flying the stars, or abiding in heaven? Sometimes, right before sleep, you may find an opportunity to nourish the soul in these ways. Other times, it is right before you arise in the morning, or in some cherished, quiet moment when no one else is at home, or on a park bench on your lunch break. But at some time during every day, your thoughts turn skyward and toward the upheaval that is to come; then your thoughts turn inward, toward your soul and its spiritual Home. In this way, you are preparing yourself for the Change Point, and the Transformation afterward. You know your soul well and reach its "heart" with serenity and contentment.

You also may receive subtle messages and suggestions throughout each day from Higher Realms. In a very real way, they are looking in through your eyes at the sad state of Earth, and at modern society's daily hassles and human injustices. Occasionally, you will receive an important directive, such as to move to another state, or change jobs. Be sure that messages like these are coming from a pure and good source, and then, follow them! Be aware that many telepathic messages come into the mind without fanfare or distinction and often we are not even aware that we are being guided!

I cannot stress enough that we will all come under criticism for our space and spiritual experiences and beliefs from "concerned" friends and acquaintances. Don't let them divert you from your appointed path! You are more important to the future than you can possibly imagine! Be strong!

DIMENSION SHIFT
A MESSAGE FROM TIBUS

Normally, dimensions are safely separate, intersecting in many infinite number of points, but in such a way that they are not overlapping and they are not entering each others' realities.

Some of these dimensions are accessible through psychic (astral) travel, but the physical molecules of these often bizarre, sometimes beautiful, occasionally frightening worlds, are comfortably fixed within the confines of each separate dimension.

However, when planet-wide catastrophes occur and when nuclear holocaust has taken place, dimensional atoms become mutated and literally transform themselves into the atomic and sub-atomic particles of new, alien dimensions.

During these times, the sub-atomic molecules and electrical/energy charges that compose the soul, and the consciousness of individuals, can be torn apart...mutated...and souls can literally be lost into oblivion.

This calamity can and will happen to those in the spirit realm, and even to Space Intelligences, as well as to you humans, if the nuclear catastrophe is a giant global one.

Your leaders do not know what they are playing with! They do not comprehend the enormity of the evil they are proposing, when they threaten rival political powers with nuclear confrontation!

May the Healing Light of Love and Goodness surround you, always,

Tibus

7

PAST LIVES AND COSMIC SOULMATES

Once you realize that your soul is you, that the electrical/energy charge which makes your mind unique, is energy that has been on Earth and in the cosmos since creation, then you can easily understand how very important past lives are in understanding yourself today, and in strengthening the soul for the Change Point. Remember, that past lives are more accurately perceived as parallel aspects of the whole self!

Imprinting is an all-important concept. All that you have been, all that you have experienced, all that you have felt, all the trials and tribulations that have been yours throughout the ages, as well as the joys, wonderment, and the happiness, are imprinted into that electrical charge which is your soul. Each time an experience occurs, it is imprinted into your soul. Oh, certainly, it is also stored in that computer called the brain, as science so dutifully tells us, but the reaction, the feeling, the consequence of that experience...is imprinted into the soul itself.

Even physical ailments or wounds can leave such an imprint on the soul that they continue to bother the individual in his or her current life. An example of this is my teenage daughter. She has always been exceptionally healthy and large for her age; however, she has always been bothered by leg and joint problems, even though doctors can find no medical abnormalities or troubles. Through past life hypnosis, it was learned that in a past life, she had been placed on the rack during the Spanish Inquisition. The torturous pain and trauma of this atrocity has been imprinted onto her soul and into her mind. It continues to "haunt" her in a very real way in her present life.

Through a past life search with Dr. R. Leo Sprinkle, I learned that I had been a very powerful ruler, a ruler with absolute power, back in the "ancient astronaut" days. In these ancient times, I was indeed one of the ancient astronauts who arrived on Earth to help humankind. We brought with us tremendous scientific knowledge and spiritual enlightenment. However, we human-like astronauts were not perfect, were not God, and so absolute power corrupted us as we arranged our kingdoms here on Earth (which was supposed to be divisions designed to expedite assistance to humankind). I ruled absolutely, with the power of life and death in my hands.

However, I rebelled at this awesome power and reminded my space brethren that we had originally come to help humankind. I reminded them that we were now ruling without mercy, inflicting our power on humans, even if it were not for their betterment. My brethren and my people (the humans I was trying to liberate) turned against me for daring to suggest that our power should not be absolute, that we should not think of ourselves as Gods.

They were afraid to kill me for I had considerable psychic powers which could be unleashed even after death, so they threw me into a dungeon and I was left to waste away. I had dared to be a "man," to speak out against injustice, and I fell from power.

Therefore, I now understand in this life certain fears and dedications that exist in my soul. I have a great and unfounded fear of the judicial system, and of prison. I have always championed "justice and equality for all," but have avoided positions of leadership even though I have leadership potential. How very important to the understanding of my soul, that I found these past life truths! I have found other lives which have added to my understanding of my soul, but none left the imprinting that my "absolute power" experience did.

UNDERSTAND YOUR SOUL: TRANSCEND PSYCHOLOGY

We must be careful not to narrow ourselves by letting psychology or other sciences convince us that their answers are the only "right" ones. Psychology tells us that we are this way or that way because our mother dressed us in pink or was overly protective, or that we have personality traits which formed when our father drank too much or was emotionally cold. However, what about the experiences from past lives? Did not they also form your personality (in other words, did not they also make imprinting into your soul)? And, they imprinted long before the experience from this life imprinted!

Perhaps you died of starvation as a child in India. Perhaps you found a near-perfect spiritual harmony as a monk in Tibet. Perhaps you died in a street brawl in old London. Perhaps, in ancient Carthage, your father whipped you daily. Perhaps you were a brave German who hid Jews in the basement as the Nazis banged on your door. Perhaps you were a disciple of Jesus or an ancient prophet. Only you can know what is right for you, only you can know the experiences you have had throughout the Ages and the effects they have had upon your soul.

Science tells us that these experiences count for nothing. It tells us that no imprinting ever took place because there is no soul. Psychology tells us that there is no life out there, no guardian angels, no space intelligences, no past lives, no enduring spirit. It is supposedly "all in your psyche...your ego, you id..." And yet, the greatest scientists like Einstein and Tesla did not prescribe to the rhetoric and dogma of science as a whole, for they believed in mysticism. They knew that there is more "out there" than science has yet found. They knew that one's soul is a very real and enduring entity. They were geniuses, they were truly evolved souls, not mere mouthpieces of the great "god" science.

Psychology fails to recognize the existence of an infinite number of lifeforms simply because these lifeforms cannot be seen by the naked eye at every moment. It narrowly and ignorantly announces that an entire spectrum of lifeforms simply does not exist; it states that angels, space contacts, ghosts, elementals, and even God/The Cosmic Force are non-entities! How very conceited and pitiful!

Atheistic analysis does not explain one's soul, does not explain the holy spark that makes each of us unique, does not explain the very essence of our being. And it is precisely this quality...the soul...that one must know well in preparation for the Change Point and Transformation. Otherwise, the soul will not be able to withstand the terrible ripping shock of natural nuclear forces which will be unleashed, tearing weaker souls apart into nothingness, with no base, no consciousness, no being.

MEDITATION: EXERCISING THE SOUL

You are a person who is very familiar with the pathways of your mind and who has practiced meditation for years, even without "officially" calling it meditation. In other words, to meditate is basic to your soul. Many of us were old and wise, even in childhood, and knew how to sit quietly, letting our minds (and thus our souls) wander and explore freely the endless cosmic worlds.

You are so busy these days, trying to make financial ends meet, and trying to function successfully in this place, that it is tempting to let your prayer/ meditation time (be it morning, evening, or late at night), slip past. You feel you must do just one more chore, work just a bit harder on business, or catch up on back-logged work, so that special, precious time for you and your soul does not come into existence, night after night (I am using night as an example, because it is my favorite time for meditation).

However, it is essential that you keep your precious moments - even if short - for your soul and your inner self. It is very easy, unfortunately, to get out of contact with yourself. You do not feel your soul any longer, nor the effects of the ageless imprinting. Nor do you have any inkling as to where your soul is going in the future. The space and spiritual messages you might be receiving, are effectively blocked by the mundane static and cannot find a pathway into your being. They "bounce off" even though they are intended for you and you alone. Eventually, your space and spiritual contacts will seek out other humans, only because you are so closed to communication! Certainly you might still know and believe that there is life "out there" and in contact, but it means nothing unless your mind/soul are fertile, and open to spiritual growth in preparation for the Change Point and subsequent transformation.

This does not mean that you should neglect your business, family, or recreational time! It does mean that one must remain actively involved in soul enrichment...if the soul is to be enriched; it is that simple! One cannot be truly happy - or survive - without this vital soul enrichment!

ENGINEERING A NEW REALITY

Have you felt a very real and urgent need to find your spiritual Home, the source from which your soul springs, in the last several years? Has your life been more complex, more hassled than ever before? Do you feel that your soul is being challenged, hurt, torn asunder at every turn of the road? Have you found solace and peace for occasional moments by seeking the spiritual satisfaction that is right...exactly right...for your individual soul? If so, your soul is experiencing "fire drills" both from natural pressures and from stresses of these days preceding the Change Point and also through planning by Higher Realms to condition and strengthen your soul. The Space Brothers, Guardian Angels, and Higher Beings know the hell that is coming and preparation is essential! However, once survival is achieved, there will be peace and beauty in the newly shifted dimension. It is then; we will become one with the Space Friends and move on to a frequency of higher consciousness. The new dimension will be opened by atomic energies; holes will be punched in the very fabric of Time/Space. The new dimension in itself will be a fresh new reality, born out of the atomic cataclysm. This new reality will not be filled with the old wrongs, injustices, bad vibrations and evils that this place has. Man has destroyed nature and our fellow beings; there have been too many wars, too many political power plays, too much greed.

The transformation following the cataclysm will be like riding a cosmic wave and washing up on a beautiful tropical paradise, because, in a very real way, we can make our own new dimension after the cataclysm. Quantum physics tells us that all is Mind. Religion tells us that our soul is the essence of our being. In this, both science and religion agree. And when the great disaster comes, our souls (minds) will be removed from our bodies...as will all souls on Earth (with the exception of the star children who will be bodily beamed up). In the panic of "death" and the joy of liberation from the body following "death," imagine the great psychic force that will be free! It will be the combined force of all minds/souls now inhabiting Earth, plus the great strength and soul of nature herself!

At that time, you will be able to pick your spot. If you wish to be in heaven with Jesus and loved ones, so be it If you wish to be among the crew of a UFO/ starship that sails the starry seas, so be it. The fabric of the Universe will be torn open and Mind will be free, Soul will at last be able to find its long-awaited rightful place in the cosmos. Remember, however, that the pressures on the electrical/energy charge that comprises your soul will be mighty! You will feel like giving up, like losing your consciousness and your soul as the cosmic tidal wave rips at your very being. Just remember the transformation that will soon follow, the beauty of the "tropical paradise" which lies ahead on your path, and be true to thine self as the devil tries his hardest to rip at your soul. Know your spiritual roots, know the place your soul calls Home and you will survive...finding your place in a fresh, new world/reality, among the stars, or in heaven itself.

The Change Point is a time we all fear and dread. However, all is in balance and the transformation will be equally beautiful if the soul can survive the great disaster. And since all realities will open up to us as this dimension is ripped apart, we have, at last, the opportunity to return to our true Home, to the harbor for which our soul longs, and has longed throughout the ages. We can return to our spiritual roots, to the cosmic well from which our soul sprang!

THE REAL LIFE UFO TRANSFORMATION OF DIANE TESSMAN

WHY DO WE INTERACT WITH THE PARANORMAL AND OCCULT?

You may have manifestations which are hints that your space guardian or other higher beings are very literally watching and monitoring you. Here are a few paranormal phenomena which many star people and spiritual contacts experience:

Many of us get buzzing or pulses in our ears and mind right before a psychic event takes place. Recently I experienced a spiritual contact and revelation in a park near my home; directly before this experience, I got a familiar "knocking" and buzz in my ears.

You may have had precognitive experiences. Have you ever know that a relative has died or been in an accident before you received official word? You should recognize here and now that you, dear reader, are a psychically gifted person. If you were not gifted, you would not be concerned about the Change Point. You would not be reading this book about the transformation!

You may have déjà vu experiences often, when you know you have been in exactly this situation, said exactly these words, felt exactly these feelings...before. These are flashes which you have had into your own future. Our beings are not confined to this time and place as our bodies are.

You may experience astral travel almost every night, yet your conscious mind may not be aware of it. And if you do travel astrally, you may travel into your own future, especially as stresses and strains of the Change Point draws near.

Being a psychically gifted person, you may sense what other people are thinking, be it good or bad and you may possess psychic sensitivity and intuition on another person's nature before you know him at all. Often your first impression is extremely accurate.

You may have had experiences as a child with psychokinesis where items flew off a table for no reason. This was caused by your, then, untrained psychically gifted mind reacting on material objects around you.

It may surprise you to know that many people have none of these abilities. You take them for granted at times and your gifts can be a factor in your alienation because you see through crystal clear eyes when society expects you to keep a "blind pose," concerned only with shallow materialism.

THE REAL LIFE UFO TRANSFORMATION OF DIANE TESSMAN

YOUR SPIRITUAL SOULMATE

Do you feel an urgent need and longing to find your cosmic soulmate? Your "twin flame" is someone with whom you can share everything, someone who knows the beauties and, yes, even the ugly corners of your soul. Your soulmate loves you completely, totally, and eternally, always touching your soul, always there to turn to, always yours in a very special way. Do you long to make a new reality with this person or to return to the beautiful world from which you both sprang?

Of course, the soulmate is always there for us if we turn to Jesus because, for many of us with Christian roots and who find the Christian path to be our true spiritual Home, He provides eternal fulfillment of the soul and spirit.

However, others of us who are also spiritually-oriented and who know the Change Point is near, and who also long for soul nourishment, do not find our roots or our soulmate along Christian paths, although we love and respect it and gain infinitely from it.

An important psychic and spiritual fact is that many of us have several soulmates or even vast numbers of soul companions who, altogether, form one very beautiful, vital, eternal soul. Many of those already in the Higher Realms are a part of a mass soul which radiates love and energy. These mass souls can pull apart and enter an individual for a lifetime or two...or more. These souls fragment as a means of growing, of experiencing, of helping humankind, for they are always advanced, loving, gentle souls when placed in individual humans. However, a fragment of a mass soul is complete in itself and always has the choice of returning to the Master Soul (the rest of the mass soul) when it wants, after one of its individual lifetimes is over (and the body it inhabited "dies"). It also will psychically and spiritually feel the pull, the desire, to rejoin the mass soul as it continues along its way by itself. It can never be totally parted from the mass soul and can "hook to it" at will through meditation and spiritual fulfillment.

Others of us have one soulmate whom we have known in a past life (or in many past lifetimes); he or she may well be in our current life in some vital, loving roll. For example, perhaps you have (or had) a grandmother with whom you are very close. The two of you always "hit it off" and can talk of your inner feelings and reactions more intimately than you possibly can talk with anyone else. It is likely that your grandmother was a loved one in one of your past lives as well, but she may have been a beloved mate in that life, or a special childhood friend. If your grandmother is "dead" now, she may well come back to you as your newborn child or re-enter your life as a dear friend you have yet to meet.

A dear friend of mine was recently killed in a tragic automobile accident. This woman had searched a lifetime for her soulmate and was finally drawn to India. She psychically felt that she was being guided to that awesome country and that she would surely find her twin flame there. Indeed, she did! He is a youngman in Bombay. They recognized each other instantly and spent many precious hours together. They did not relate on a physical basis because, in this lifetime, he is married. However, the relationship was all that they had both dreamed it would be. Now she has gone on to Higher Realms and I know that she is lonely for him...and he for her. However, in future lifetimes, they shall once again find each other and know the pure joy of togetherness.

Sadly, some us are going through this lifetime without our soulmate. We search, and our longing is great. Sometimes we feel we have identified the soulmate but in fact, we have made a mistake, blinded by our urgency and need. This can lead to great hurt which is imprinted on the soul forever...but the soul grows from all experiences. One must feel one's way along, follow instincts, and not be afraid to take a chance in identifying the soulmate. Make the leap. Probably your psychic and spiritual instincts are correct and great joy and fulfillment will come into the otherwise lonely lives of you and your soulmate, for he or she is seeking you as well!

If you are from a mass soul, you may have found members of your Home Soul in this lifetime who are, in a very real way, a part (mirror reflections) of your soul's companions and counterparts.

Some of us are lone entities with no soulmate or Home Soul. Lone entities are of equal worth and are very strong, magnificent souls.

For reasons unknown to us at this time, some of us are totally alone in this time frame but know that there is "Home" with other souls who are our twin flames. Some of us have not found other members of the Total Self in this lifetime. This is very sad, but be patient.

Some of us feel a warm relationship with our beloved pets. It is comforting to know that if your ties with them are strong enough, you may take them (or their pure, loving souls) with you as you survive the Change Point. Their life forces are not as strong as yours and they will panic. With the strength of your mind, command them to cling to you, their loving human, and they will be with you as the transformation occurs. Nature is a vital part of The Creator and animals are loved and cherished by the Creator of All Spirits. It is not "foolish" to hope to take your pet with you to the transformation!

Of one thing we can be sure! When the Change Point comes and the transformation is at hand, and as new dimensions open up under the tremendous strain of natural and nuclear forces, soulmates will be reunited, mass souls will come together in full joining again. That combined strength will help all of us to survive the cataclysm and to be transformed into a beautiful new world!

10

WE ARE AMONG YOU NOW

STAR PEOPLE

Author's Update: As I read THE TRANSFORMATION along with you, which was written thirty-eight years ago, I am amazed that the essence of what Tibus transmits, remains the same today; however, there are a few variations in how I interpret it; at times I add what I know in the 1980s rather than allowing his message to be his basic message.

An example: He refers to the Federation, which we now call Space/Time Intelligence. When I wrote this, I realize I gave his group a Star Trek-referenced title, when in fact the simple message he sent was, "the group of good beings to which I belong."

Another example: I mention his brothers-in-service, Ashtar and Monka, when in fact he was referring only to "my brothers and sisters with whom I serve." It is easy for a channel to assign a name or title from her current point in time, rather than taking the message exactly as received, which did not reflect 1983.

One more comment: Today we know that anyone is a star person who is of good intent and seeks enlightenment. I have friends whom I would feel are "star people" but they have never had an encounter or sighting. They are "simply" an enlightened human being. This is what counts, this is our goal! On the other hand, someone can have actual UFO experiences and not be a person of good intent.

This chapter is an introduction for the "star people" out there. Who are we? Why are we here? When did we come? How long will we stay? How do we relate to you? Might you be one of us?

THE REAL LIFE UFO TRANSFORMATION OF DIANE TESSMAN

What is space channeling? Is it a new phenomenon in the history of the human race, or has channeling been done throughout humankind's history? How does channeling work? Might you be able to do it (would you want to)?

What of The Federation? Who exactly are the Space Brothers and Sisters? Are they the same as star people? Do the two know each other? Do they work together? Are contacts with UFOs a prerequisite to being a star person?

In my work as managing editor of *UFO REVIEW* and *INNER LIGHT PUBLICATIONS*, in my mission as spiritual leader of the Starlight Mystic Church, and in my counseling/guidance work with my fellow star people (and others), through *THE STAR NETWORK HEARTLINE* and private channelings/readings, I have encountered many beautiful people who also want to know the answers to these and other similar, urgent questions. Telepathic contact (channeling), and face to face contact with The Federation occurs more and more with each passing year. The star people movement also grows by leaps and bounds as "time" in this 20th Century period flies by so quickly. It is all leading somewhere! This manuscript will tell you the promise, the goal, the mission...of all concerned in this movement (both those in space and those who live on the planet Earth for now).

I am asked so often to explain the definition of star people; almost invariably it is because the person asking the question has good reason to suspect that he or she may well be a star person who has not yet fit the pieces of his or her personal puzzle together, has not yet remembered consciously...the star mission. Also, though the term space channeling is used frequently, many people wish to understand this term more clearly. Seldom is it truly defined or explained. I (and my space contact, Tibus) will explain this to you, in detail.

There are lists of star people's physical characteristics. How relevant are these? Have more traits been discovered? Are there also mind/soul characteristics unique to star people? Is there a common thread in the behavior patterns of star people from babyhood onward?

The format of this chapter is unique. Tibus, my space contact, and I will both approach each subject in a kind of point/counterpoint. The knowledge you will gain will be from the space brother prospective, and from the star person perspective. In unison, balance, and harmony, we strive to make this more than a "primer" on star people but also a handbook for all those concerned about the future of planet Earth, for all those fascinated with the future, the stars, the higher planes of existence!

THE REAL LIFE UFO TRANSFORMATION OF DIANE TESSMAN

In the first section of this book, I detailed the encounters and events of my life and so will not review them here. Suffice it to say, that my life's path has not been an "average" one. In childhood, I was contacted three times; these UFO encounters were not frightening, but instead, quite the opposite: I felt as though I were truly HOME during these experiences.

During these contacts, I met and communicated with my "Special One," Tibus. Through psychosurgery (a medical field which 20th Century medicine is exploring even today), he and I share consciousness. This phenomenon has also been described as: "sharing brain/mind waves;" "on-going telepathic contact;" and sharing an "implanted essence." These terms, and our explanations of them, will be explained fully within these pages.

Not all star people have remembered contacts with UFOs, and still they are very much star people. They have always felt out of place and painfully different in the 20th Century, on planet Earth. They do not know how to - nor do they care to - play the "games" which must be played for survival's sake on 20th Century Earth. They cherish all life, holding animal and plant life sacred and finding great joy and comfort in nature. They veer away from organized religion, realizing that it is much too narrow for the universal wisdom and law and for the cosmic God-force which is "out there" (and which also exists on Earth)! Star people do have special ones; just a Tibus is my Special One; not all special contacts are UFO occupants. Some are "guardian angel" energy beings. One thing is sure: all special ones are co-workers who supervise and guide the star person through his or her Earth lifetime.

Star people deplore cruelty and violence in any form, finding the "low vibrations" on 20th Century Earth almost unbearable. They foresee nuclear catastrophe and the pollution/contamination of this beautiful planet if there is not a spiritual awakening and upgrading to a completely new and higher dimension/frequency (these terms will be explained!).

DIANE: STAR BEGINNINGS

In looking back on my own childhood and in learning about the childhoods of other star people, I have found that a star identity and a star destiny cannot be escaped - nor do we want to! We have been on a different "wave-length" from the rest of our families and from the world, since the beginning of this human lifetime!

THE REAL LIFE UFO TRANSFORMATION OF DIANE TESSMAN

The supraconscious knowledge that there is a mission to be performed, a destiny to be fulfilled...is with us from the beginning.

We are wise and helpful, even as small children; there is an "ancientness" about us. At the same time, we retain an innocent and child-like quality as adults. We value more a hike in nature than a sophisticated trip to Las Vegas. We value more a kitten with soft fur, than a "priceless" mink coat; as a matter of fact, the hunting and killing of nature's lifeforms is abhorrent to us and is one of the few things which will cause our tempers to explode!

We enter "slide zones" and dimensional overlaps easily without being traumatized or enveloped by fear. For this reason, we have had many encounters with the Space Brothers (our co-workers of the Home Dimension) - particularly with our own special one (space contact or guardian angel). We also have experienced psychic phenomena at various times in our lives, be it precognition, clairvoyance, sightings of ghosts, telepathy, telekinesis, sightings of UFOs or experienced the beeps and electromagnetic effects brought on by UFO activities near us.

However, some of us have been spared the truly spectacular paranormal experiences, living lives which instead interact with other dimensions in the dream/sleep state, lives which are full of symbolism and enlightened thinking, living lives which have a driving need to find out more universal knowledge, lives which pursue the star purpose and mission. Many star people experience both spectacular paranormal events and live lives which are subtly guided and inspired. We recognize and accept all types of star paths as equally valid and of worth.

Ultimately, realizing that you are a star person dawns - form compelling inner feelings, a lifelong search, a feeling of universal essence which will not let you go, no matter how hard you try to be "normal" or mundane. While UFOs or parapsychological experiences may be catalysts, the star person's inner difference is the "bottom line."

As I have told so many star people, it is not what has always been wrong with you (though the world around you informs you of this!) but rather what has always been right with you!

MESSAGE FROM TIBUS

This is Tibus. I come to you in Love and Light.

THE REAL LIFE UFO TRANSFORMATION OF DIANE TESSMAN

In the late 20th Century, in which you now find yourself, research is beginning into mind waves/particles, unified fields, co-existing other dimensions, and into the very state of Life itself (called consciousness/being); also, at this very moment in your history, humankind has the technology to develop starships which fly Space/Time. Most humans do not realize that these fields of research are as far along as they are (though they are still in the "caveman" state in comparison to other civilizations). The Earth governments prefer to deal in secrecy and hypocrisy, keeping knowledge and inspiration from the people.

20th Century Earth researchers are finding that different realms (these may also be called dimensions, planes, or worlds) exist on different frequencies, just as your radio stations can be reached on different frequencies of the dial. Mind waves/particles are analogous to radio waves is this example.

To continue our analogy, let's say that everyone in the neighborhood receives a certain radio station at a particular place on the dial. However, one person in the neighborhood receives a different station when his or her dial is seemingly at the same place. This might be because of a variety of alternatives. Perhaps this person picks up "ham" radio signals; perhaps this person's radio is very complex and is set up so as to receive distant signals instead of the closest ones, or perhaps this person's dial is slightly "off" and so when it seems to be set on the regular station, it indeed picks up a station near the regular one, but not on the same frequency.

Our star people exist on a different frequency of mind wave, a different vibratory rate, they interact with a different dimension. How do they do this? Both because their "radio sets" (their minds/souls) are basically a different "make" than the typicalradio and also because, in most cases, there have been "adjustments" made during experiences and encounters (perhaps not remembered consciously) with us of the Home Side (UFO occupants, guardian angels, beings further up the mountainside than 20th Century Earth).

Does receiving a different station cause our star people not to fit into the neighborhood as well? Yes, sadly, this is true. Our star people do not "fit in" - ever - in their lives. However, the neighborhood frequency is one which involves egotism, violence, materialism, pettiness. And so, it is good not to receive that "station," no matter how difficult the star frequency/path may be!

And so, when Diane explains that star people feel out of place and that the star identity and destiny cannot be dismissed, she is essentially saying that the star person's mind/soul simply is of a different frequency. The mundane dimension is not their soul's home!

I would like to address the mission and destiny subject in a later chapter.

Being an "essence" (may also be referred to as "soul" or "consciousness") from a different frequency, our star people do experience many "slide zones," as Diane puts it. The mind/soul longs to return home; it does not find the unknown as frightening as the violent mundane reality in which the Star Person lives - and so many parapsychological occurrences happen.

Also, we monitor our star people carefully; many experiences either in the dream-state, or in the waking state, occur because it is time for them to do so.

I am Diane's co-worker on the home frequency. At certain times in her human life, I have interacted with her, so as to nudge her along her star path, so as to re-vitalize her star energy, so as to remind her of her star mission/ destiny. This is my responsibility.

She may or may not remember a particular encounter in her conscious memory. Often encounters are remembered, such as several of hers were, during hypnosis (see transcript of Dr. Leo Sprinkle's hypnotic regression session with Diane). Whether the experience is remembered consciously, remembered through hypnosis afterward, or not consciously remembered at all, the mind/soul remembers; the joy, the wonder, the feeling of being home again is remembered in the being, in the heart!

This is all we require. The other puzzle pieces will fit together as time passes. This we promise you!

When a group such as our Federation (the Space Brothers as we are commonly known) find the technical and spiritual "secrets" to mind waves, essence frequencies, other dimensions, it is possible to spend lifetimes in these parallel realities (dimensions) and then to return to the home dimension - all remaining as it was when the essence (soul, consciousness) first began his or her journey.

In this way, it is possible to gently nudge a primitive race such as humankind, 1988, toward a more peaceful, elevated reality. These essences (star people) who are "out of place" are very brave volunteers for human lifetimes. Our star people pass as humans; they are on Earth but not of Earth. Anytime any mind/soul elevates itself past the lower frequency, it is indeed a star soul, an enlightened one.

THE REAL LIFE UFO TRANSFORMATION OF DIANE TESSMAN

DIANE: WHO ARE THE 'SPACE BROTHERS'?

Even the hardest skeptic would have to admit that humankind's history has been greatly influenced by the mystical, the spiritual, the unseen. This influence has been intended as a positive one, but it is sadly true that the human race has taken many beautiful spiritual philosophies and turned them into self-serving, hypocritical, and even evil doctrines. We will not be concerned with these warped positive energies here, but rather will concentrate on the purely positive.

Many people accept that Biblical times were special times; these were times when the Son of God walked the Earth, showing humankind The Way. These were times when various people "channeled" The Word of God, when many people became inspired to find Christ Consciousness within themselves as they related to Him.

The Space Brothers have told us that these also are special times. Virtually all prophesies of all religions (and individual prophets such as Nostradamus) have told us that the latter half of the 20th Century is to be the test for the human race.

Is it so unusual, then, that certain individuals receive channeled messages from the heavenly realm, just as people in Biblical times did?

It is downright logical (as well as spiritually inspiring) that Jesus (also named Sananda in Space Brother channelings) and His heavenly hosts still reach humankind today (of all times!).

The concept of angels having wings seems to have grown from humankind's attempt to explain angels' instantaneous appearance and disappearance in various encounters. Always, angels have been described as human-like; they manifest as beautiful humans, flawless humans. Now, it may well be that there are higher beings who have wings...but the point is, humankind has had experiences with "supernatural human-like beings who come and go in the wink of an eye" since human history began. These higher beings' presence is accepted by many people only in the context of ancient times. The Space Brothers are these same heavenly beings appearing in modem times!

In ancient times, the human race was less scientifically oriented. They merely accepted that these beings were "heavenly angels." Now humankind refers to space as the "the final frontier" and believes that one day, he will be able to go "out there" (and this also is the Space Brothers' fervent hope for the human race). Now, these angels are called space beings or Space Brothers. It may well be that this description is only slightly more accurate or specific than the ancient definition.

MESSAGE FROM TIBUS

This is Tibus. I come to you in Love and Light.

I wish to channel some additional information on the subject Diane is covering.

To put it succinctly, our star peoples' mind/souls (remember the radio set analogy) are capable of contact with us, the same heavenly hosts who worked with the human race in Biblical times, in ancient times even before the days of our blessed Sananda, and in times since. We have never left you!

We never tell you that our star people are a "closed group" or a "chosen group." Anyone can have the key to the kingdom of heaven. Yes, our star people are souls whose home frequency is our frequency, but as I have said before, any soul which elevates itself, which seeks enlightenment...becomes a star soul!

Our star people are chosen in that they are answering a call to serve and to seek a higher, more spiritual nature (instead of catering to mundane, cruel, narrow behaviors).

And so, if you, dear reader, feel a surge of inspiration at this point, do not tell yourself, "Oh, that's nice, but I certainly am not a "chosen one" or a "star soul." You have merely to open the door to find the higher realms! (Remember Jesus/Sananda's words, "I stand at the door and knock.")

Because humankind is involved in elementary space exploration at this point, we are referred to as the Space Brothers. This is very accurate for some of us, but not as accurate for others. However, we like and accept this term.

Because man was of a more fanciful, innocent nature in ancient times, he called us angels. By angels, we know that he meant "pure energy beings of God and of goodness." We accept this as accurate; in fact, ancient man's term for us did include all within the Federation, whereas "space-going" refers to some of us.

In order to comprehend what I am about to channel, you must remember that the universe is made up of an infinite number of intersecting dimensions; even man's quantum physics states this fact. And so, not only is space infinitely vast (that which you view at night) if one goes straight out into it, it is also infinitely vast if one explores even the myriad of intersecting dimensions around planet Earth alone!

Outer space is much more vast and much broader in definition that science fiction stories indicate.

Keeping this in mind, I will tell you that some of our Space Brothers (I will call them Federation members from here on in) are from the myriad of intersecting dimensions around planet Earth. In times past, these have been called the spirit world. The Spiritualist Church has channeled these beings for many years; they have guided people individually, giving messages of impending danger, messages of hope and love. These spirit world Federation members usually work with personal human matters for they have recently spent a human lifetime and can relate to human problems. Many paranormal occurrences which star people experience are caused by communication with this spirit world Federation contact. An example of this is the on-going communication that one of our beloved channels (star people) feels with his wife who passed from the human plane of existence and now works with us Space Brothers (she is one of us).

The question usually arises, "Well, then, is the idea wrong that The Federation are aliens from other planets? Are they really the traditional spirit world which has been reached in séances and in psychic ways for many years?"

The answer is, "We are the spirit world, we are aliens from other planets...and more!" Do not ever make the mistake of limiting us to one exact source! We are many beings of great diversity! However, all of us are beings of God and goodness who are concerned about planet Earth at this time!

Yes, some of us are beings from other planets which circle other stars; some of us even look like E.T. of Hollywood fame! As you know, Steven Spielberg based his little alien character on actual sightings of the "alien" bodies which have been retrieved from UFOs (our craft) which have malfunctioned and crashed.

Other extraterrestrial (outer space) Federation members are not nearly as humanoid as E.T. types; of all the science fiction which has been written about variations on life (gray masses of protoplasm, tiny multicellular, sentient lifeforms, rocks which have consciousness, lifeforms which are pure energy/light, etc.), please believe me that it is all "out there," and then some! The encounters which await humankind when he enters The Federation are not only more diverse than he imagines but more diverse than he can imagine!

However, as man explores outer space, he also explores inner space.

Many of the angels of whom we spoke earlier are spirit guides (Ascended Masters), who are not technically of extraterrestrial origin, not technically of the spirit world (those who have recently passed from the Earth plane). These are beings of the Higher Realms - energies - who call no one planet home but rather serve God directly. These beings are also Federation members, having worked with humankind since time immemorial (the Eastern religions and philosophies have known them well, as have Christianity and other inspired religions).

These angelic beings/Ascended Masters send much of the channeling received by our star people. They are dimension travelers of sorts but their mind/souls are so powerful and so good that no technology is necessary, as God reaches all dimensions, all planets, all worlds.

Another group which belongs to The Federation is, in science fiction terms, time travelers. These are humans of the future conscious level who, through the help of technology (space and dimension craft), journey back in time to guide their human brothers and sisters - before it is too late.

This group is, in one way, the most important Federation group who now works with humankind, for the Future Human Consciousness is exactly what modern man must aim for.

Time may be traversed; it is not a one-way street. Time may be "hopped," various points in time may be visited, for time is made up of multiconsecutive points, all intersecting with multi-dimensions at which we can "Space/Time interphase" (intersect) points (warps).

There are alternate realities to all timelines. Those Federation members of the Future Human Consciousness are those who belong to a timeline where Earth survived the late 20th Century and flourished, spreading her seeds out into the galaxy and to other dimensions. Earth, in this timeline, has become a valued Federation member; we have found that - through mind waves and technical devices which help translate "alien" mind waves - we can communicate freely and with love to the spirit world, the angelic beings, the extraterrestrials, and a host of other intelligent lifeforms including Earth's special natural energies frequently called Mother Earth, and the beloved animal intelligences on planet Earth. In 1988, humanity is just beginning to realize that the whale, for instance, is a wise and sentient lifeform which communicates in intricate ways.

THE REAL LIFE UFO TRANSFORMATION OF DIANE TESSMAN

As our beloved Jesus/Sananda said, "I stand at the door and knock." The Federation now knocks at humanity's door. The time has come for humankind to grow up. He is not the only fish in the sea! Spiritually, also, man is not alone!

MESSAGE FROM TIBUS

This is Tibus. I come to you in Love and Light.

First, you must realize that one may transcend the river called "time." Most people on 20th Century Earth accept that time ticks along just as the river keeps flowing downstream and that this is an absolute which can never be overcome. However, with advanced technology and/or with a mind/soul of a higher frequency, one may head upstream just as if you had a motor boat to help you go against the current. Or, one may simply stand on the bank of the river and observe what was and what will be, as well as what is. Also, you must realize that there are other rivers (other timeframes, other dimensions/ frequencies) flowing consecutively with the 20th Century Earth "river".

We of the Federation have stood on the bank of Earth's timeline/history since human life began on Earth. Just as the U.S. citizen should not have gone into the Aboriginal tribe's culture and totally changed it, so we have not overtly interfered with the karmic path of planet earth. However, we do urgently offer warnings of impending danger, we do offer wisdom and insight on the beauty which can be, and we do send in "pre-made" interpreters!

In other words, there are souls among us whose unique essence very much belongs to our frequency/dimension - who volunteer to live on Earth for a lifetime, awaiting contact from us (for this promise from Home never leaves their hearts and souls). This is the only way which we can find interpreters (or bridges) between our dimension and the Earth (mundane) dimension. Unlike the Aboriginal interpreter, Earth simply does not offer a way for tribal residents to get away (leave Earth) for training/experiences elsewhere. Can you imagine a person who had been taken into space by aliens being accepted back on Earth and allowed to advise/help the Earth "tribe" in its problems? The governments of Earth would not even let the "interpreter" out of confinement after his or her experience in outer space!

In a sense, we infiltrate; our star people are on lifetime "espionage" missions. However, these missions are ones which are only to enlighten Earth, to gently guide her, to quietly raise the frequency level, to pave the way for a higher dimension but within Earth's historical timeline. We do not overtly interfere or change history or meddle unless individual crises do not allow otherwise; and even then we often choose to allow the mundane dimension's karmic debts to be enacted, lived out, fulfilled - so that the higher dimension may occur naturally.

And so, occasionally a star soul is born into a family whose other member's essences belong exclusively to the mundane dimension's frequency. (Once in a while, the star soul is born into a family who has another star person within it)

This baby, whose unique essence is not at home in the dimension in which it finds itself (a stranger in a strange land!) frequently experiences serious health problems in its early years for the dimension is literally poisonous to him or her.

This baby often has an odd blood type, low blood pressure, low body temperature. However, this is not always the case. An essence from outside the mundane reality simply has trouble adjusting its unique energies to a human body. We do not stress these physical differences nor do we stress the unexplained scars which many of our star people have (the result of medical procedures by us during encounters with us, for specific purposes...usually to protect the star person.) We do not stress these characteristics of star people for the simple reason that these are physical differences which could be recognized - and acted upon - in a Nazi-like way by a frightened Earth government, military group, or smaller subversive group. We do not want a finger pointed at our star people; their entire mission is one of "low profile" until the return Home can be embarked upon.

The star child reaches early childhood as a human but finds that she (or he) looks at the stars with tears in the eyes - tears which are not fully understood at the time but tears which come from the very heart and soul of the child. These are the stars of Home.

The star child finds that other youngsters function on a more brutal, non-sensitive level than she does. She wonders what is "wrong" with her. She turns to Nature for its precious animals, forests, streams, oceans, mountains for comfort and companionship. The star child feels very much alone, very much a stranger in a strange land.

The star child interacts (usually this is not consciously remembered for the child's own good) with unseen companions/playmates; she has dream experiences with the home dimension. Usually, there are also physical encounters with "paranormal beings" and/or UFO occupants. As mentioned before, these are necessary visits by us to our young brother or sister. They are necessary to activate, to awaken the child. The memory of these visits is usually blocked by us from the child's conscious mind (again, so as the child will not stand out as "too strange.")

The star child has a great sense of justice, often becoming involved in human rights and environmentalist causes; however, eventually the star person becomes convinced that a spiritual/vibratory change is the only thing which will move planet Earth forward, for the established governments are too corrupt and complex to change effectively or to change in time to stop global destruction and contamination.

Perhaps the most confusing thing about the star people concept is that no one seems to know how narrow or how broad to make the definition.

Is a star person only one who channels a space intelligence, just as Diane is channeling me at the present moment of this writing?

Is a star person only one who is extremely wise in metaphysics or UFO data or one whose life is so perfect as to allow an almost total spiritual involvement?

Is a star person only one who has an odd blood type, low blood pressure, sinusitis, low body temperature, an extra vertebrae, who was an unexpected child? (I must explain here that often our star people's conceptions occur under impossible conditions, such as their mother being unable to conceive or their father being sterile.)

Is a star person only one who has always felt they do not belong to their family? Or, must a star person want desperately to fly in a starship?

The answer to all these questions is "No!" There is no one "requirement," no one list of characteristics.

It is true that a star person will probably relate to one or more of the paragraphs above.

It also must be remembered that star people's sources (though all of the Federation, a coalition of beings of goodness and God who share a great concern for planet Earth at this time) are not all the same! Some star people do remember, within their very soul...being a crew member aboard a "nuts and bolts" space craft (starship.) The longing to return to this home craft is much like a swallow's instinct to return to Capistrano. However, other star people come directly from the "pure energy beings" (angelic presences/ Ascended Masters) who do not use starships.

THE REAL LIFE UFO TRANSFORMATION OF DIANE TESSMAN

This example is true for the other characteristics mentioned above. If you do not possess most of these characteristics but if you have a deep longing in your soul for "elsewhere" and for a bright new day for planet Earth, then do not dismiss yourself as most likely not a star person. You do not need any exact "qualifications;" what you feel within is the true test, the true definition. It is very difficult to draw lines between star people and star helpers. In the final analysis, the soul of goodness who seeks, who wishes to make a better world...is our brother, our sister. Yes, some star people are distinctly "alien," others are not so distinct. It is the spirit which counts!

DIANE: THE SPECIAL ONE CONNECTION

In metaphysics, spirit guides have long accompanied the voyager on his or her journey through the inner reaches of the mind and the outer reaches of the universe.

In spiritualism's communication with the spirit world, other worldly presences have long given advice and comfort (often a trance medium can channel for a loved one who has passed into the spirit world, giving a special message to the relative or friend left behind in the mundane dimension.)

Many people know that they have a guardian angel who guides and protects them throughout their life's path.

Those who are drawn to seek contact with "outer space intelligences" or extraterrestrials often channel the wisdom and advise of those higher beings.

Do these descriptions also fit the Special One who abides with each star person in a shared consciousness, shared mind waves situation.

Yes, the Special One may be thought of as a spirit guide, a good presence from the spirit world, a guardian angel, and/or a "voice" from outer space, or more accurately, from The Federation/The Space Brothers.

However, the Special One may also be described as the co-worker of the star person, the soulmate, the companion who stays on the Home Frequency and whose responsibility it is to contact, to monitor, to guide, to stay with the star person in his human adventures.

In many cases, the Special One is simply a crew member aboard one of the home starships. In other cases, the Special One is very much of the angelic realm, truly fitting the guardian angel definition. Again, the Special One's exact source depends on the star person's exact source. The Federation's members are varied; the diversity is beautiful, but all beings of the Federation are of God and goodness. All members of the Federation believe in universal law, wisdom, goodness, integrity and in serving the creative God-force.

The star people I work with all know within their hearts that they do indeed have a co-worker, a Special One. Not all have found the clearest channels to him or her yet, but spectacular leaps have been made toward this - our most important mission at present if the larger, overall mission is to be fulfilled.

MESSAGE FROM TIBUS

This is Tibus. I come to you in Love and Light.

Again, please remember that all unique essences (minds/souls) function on a certain pattern of energy. The type of energy on which they function is determined by the frequency (dimension/vibration) to which they belong.

In other words, "A.C." electrical current might be the type of energy for one dimension, whereas "D.C." electrical current might be the energy for another dimension. This is an over-simplified analogy but it gives you a concept of that of which I speak.

Each mind/soul is unique; however, through spiritual advancement and through technical advancement, we have found that a mind/soul can exist independently in two or more dimensions at the same time. Thus we remind our star people that in a parallel (not "past") lifetime, they are one among us, our brothers and sisters, our esteemed and loved colleagues.

We have also found that, through the advancement of the psychic powers of the mind and through technical/medical implants, a mind/soul can be in communication with a co-worker from the home source at various intervals throughout his or her life. This communication can be constant (and we call this a shared consciousness with the co-worker/Special One) or it can occur only when necessary (we also called this telepathic contact channeling).

You must also realize that this shared consciousness and/or channeling allows you to be empathetic with the co-worker/Special One from the home dimension. And so, this is not a mere sharing of cosmic wisdom or facts on possible global destruction, it is an emotional contact as well.

THE REAL LIFE UFO TRANSFORMATION OF DIANE TESSMAN

The young star child feels this emotional contact first. The Special One who often times have met with the young star child during (what is called on Earth) a UFO encounter - is as a parent to the child. More than parent, the Special One represents the link to Home. The star child lives on two sides of the mountain: one is his or her life on Earth and the other side is the home side of the consciousness (which is not usually remembered in conscious detail but is remembered always in the heart and soul). The emotional link is the most important connection which the star person has with the Special One. This link is felt even if crystal clear communication/channeling is not achieved. This link is all that is truly necessary, though the more finely tuned communication is of course preferable.

The childhood contact may also be termed a spiritual vision or experience. UFOs need not be involved!

There are pre-planned stages which each star person goes through. These stages are known and approved by the star person in his or her parallel life in the home dimension before embarking on the human lifetime. Other facets of the human mission are also known and agreed upon. We stress that our star people are much admired and respected for accepting these missions; there is no punishment involved in living a lifetime on Earth but rather it is looked upon as a noble mission to help save a faltering planet.

In early childhood, the star nature of the star person is very evident. Many interactions with the home dimension occur at this time. The star child usually has three major encounters/experiences with co-workers from home. These may involve UFO experiences or spiritual/paranormal experiences. Usually these experiences are almost totally blocked (by us) from the star person's conscious mind for their own protection; the star nature is sufficient - that which beats in the star person's heart and soul - without their reciting, childlike, an experience which they have had but which no one else believes. This only alienates the star child, hurts the star child...and does not help with the lifetime mission.

The star person does not have an easy time of it in ordinary schools; other children are usually mean to the star child much as chickens mistreat a quail which wanders into the henhouse. Small beings of any dimension are more "psychic" than adults and sense the different frequency which operates within the star child's mind/soul.

Being more gentle, kind, sensitive, and tolerant than those around you is difficult and results in many hurts and emotional scars. The Special One often appears to the star child as either a "presence" which can be felt (a very loving presence) or the Special One fortifies the star child's mind/soul, allowing the star child to know that there is truly nothing wrong with him or her...that there is great beauty and intelligence within.

The Special One opens the star child's mind/soul to a very pure communication with nature and with God. Usually organized religion is found to be dreadfully lacking in depth and universalism by the star person, who studies, meditates, experiences on his or her own terms. The star person is basically a mystical being from babyhood onward.

Usually in young adulthood, the star person makes an attempt at normalcy within the mundane dimension. This simply does not work out because it is like trying to get a radio station while tuned to another station; one cannot change the basic frequency of the essence!

There is a time of re-awakening, a time when pieces of the puzzle fit together...after the young adulthood phase is over.

At this time, the Special One re-contacts the star person in a "re-awakening." Sometimes the star person undergoes hypnosis, seeking out a reputable medical hypnotist, in an attempt to solve the puzzle of his or her life. Suddenly, the star person knows there is a star identity, that there are hidden encounters and experiences, that there is a star mission to be performed. A flame grows, telling the star person that the truth must be found, that mystical secrets must be unfolded, that the home dimension calls.

Often at this time, the star person changes professions or living locations, making an abrupt change in his or her life. This move is very definitely guided and protected by the Special One; a new profession is found which better suits the star nature and the star mission.

At this time, the Special One is sought out in meditation, in channeling, even in seeking out UFO contacts.

Once the full star nature is freed, there is very little which the star person cannot do within the Earth dimension; also, a major step is made back toward the "stars of home." The star nature must be recognized, valued, loved by each star person! Scars from the mundane dimension must be healed, walled off - not allowed to offer a barrier to the star mission.

THE REAL LIFE UFO TRANSFORMATION OF DIANE TESSMAN

As the life of the star person unfolds (almost always not along conventional lines!), the star mission is being fulfilled and the Special One smiles.

However, our star people (though many have lived on Earth in all time frames) are on Earth in great numbers during this time frame due to the impending disaster of nuclear confrontation and destruction. Also, Mother Earth (a personification of the Divine Cosmic God within this planet's atmosphere) has been polluted, murdered, maimed by man's careless, cruel hand. And so, the star mission has three phases: one before the Change Point (called the End Days by some), one during the Change Point, and one following the Change Point.

I will elaborate on the Change Point in a moment, but I wish to stress now that the Special One is with the star person at all phases of the star mission!

1) The Special One is a loving companion and equal co-worker in the star persons parallel life in the home dimension.

2) The Special One is the contact in the star person's childhood experiences.

3) The Special One is the on-going protector, monitor, guide throughout the star person's lifetime on planet Earth in the pre-Change Point era.

4) The Special One will be the bridge between the star person and the home dimension as the star person returns home at the Change Point

5) The Cycle is complete. The Special One is once again as he or she was in the #1 phase.

DIANE: EARTH CHANGES

Author's Update: As my mission has unfolded over these many years, it is plain that our primary mission has been to try to help the life-forms of Mother Earth and to wake up humans about how we are hurting our unique, magnificent planet.

Tibus has sent messages and waged ongoing campaigns to educate and awaken people spiritually not only to the nuclear threat, but to how we are altering the climate of our planet so as it is less hospitable and, eventually, non-inhabitable.

Along this line, we have talked about the coming of superstorms which were unheard of in 1983 (Whitley Strieber first wrote of "superstorms"

in 1987), we have predicted floods, droughts, the increase in size and frequency of tornadoes and hurricanes, and the deadly rise in temperatures to the point where in areas of "hot climate" are now nearly unlivable in the summer season, and more.

Tibus' urgent messages regarding "Mother Earth and her living spirit Gaia," have gone out to subscribers without fail. Another of our special topics is the plight of Earth's animals, whether they live in the oceans or rivers, or on land, whether they fly or run or crawl, we have warned of their coming extinction. This goes for Mother Earth's pollinators (from bees to butterflies) and for the wondrous trees of Earth which are also threatened.

We have urged star people to be activists as well as to meditate in order to help spiritually. In 1983, Tibus and I had a huge assignment ahead of us, and we continue this Assignment: Earth even today.

Any intelligent person is very worried about planet Earth at this time. The End could come tonight, tomorrow, next week. Never before have we had the killing capabilities that we do today; the "overkill" factor is staggering! Not only can the human race kill all life on planet Earth for billions of years, but it can overkill all life on this planet many, many times over!

Remember also that the unleashing of nuclear radiation will affect not only this world but worlds/dimensions/planets which share intersect points with this one (an infinite number!). Nuclear radiation warps, destroys energy/life itself. What happens to the very soul itself which is caught in a nuclear holocaust (or even a smaller nuclear "mishap" like the meltdown of a nuclear reactor?). Is the soul damaged or destroyed? What does this mean to, for instance, the spirit world?

All star missions of all star people are aimed at the point in time when the choice will be made between life and death on planet Earth. The foremost mission (overall) is to help raise the frequency so that a new, higher dimension maybe entered without nuclear destruction! This is possible, even now. If this cannot be achieved, we will work for a brave new start after limited destruction occurs.

And if there is full scale destruction, we will join hands with our Special Ones and co-workers on the home side in an attempt to salvage some life from the once beautiful Earth...to nurture it far from Earth, and to help it flourish once again.

THE REAL LIFE UFO TRANSFORMATION OF DIANE TESSMAN

The point is, we are as ready as we can be. Through our self-explorations as flowering star people, we are not only aware of the home dimension, but we love it and long to return to it. We also know Mother Earth well and would do all in our power to save her. We abide in Christ Consciousness, the home frequency, having not compromised to the colder, crueler materialistic dimension in which we live this human lifetime.

As Tibus has stated, there are alternate time lines, alternate eddies and currents in the river Time. We must never assume that the End Days are a foregone conclusion and simply wash our hands of the whole matter, choosing not to champion rights, environmental causes, or nuclear awareness causes. We can make the future positive, it need not happen!! It may be your individual belief in this which will engineer Earth's reality/time line away from nuclear destruction.

If "it" does happen, either limited or full scale, we are as ready as we can be!

MESSAGE FROM TIBUS

This is Tibus. I come to you in Love and Light.

One thing is certain: a change in frequency/dimension will occur for planet Earth. It is simply a case of change or perish!

Our star people are living human lifetimes during this time phase for exactly that reason: to assist Earth through this Change Point.

The "radio station", the point on the dial, must be changed! A new frequency of Light and Love must be received!

I stress that this does not mean that Earth cannot go forward in technological ways as well, cannot travel to the Future Human Consciousness in proud silver starships. In no way does the Change Point mean that Earth will become a place where "angels tread." Our star people who hail from the angelic realms will return there...but Earth herself will go on her own path at her own rate of speed...toward The Future.

The nuclear cloud hangs heavy, but rest assured that there is a silver lining. If the nuclear catastrophe occurs (and it will in some time line), then from these ashes will rise a brave new phoenix called Future Humanity. We will still take our place as valuable beings within the universe, but the path willbe much harder. We hope to avert nuclear disaster in the dimension/time line in which you find yourself.

And so, the means by which the Change Point occurs is not the main issue here (though one of grave concern). The mam issue is that a new wave length of energy called the Change Point will "flood" the mundane dimension. This newenergy/wavelength will seem as a tidal wave at first, particularly to those who are not flexible, adaptable and who are not familiar with star nature and spirituality. At first, it will be a "sink or swim" proposition for each essence/ soul/mind.

Once the time of turbulence is over, a new, higher dimension will dominate and will become the "home dimension" for all souls formally of the mundane dimension. Our star people will assist those who are not familiar with the new, higher energy...for our star people have worked with it all their human lives, and it is indeed their wavelength, their home energy!.

In this way, our star people are the bridges between dimensions. They are as electrical adapters which take one wavelength of energy and translate it into another wavelength. They are special...more special than they have yet imagined!

They will lead you in the evacuation of planet Earth when and if that becomes necessary!

DIANE: RESPONSIBILITY OF A STAR SEED

There are many goals and truths which all of us have in common, be we defined as star people or as humans seeking enlightenment and a new path for our planet.

None of us wants nuclear war. None of us wants to pollute or kill nature. None of us wants to hurt another human nor another living being. We all seek spiritual fulfillment and a raising of consciousness level.

The star person has an added spark to this universal goal because there is a direct link to a higher world. Many souls follow the "regular" evolutionary paths of a planet in terms of karmic development and the soul's progression. The star person's soul comes from outside the regular soul development as it unfolds on this (or any) planet. The star person is a volunteer soul who did not have to follow the karmic progression but who chose to, in order to help.

Never does a star person brag about this fact. And never do we claim that there are not many, many souls from outside the regular karmic path now living, working, helping, on planet Earth...for there are!

Being a star person brings responsibility. It is not enough to earn a living and to not participate much in the cruelties of the mundane dimension. We have a responsibility to play a more active role!

Currently, one does not go down the street telling people that you are from another world. However, the day will come soon when we will be sought out to explain what is happening (at the Change Point), when we will be pressed into duty, when we will have to be the best we can be.

Many of us have great healing abilities. Other of us have the ability to be brave in the face of the unknown, to actually feel that it is our friend. There will be much bravery and courage needed! Many of us will be the psychological healers of traumatized minds, others will have the ability to lead into the New Age (past the Change Point) for we are experts in it through our quiet studies and experiences!

The star people movement will come out of the closet soon. It is an idea whose time has come, a people who will pave the way for a New Humanity. We will be proud to be humans...and thrilled to go out into the galaxy, to traverse dimensions, to explore new worlds...and meet the life which is out there, learning from it, offering a helping hand if necessary (just as is being done for us at this time).

The future is ours.

MESSAGE FROM TIBUS

This is Tibus. I come to you in Love and Light.

I do not channel pages and pages on the Change Point to Diane for this is not for me to "dictate." Each reader must comprehend its significance for his or her self and meditate/think/feel...that which I communicate. Details are not necessary and are detrimental in many ways. If I could fully communicate through human words the enormity and the significance of the Change Point which lies ahead, I would be very tempted to do so. However, it is for each of you to internalize and fully comprehend.

In conclusion I transmit to you that our star people are among you now in greater numbers than at any time in human history (even Biblical times).

THE REAL LIFE UFO TRANSFORMATION OF DIANE TESSMAN

They are among you in order to guide you through the Change Point into a new, higher dimension/world which has not the shallowness, the emphasis on money, nor the brutality of the current consciousness.

Some of you who are reading this know already that you are indeed star people. Diane, myself, and others have confirmed this to you but indeed you have always known it within your heart and your memory echoes.

Some of you reading this suspect yourself to be a star person. Do not ever underestimate yourself, do not be humble in pursuing this possibility to its fullest. Follow your inner feelings more than any overt UFO contact (or lack of it). The details of your star path (such as UFO contact or the lack of it) will become clear as your path continues.

Some of you reading this are educating yourself as to the existence of star people. We urge you to be the best humanity has to offer. One can simply raise his or her awareness level to such a point as to be on the higher frequency. This is within reach of all intelligent (sentient) life.

Our star people are among you now! Yes, they are aliens in the literal sense of the word....but they are also humans. They have lived lifetimes as human, have been initiated into human ways in painful learning experiences. They stand ready to help Earth through the Change Point just as they did when they accepted their star mission in their parallel life among us. Theirs is a love...a universal love...which transcends dimension. Theirs is a mission which abounds in the unconditional joy of helping an entire world/dimension through the most challenging and dangerous time in its history. Please love them as much as we do, we who are their co-workers of the home dimension, and search your inner being for the highest of star/spiritual qualities...for this will be your home frequency as well in a very short time!

11

MESSAGES FROM TIBUS

PART ONE

TIBUS CHANNELS REGARDING REINCARNATION March 1987

Author's Update: ***THE TRANSFORMATION* of 1983 was an 8x10 booklet, but in 1987, my publisher and friend Timothy Green Beckley of Global Communications, asked me to enlarge *THE TRANSFORMATION* so he could publish it as a paperback I was happy to share transmissions from Tibus which I had recently been receiving.**

I would like to use this channeling to discuss certain aspects of reincarnation with you; but before I begin, I would just like to remind you that the negativity which has been so prevalent recently is not a permanent aspect of your life. Rather, it is my opinion that much of this negativity has come into Earth's sphere because of a current "downward trend" - politically, technologically, and spiritually.

To explain, let me simply say that the star person such as yourself is sensitive to any and all changes in the Earth's magnetic fields - and those fields are, of course, comprised of living energy as well as of static energy. At any rate, it is interesting to note that your world has recently found itself in the grips of many problems - the Iran hostage situation, the continued trouble in the Middle East, the loss of the Challenger over a year ago, and a series of other, perhaps smaller problems which have all contributed to the general sense of negativity which has been affecting your world lately.

What is important for you to remember is that you can overcome this negativity by simply refusing to participate in it. While it isn't always possible to escape it or its influences completely, it is always possible to use your own spiritual awareness in order to side-step any personal involvement with it. In other words, by being aware of this negativity and by being even further aware of its cause, you gain the ability to view the situation from a much higher standpoint - that is, you develop the ability to understand the negativity, the depression which seems so common in the general populace recently, and the feeling of hopelessness which some star people have mentioned recently. As always, the key to defeating this negative energy is through your own awareness. With that awareness, you then gain the option of not participating and/or contributing to the negativity. And, of course, as energy is taken away from this negativity little-by-little, the negativity will slowly dissipate and eventually be gone. Add to your nightly meditations a mantra for harmony and well-being - for yourself, for your planet, and for all creatures with whom you share your world.

Additionally, awareness is what this reading is all about - your awareness not only of situations and circumstances in this Earthly incarnation, but awareness of previous - and even future - incarnations as well.

As Diane has mentioned many times previously, most people on your planet today have lived a variety of previous lifetimes - some in Rome, some in England, perhaps even some in Atlantis, Lemuria, or other so-called "mythical" societies. Wherever you lived, it is important to know that you have lived, and that you will live again even after passing through this current lifetime.

Many non-believers in the phenomena of reincarnation would attempt to tell us that past lives cannot be verified except under the questionable process of hypnosis. And yet, I transmit to you at this time, that such is simply not the case. Any person who truly wishes to gain an awareness of his/her previous incarnations can easily do so - through meditation and, surprisingly enough, through simple psychic/spiritual awareness.

Many times, you have undoubtedly experienced the sensation of déjà vu - a feeling of "I've done this before." As I have mentioned in previous channelings, the deja vu phenomena is a very important one to the star person as a means of comprehending the nature of time travel. But it is equally as important in developing an awareness of previous lifetimes. The feeling of "I've done this before" is one which scientists cannot accurately explain anymore than those same scientists could explain the theory of reincarnation. And yet, it is a relatively simple phenomenon - one which everyone (even "unpsychic" individuals) has experienced at some time in their life.

Since I have discussed the déjà vu experience many times in the past, I will not use it extensively here; yet I wanted to you to be aware that it is one more way that we can begin to verify previous lifetimes. For example, when passing through a certain area of the world where you have never visited before, you suddenly know exactly what lies around the next bend. Perhaps this is not because your mind "races ahead of itself' as scientists would attempt to have you believe, but because, in a former existence, you travelled that same road- whether the road was a freeway, a horse trail or nothing more than a rabbit path through dense undergrowth. Perhaps you seem to be born with certain knowledge because you have been here before, or because you were drawn back to that location because of a former incarnation.

For instance, the succession of individual lifetimes is no accident, no simple matter of coincidence. Each lifetime is part of a natural progression – yet each individual lifetime need not follow the one which, logically, should have happened just before. To explain, please bear with me.

It is entirely possible - even likely - that you have lived just as many future incarnations as past lives. And yet, since the human mind can only comprehend time as a linear flow of events, spiritualists, astrologers and psychics tend to refer to these other lifetimes as "past lives" for the matter of clarity. In other words, chances are that you have lived at least one life time in the past - perhaps in the Old West, or perhaps during the time of Queen Elizabeth I. But it is equally as likely that you have lived in the year 2010, for example, or in the year 21,110, for that matter.

In short, we are capable of skipping around in our lifetimes - for several very good reasons. Essentially, there are many lessons to be learned in each different time period, and it is often necessary that we learn a lesson which can only be taught in the year 2010, for example, before we can complete our "life's mission" in our lifetime in the year 1900.

For example, perhaps you have never considered that the technology your world is utilizing today is a gift from the future rather than a progression toward the future. In other words, it is conceivable that you lived a life in the year 2500 A.D., for example, and that during that lifetime you studied spaceflight extensively - for the express purpose of coming back to live a lifetime in the year 1995 A.D., and bring the future "lesson" back to the past. In short, this is called "circular lives" - and it is the only theory which can adequately explain leaps in technology, the raising of spiritual awareness, and so on.

As an easier example, consider that women, Blacks, and other "minorities" have only recently been gaining rights which have always been available to White Anglo-Saxon Protestant men. Could this be because someone who had lived in an ideal future society - either on Earth or on another world - came back to live in the early 1900's, for example, and "brought back" her knowledge of a society where men and women were equal? The same theory works quite well for any other minority.

THE REAL LIFE UFO TRANSFORMATION OF DIANE TESSMAN

Perhaps a black man was born in the year 2200 A.D., and was able to live as an equal brother to the white man, the Oriental, the Hispanic and so on. And yet, that black man, being aware that his forebearers lived in slavery, was compelled to enter a "past life" in order to start the wheels of freedom in motion.

And, of course, there are the lifetimes we have lived on other worlds - also for the sake of learning - both for one's own individual spirit, and for the sake of bringing that acquired knowledge into whatever new lifetime he/she enters after death. The majority of all star people have lived at least one other lifetime on a world other than Earth - which often leads to the feeling of "I want to go home," or which contributes to the sensation of loneliness or "awe" which can overtake you when you look at the stars. This sense of homesickness is, of course, the result of having lived elsewhere - and the pull of your immortal spirit to return to that home which exists in the far reaches of space.

At any rate, whatever lifetimes you have lived and wherever you have lived them, the most important thing is for you to develop your awareness of these lifetimes more fully. This is critical to the star person, for it will enable you to more fully comprehend your sense of personal direction and, additionally, it will help you to more fully understand the nature of your cosmic mission. Each soul has two specific purposes in each lifetime: (1) To add to your spiritual knowledge on a personal level and; (2) To advance your cosmic mission on toward its eventual completion. Your personal spiritual development, of course, is equally as important, yet you should know that each individual lifetime furthers you on a vast, cosmic mission. Everyone who has lived or whoever will live does so for one large purpose and several smaller purposes - and by developing a greater awareness of your past lifetimes, you will gain a deeper understanding of both.

Finally, remember that you are important in the scope of things. You are an integral part of the cosmos itself, and you are here for a very important reason. As a star person, one part of your cosmic mission is to bring enlightenment to those around you, as well as to continually involve yourself in spiritual mysteries which are perhaps the food of your very soul. This food is part of your joy of living, part of the fuel which helps to stabilize an often "crazy" world, and which keeps your own spirit afloat.

Remember that we are with you, and that we will be together always. Through the common bond of other lifetimes, we have all been drawn together in this incarnation for a great purpose, and I am so very pleased to know you now, as I have known you before, and will know you again.

May the healing light of God and goodness surround you always, **Tibus**

Comment: As Tibus indicated, it is often the unknown (or mystery) which feeds the soul of the star person. And as long as we continue our search, I am confident that those questions will lend themselves to answers - and more questions. Additionally, as Tibus has said before, perhaps the question is of far more importance than the answer - and I now feel that I have a greater understanding of why this is so. D.M.T.

TIBUS CHANNELS REGARDING CREATIVITY, IMAGINATION AND "POETIC TRUTH "

April 1987

The creative process of thought is as valuable to them as are facts which can be learned through study. Star people are also being encouraged to utilize our creative thought processes for a variety of reasons. By using our imagination, it becomes possible to see things which otherwise might remain forever hidden. It becomes possible to speculate on the birth of a star or the death and subsequent transformation of an entire universe. It has been said that "Life itself exists within the limitless space of the mind itself." We live our solitary lives in the confines of our own head; and yet, through creative thought process, we begin to reach out - for the stars, for enlightenment, and for Ultimate Truth.

I would like to talk to you at this time about what we star guides call Poetic Truth. In essence, this is a concept which is as ancient in the Home Dimension as the concepts of life and death are here on your Earth. For the most part, the idea of Poetic Truth has not yet been "born" onto your world, and through this reading, it is my hope to inspire you with the knowledge and the intuition which will give you the ability to help awaken that Truth here on your own planet.

Essentially, Poetic Truth is a combination of imagination, creativity and intuition. It begins, of course, with Intuition - one of the basic psychic gifts of the star person such as yourself.

What is Intuition? It is primarily the ability to sense truth or a lack of truth in something - whether it is a concept, a statement or a condition. For example, you have obviously had an opportunity to travel to some new place at some time in your life. Upon arriving at your destination, you have had feelings about that place - either good or negative, usually. Your Intuition tells you a sort of "history" of the place you are visiting. You know, for example if you are visiting a house you have never seen before, something about the people who live there. Your Intuition tells you that these are warm, loving people; or, contrapuntally, your Intuition could warn you that the people living in the house are not what they seem.

At that point, your Imagination comes into play - in the form of mental scenarios acted out on the stage of your mind. For example, if your Intuition tells you that the people living in the house you are visiting are warm and good, your Imagination encourages images of a mother and child sharing cookies and milk in the kitchen. Or, if your Intuition gives you a warning, your Imagination may well dredge up a scenario of someone having died unexpectedly in the house. You see these images on the viewscreen of your mind's eye.

And, surprisingly, if you were to research the history of the house, you may well discover that your Intuition and Imagination were "right on." Perhaps the details may have been slightly different, but in essence, your impressions turn out to be correct.

This is the first part of the phenomena known as Poetic Truth - the ability of the star person to combine Intuition and Imagination in order to garner a certain truth about people, inanimate objects or physical, geographical locations on a map. You know intuitively if you should or shouldn't travel into the desert, for example. You know intuitively that you are going to like your new boss or your new employee. And with the added dimension of your imagination, you begin to project your own imprint into the situation - which is where the third ingredient of Creativity comes into the picture.

All creatures are capable of Intuition and Imagination. But Creativity is an art form reserved for a select few - including star people such as yourself. Creativity is exactly what the word implies - the ability to create, to form and mold reality in accordance with your own wishes and desires. In essence, Reality Engineering is something all creatures do to one extent or another - but Reality Engineering is not exactly the same thing as employing your Creativity. You engineer your reality through unconscious actions - such as walking down one side of the street as opposed to the other, for example, or having vegetables for dinner as opposed to fruit. These more-or-less "subliminal decisions" are, of course, vitally important to your personal destiny, yet they do not employ your Creative ability to its fullest extent.

Which brings us, of course, to the concept of Poetic Truth. Poetic truth is, in a very simple explanation, the ability to combine Intuition, Imagination and Creativity in order not only to bend destiny, but actually to create it. It has often been said that everything which has been thought of now exists on some physically real plane. For example, far-flung star civilizations exist because writers have "created" them on paper and have subsequently made their writing available for others to read. Upon reading those works, others become involved in the creation/maintenance of that one writer's original "universe." A good example of this would come with a very popular television program known as Star Trek. It began in the mind of one writer, yet now it is a part of world culture. Everyone has heard the phrase, "Beam me up, Scotty," and almost everyone has some basic knowledge of the journeys of the USS Enterprise. And I transmit to you at this time that this is no accident. Essentially, every reality begins in the mind of one entity. The Divine Creator thought of the universe, and now the universe does, in fact, exist. The first man thought of his aloneness and longed for another such as himself. And now two sexes exist. Man thought of flying, and eventually air travel came into being.

The list is, as you can see, endless. And it applies very strongly to the star person. Why? Because everything must first be conceived before it can exist. As a star person you can conceive of things far beyond the ken of most people living on your planet today. You can conceive of far-flung stars supporting peaceful civilizations. You can conceive of star-flight capability which would bring the stars within the reach of your world today. You can conceive of world peace and the harmony of Man and Animal.

And in your conception, you will learn to employ the art of Poetic Truth. In essence, by utilizing the full potential of Imagination, Intuition and Creativity, you will begin to spark the flame of realization in the minds of others. For example, it's one thing to say, "I believe that man will eventually go to the stars." It's another matter entirely to say, "I know man will eventually go to the stars."

Belief is a matter of choice. I might "believe" that the moon is made of green cheese, yet that does not make it so. But if I know the moon is made of green cheese, if I truly know it as a matter of Truth, then in some reality, the moon is made of green cheese. Of course, in this reality, the moon is the moon - composed of rock and soil and the other elements. Why? Because the majority of people know that the moon is, in fact, a physically real body just as your Earth is a physically real body.

But you can see the possibilities that this opens. If the majority of people on your Earth began to believe that the moon was made of green cheese, is it possible that the chemical structure could be changed? This is, of course, a crude example, yet it illustrates what we mean by Poetic Truth.

Existence begins with Knowledge - and Knowledge leads, eventually, to Truth. There would be no logical reason why people would want to believe the moon is made of green cheese, yet there is every conceivable reason why Mankind would want - need - to believe that your people will eventually travel to the stars and beyond. And as a star person, part of your important earthly mission is to inspire that need/belief/knowledge in the minds of your fellow Man.

In your heart, you certainly know that life exists on planets other than Earth. And though this is a simple concept to you, you must understand that the majority of your fellow humans never even bother to consider this idea. Through your Intuition, you know that you are not alone in this vast universe. Through your imagination, you can see how life might be lived on some other world. And through your Creativity, you are charged with the task of inspiring that absolute knowledge within others.

The next time you are talking to someone of the mundane dimension, you might casually ask, "What do you think about the possibility of life on other planets?" I think you'd be surprised at the answer. Some people will say they aren't interested. Others will become very uncomfortable at the question. But the majority will show some type of interest. And as you begin talking, you will start to realize that these mundane souls are actually inspired by your enthusiasm, by your absolute knowledge that you are not alone.

This is only one manner in which Poetic Truth works. It is, for the most part, a matter of knowing something within your own mind - and not only knowing, but accepting what you know as Truth. Your Intuition gives you the ability to sense that Truth. Your imagination gives you details of how that Truth functions. And your Creativity enables you to give a spark of your star nature to others. Also, your Creativity allows you to more accurately see one of those far-flung worlds, and to know the people and cultures existing on that world. Open yourself to your Creativity, my star friend, and it is my heartfelt belief that you will find another part of your own personal Answer.

THE REAL LIFE UFO TRANSFORMATION OF DIANE TESSMAN

We encourage you to meditate further on this concept, and to contemplate the three ingredients of Poetic Truth in conjunction. Remember that Intuition, Imagination and Creativity are all a part of the process of creation of any reality.

"To exist is to be perceived." We perceive you, my star friend, just as you perceive us. And this is, of course, only the tip of the iceberg. There is an infinite universe waiting to be explored - and that exploration must begin with a thought.

May the healing light of God and goodness surround you always,

Tibus

Comment: Sometimes, it's easy for us to overlook our creative nature in our haste to survive and succeed in the mundane world. And yet, as Tibus has pointed out, only through the combination of Intuition, Imagination and Creativity can we hope to achieve the goals we all perceive. It must be through the development of spirituality combined with the instinct for survival that we continue our trek toward Oneness with the Cosmos, with Nature, and with our own human/star nature. D.M.T.

TIBUS CHANNELS REGARDING "BELIEF" AND "KNOWLEDGE"

May 1987

I would like to cover several topics with you at this time - most of them being of a somewhat ethereal and contemplative nature. Many times during one's day to day existence, there is a tendency to overlook the greater mysteries of Life itself; and only by allowing one's mind the freedom for that contemplation do we live up to our full potential as spiritual beings.

Meditation is perhaps one of the most critical aspects of a star person's life- not only the formalized meditation which requires silence, solitude and focus, but the more obscure forms of meditation which occur spontaneously. When you are alone with Nature, for example, or when your mind simply begins to drift as you are working, are also forms of meditation - the type which happens naturally whenever your mind feels a need to momentarily escape from the trials and tribulations surrounding you in your environment.

Which brings us to the point of personal survival in a troubled world. One of the first steps toward insuring the survival of your own serenity is to make a commitment to meditation, to remember at all times that your Mind and Spirit are of far greater importance than the self-serving needs of the Body. And while we strongly stress attention to physical needs as well, those needs can best be served when the Mind and Spirit are fulfilled and at rest.

Additionally, through your meditations, we encourage you to remember that the peace of the world begins in your thoughts, in your heart and mind. Remember that all thoughts and ideas are a form of energy - and that when you project or internalize those energies, they become forever a part of the unique fields surrounding this planet and all her people. Since you are obviously aware of the specifics, I will not go into further detail at this time, except to say that it is important to remember to project a calm, centered attitude at all times, to overcome the more base emotions of anger, possessiveness, jealousy and fear, and to subsequently replace those feelings with love, warmth and a spirit of sharing. Remember, my star friend, you are a part of this planet, too, and the energy of your thoughts and desires is an important part of the Whole. If the first step toward peace begins with a thought, then let that first thought begin within the serenity of you.

On another subject, perhaps not too closely related, I would like to discuss with you the abstract concepts of Belief and Knowledge, and how these two divergent ideas mesh with your own intuition to influence not only your own life, but the lives of those around you.

At some point in your life, you have probably encountered the universal riddle which asks: If a tree falls in the forest, but no one is present to hear it, does the falling tree make a sound?

On the surface, this may appear to be a somewhat "silly" pursuit. And yet, when we consider it in a broader perspective, it becomes possible to realize that there is no single definitive answer. For example, science tells us that the : physics of the falling tree are not altered regardless of whether anyone is there to confirm them or not. Theoretically, the tree does make the same sound it would make in the presence of hundreds of people. We believe, because of what we are told, that the tree falls and an answering crash resounds through the forest. But, I ask you at this time, do you personally know this to be true? Can you, without a doubt, say with absolute Knowledge, that the tree falling in a deserted forest made any sound at all? Can you know that physics work the same without the presence of human beings to confirm them? Or are you left to wonder if indeed there are still mysteries beyond human ken?

THE REAL LIFE UFO TRANSFORMATION OF DIANE TESSMAN

Of course, the example of the tree and the forest is somewhat extreme, yet we star guides feel that this riddle adequately demonstrates the difference between Belief and Knowledge. Only through personal experience can one be imbued with Knowledge, thus it is critical for the star person such as yourself to continue to amass a variety of experiences, to explore the mysteries which surround you, and to inevitably draw your own conclusions based on what you know to be true. At no time should the star person simply follow blindly. Instead, it is within your Earthly mission to continually question, to analyze what you have been told, what you have come to believe, and to subsequently apply all aspects of your Whole Self as you search for your personal answers as well as for Cosmic Truths.

Mainly, the star person such as yourself is encouraged to learn the difference between a fleeting belief and the absolute certainty and power of Knowledge itself. For example, no matter how much we may want to believe that this world will eventually find peace with itself, we cannot know that until that Knowledge becomes a part of our personal experience. And for that reason, it becomes imperative that you do amass the experiences and the Knowledge which will enable you to know rather than to simply believe.

Secondly, I ask you at this time to contemplate the proverb of the butterfly and the man. Many years ago, a man fell asleep and dreamt he was a butterfly. Then, upon awakening, he was no longer certain whether he was a man who had dreamt he was a butterfly, or a butterfly who now dreamed he was a man.

Again, this is illustrated in rather simplistic terms, yet it is our hope that the hidden complexities will encourage you to apply this type of thinking to your daily life. At some time, you have undoubtedly said, "This can't be happening to me. It's all just a bad dream from which I'll wake up in the morning." Or, in direct opposition, you may have had a profoundly beautiful experience at some time, at which point you said to yourself: "If this is a dream, I hope never to awaken."

And while we cannot live our entire lives by such a philosophy, it is occasionally enlightening to step back and ask ourselves, "What if what happens today is a dream?" By doing so, it becomes possible to visualize how an alternate path might have led to a different outcome, and how embarking on that different path might still effect the balance of the situation. For example, let us assume that a man is fired from his job and that, after the fact, he steps back with the attitude that the entire incident was nothing more than a bad dream. By gaining the perspective of distance, by sometimes telling yourself that daily experiences are of no more consequence than a simple dream, it becomes possible to gain a greater understanding of one's place within the Cosmic structure of the Universe itself. By realizing that no job is permanent, by understanding that even the nature of the most loving relationship is subject to change (positive or negative), we begin to realize that all we have been led to believe throughout our lives is really insignificant when compared to the majesty and scope of the infinite universe. By accepting that our lives are perhaps nothing more than a dream in the mind of God, we begin to understand that our primary function in each individual lifetime is to learn, to amass experiences through which we gain a deeper comprehension of our function and our goals.

Of course, these same philosophies can be narrowed down to a more personal field at any time. Rather than viewing the subject on a Cosmic level, it is possible to view the same circumstances on a day-to-day level as well. Then, as you begin to realize both the significance and the insignificance of the mundane world, your mind will automatically seek the serenity to be found on higher, more spiritual levels. By abandoning beliefs for the pursuit of Knowledge, the star person such as yourself is filled with understanding, serenity and ultimate harmony with oneself and with the greater universe.

Finally, remember that the path to Knowledge and Awareness is never an easy road to follow. It is a path which requires commitment, dedication and perseverance. And yet, I transmit to you at this time that the rewards of following this path will far outweigh the obstacles and even the occasional pain which is a part of any genuine desire to accomplish a new task.

Remember that what you believe to be true maybe nothing more than an illusion, a concept which is shattered under the light of scrutiny and personal examination. But what you know to be true - those truths which resound in your heart and fly free in your spirit - those are the eternal truths which will bring peace in times of trouble, serenity in times of turmoil. And it is those truths which will see you safely Home to the stars and finally beyond.

May the healing light of God and goodness surround you always,

Tibus

Comment: I realize that many of these concepts are perhaps strange and unusual, yet it is Tibus' desire that you should continue to ponder the mysteries of Life as well as those safe paths which we all tend to choose at times. Only when we abandon the "safe and easy" path for the spiritual pursuits of enlightenment and awareness will we achieve Balance within ourselves, and with the Cosmos as well.

When we remember that the Star Person chose this lifetime and this Earthly mission, we begin to understand that we are here for a very important reason, and that only by applying ourselves with full Knowledge will we be able to defeat the laziness which accompanies a simple "belief system." We must know that we are; only then can we truly be. D.M.T.

TIBUS CHANNELS REGARDING "THE BALANCE" YIN AND YANG WORKING TOGETHER TO CREATE A BETTER, MORE PERFECT WORLD.

July 1987

This is a time of great energy on your planet - some positive, some negative. But what is important is that you avail yourself of all aspects of this energy. The positive energy can, of course, be utilized in your daily life, through meditation, enlightenment and your own growing awareness. Negative energy, on the other hand, cannot be ignored either, and must first be incorporated into the positive energy before it can be of positive benefit to anyone or anything.

Briefly, it is possible to work with negative energy in two ways. The first method is simply to make a conscious effort to dispel negative energy through the positive powers of meditation, prayer and creative visualization. To do this, one needs only visualize a void of darkness being penetrated by the pure goodness of the White Light of Healing. This seems simple, but it does indeed work - particularly if you can visualize the healing light surrounding and eventually absorbing all negativity until only goodness remains.

The second method of ridding oneself (or one's planet) of negative energy is to make a conscious attempt to turn the negative energy into positive. For example, a rainstorm is viewed by many people as being a negative thing, i.e., it may serve to ruin a planned picnic or outing to the beach. But on the other hand, when one attempts to see that the rainstorm is necessary to cleanse the planet, nourish the trees, and breathe Life into a desert (for example), one begins to see that what one initially viewed as a negative aspect is, in fact, a very positive aspect instead.

Additionally, try to visualize the same "void" of darkness as described above. But instead of visualizing the White Light of Healing absorbing that darkness, try to imagine what might happen if that "void" was simply turned wrong-side-out. Since it is a universal constant that all things have their opposite (love/hate, light/dark, slavery/freedom, etc.), it is certainly true that positive and negative are also two sides of the same coin. Thus, instead of visualizing that negativity becomes absorbed by light, focus your meditations on the possibility of light and darkness working together.

As you know, your planet is highly dependent on cycles of day and night (light and dark). Typically, the night has been viewed by certain religious sects as being "evil" or "negative." But, like the rainstorm, periods of Earth– darkness are necessary in order to preserve life on your planet. For example, consider what would happen if there was no nighttime. Your world would exist in a perpetual state of sunlight - which would eventually cause the trees to perish, the nocturnal animals (such as bobcats, coyotes, owls and other species) to become extinct. On the other hand, a state of perpetual darkness would destroy the trees just as quickly because of the lack of light to complete the chlorophyll cycle. Many human beings would suffer irreparable psychological harm, and your planet would, again, be plunged into a state of chaos.

I use these examples primarily to illustrate that all things must work together in harmony and balance in order for Life itself to flourish. This is equally as true of positive and negative energy. Consider your planet as a gigantic battery - and, as with any battery, it must have a positive charge and a negative (grounding) charge. Without the ground of negativity, the battery would not function. And without the positive spark to ignite the flame, the planet would remain grounded in utter negativity.

Please understand, my friend, that we star guides are not advocating the use of negativity to attain personal goals or long-term desires. Rather, we are pointing out that each aspect always has its opposite. Death is the temporary resting place after life. Life is how we begin anew after physical death. This is true for the spirit as well as the flesh - and although the spirit itself can never truly "die," it does go through periods of dormancy (or rest/hibernation) before embarking on its next physical incarnation. This is part of the spirit Life Cycle, and a part which we encourage the star person such as yourself to meditate upon whenever possible.

Aside from the subject of positivity and negativity, another concept I would ask you to consider at this time is this: What is the sound of one hand?

THE REAL LIFE UFO TRANSFORMATION OF DIANE TESSMAN

In ancient times, the Zen religion asked this question of many pupils - to meditate upon the sound of one hand clapping. Now, we as your star guides pose this same question to you, in the hopes that your meditation will lead you to discover that the universe holds little of "logic" in its sphere.

Additionally, as you ponder this concept (the sound of one hand clapping), we ask you to consider the topic of silence itself. What is silence? At any time, anywhere on your Earth, there is some sound - either that of the wind or a stream, traffic or the shouts of children at play.

In the mind, however, silence can and should dwell - as a form of meditative serenity, and as a retreat to which the star person such as yourself can flee from the constant turmoil of the mundane (Earthly) world.

Only when the mind embraces silence can full awareness be achieved - and only in the mind can full silence be discovered. This is not simply a matter of meditation to achieve silence. Rather, it is a matter of putting the mind, body and spirit in balance - and allowing the spirit to lead the mind and body into the silent places where true awareness begins.

This is an exercise which should be done on occasion, though one which should not be overdone - for the simple reason that the conscious mind requires the noise of Life in which to complete its mundane journey. However, when the star person such as yourself can begin to gain control over that conscious mind, thereby allowing the subconscious mind its "freedom" as well, a giant step toward spiritual freedom has been taken.

It is our belief that the Silence of Spirit Meditation will enable you to more fully understand the chaos which surrounds you in your mundane (Earthly) life, and to gain a greater ability to cope with the negativity which often invades one's day to day existence. Remember that chaos and negativity are natural states of existence in this universe - just as spirituality and serenity are natural states as well (all things in balance). In order to understand one, a commitment must be made to understand all. Only in this manner will true awareness be achieved.

Finally, as you begin these simple exercises, I advise you to seek the counsel of your Special One. The star person, as you well know, is served by an individual star guardian (just as I serve Diane). It is this "bonding" between the Earth-spirit (the star person) and the Cosmic Spirit (your Special One) that allow both parties to learn from one another and to grow in a mutually beneficial direction. Remember also that we star guides seek to learn from you just as you seek to learn from us – a balanced goal which will have much greater rewards than a more typically one-sided venture.

As you conduct your daily meditations, call upon your Special One to guide you toward the Silence of Mind - the condition of non-thinking wherein the Whole Spirit is allowed its freedom, thereby allowing you a deeper sense of awareness and enlightenment. There is perhaps no deeper commitment than that between the star person and the Special One, and though we may not stress this aspect often enough, it is profoundly true.

Remember always that you are unique; you are a creature of balance and harmony, a spirit on a quest for enlightenment and freedom. Purify your heart through meditation, strengthen your body through spiritual healing and the correct herbal teas which your Special One can recommend, and prepare your Spirit for the most important journey thus far.

May the healing light of God and goodness surround you always,

Tibus

Comment: My best possible guidance for star people at this time is to ask you to remember that no path is an easy one save that which is not a path at all. In simple terms, we must commit ourselves to a goal, set for ourselves certain long-term goals. If we sit back and simply "wait" for enlightenment to come to us, it never will. It is only when we seek awareness - and make a commitment to achieve that awareness through our labors - that awareness becomes possible.

As star people, we must always strive to remember that all things must exist in balance - light cannot exist without darkness, hate cannot exist without love, good cannot exist without evil. Then, by striving to accept the balance of the Cosmos into our daily lives, we will be able to see that we cannot right all wrongs (but we can right a few); we cannot always feel only love (but we can make the love we do feel work for the betterment of Humankind); we cannot exist in a world without evil (but we can make our own goodness count as we let our star-light shine).

We can achieve this Balance - both personal and spiritual as well. It is, like any other path, a difficult one. But Knowing that it is possible makes it work - for ourselves, for our planet, and for all the lifeforms with whom we share this immense universe. D.M.T.

12

MESSAGES FROM TIBUS

PART TWO

TIBUS CHANNELS REGARDING SIMULTANEOUS LIVES

Author's Update: Time is simultaneous, not consecutive. Tibus and I have zeroed-in on "time" as the years go by, knowing that humankind will be unchained from the prison of "marching to time" in the future. Time is relative indeed, and Now is eternal. We were already working on the simultaneous nature of time and life in the 1980s.

This is Tibus. I come to you in love and light.

Recently a question was asked regarding whether star people are also simultaneously on the ships with their star guardians.

I wish to communicate with you on this very vital and wonderful subject. First, I would like to offer a quote from Kahlil Gibran:

"All things in this creation exist within you, and all things in you exist in creation: there is no border between you and the closest things, and there is no distance between you and the farthest things and all things, from the lowest to the loftiest, from the smallest to the greatest, are within you as equal things. In one atom are found all the elements of the Earth; in one motion of the mind are found the motions of all the laws of existence; in one drip of water are found the secrets of all the endless oceans; in one aspect of you are found all the aspects of existence."

There is an inclination on the part of the human race to take matters literally, in a mundane sense - and this warps these matters beyond recognition of Truth. This is not a fault on the part of the human race. It is simply a phase in their "adolescent" development. Teenagers tend to seek immediate gratification; they feel they will never grow older or wiser. They live for today. This is how the human race is, at this point in their evolution.

Therefore, if we transmit to our friends that they are with their star guardians simultaneously or that they are UFO occupants, or that they are at Home...we have found that this tends to translate as, "Last night I went to Venus on a spaceship," or, "I am simultaneously the high commander of the fleet."

This is why the contacts of the 1950s did not work out better as time went on. As with a child perceiving Christmas, humankind perceives one present under the tree or one light on the tree, but the concept of all that Christmas is, tends to elude the child until he is older (there are so many levels to understanding, all are equally a valid part of The Question and The Answer).

With this said, we quote our friend, Dr. Leo Sprinkle: "Us folk will become UFOLK."

It is a truth that our star people will become - and simultaneously are - we of the Home Side.

However, this is not simply a case of one aspect of a star person reaching out to another aspect of the same person...if this concept were understood as this, it could be argued that we of the Home Side are not really "out there," that UFOs are not real, that there is no higher contact...because what we would then be saying (in most of humanity's perception), would be that some "spacey" people were dreaming of the future, and that even though they were wrong in their perception that there are space intelligences, their dreams will nonetheless become catalysts toward humankind evolving spiritually and in humankind going into space one day.

Now the outcome of such dreams is a worthy one and in essence the same one as we champion; however, not I nor anyone else on the Home side is willing to concede that we are not real.

The simple truth is, that we are "out there," UFOs are real and there is higher contact!

A similar concept is that of past and future lives. In human perception, they are viewed as linear on the timeline. We find that they are more accurately perceived as "bubbles in time" and therefore, we use the term "parallel aspects of the Whole Self" in an effort to make that concept a more clear and pure one.

THE REAL LIFE UFO TRANSFORMATION OF DIANE TESSMAN

When the concept of our star people becoming - and being - us is purely and clearly perceived, this cements the relationship between the Special One and the star person.

We have discovered that the human race is shackled with the perception that TIME is an absolute. Reality can therefore only be viewed from a limited view. We have discovered that the greatest liberating event which can befall a race occurs at the moment that the knowledge of TIME BEING RELATIVE enters into the mass consciousness (of that race). This cosmic revelation must happen only when a race which is spiritually ready (unconditionally loving and peaceful).

We would be wrong to simply spring this knowledge on the majority of humans that many of us are humans from the future. Y es, there sure aliens here from far distant planets circling far distant suns...but that concept would not be as upsetting to the human race as the knowledge that others of us are Future Humans. However, this and other "earthshaking" knowledge will have to be made known to humanity before it is spiritually ready to know these things due to events of the Change Time/Point. We/you can only work as hard as we can beforehand to prepare humanity...

Even though star people like yourself are used to the idea that time is traversable and relative, we realize that it is still hard to truly interiorize the idea that you are us and yet that we are separate beings, real unto ourselves. In the present reality, some of us have gone to live human lifetimes (you) while others of us have stayed behind to protect and guide (us). However, in a parallel and equally valid reality, we are all here. You have made this fact a reality by your noble work in your present lifetime. You have created a path home for yourselves and for all Earth.

As you can see, these concepts become confusing and nonsensical to one who has not achieved a certain level of awareness. Therefore, we do not approach this subject directly with all people. The worst that can happen is that the person declares that he himself flies to Venus in starships when no one else does or that he, himself is, in a parallel aspect, high commander of the fleet when no one else is. This is a perception which has the human ego very much involved in it. This is not wrong, it is merely a stage of adolescence, but it can lead down a false path.

We await you along the true star path!

May the healing light of goodness surround you, always,

Tibus

THE REAL LIFE UFO TRANSFORMATION OF DIANE TESSMAN

TIBUS CHANNELS REGARDING SENSITIVES

In a meditative session, Diane asked Tibus, "My dreams, like those of others, are very interesting and I've often thought that they are memories of mine from some past/future life or that they are perhaps are they your memories. Just what are they? I am especially inclined to actually remember what a starship is like, feel I belong there. Fm not alone in this starship feeling, of course, as a good many star people have it (and even some science fiction fans if they would admit it). Tibus, can you give me a "more official" answer(I don't have one at all, actually. I just know this strange memory/feeling exists)? Sometimes it's like I am watching a sequence like an old news reel."

This is Tibus. I come to you in Love and light.

Sensitives have "memories" which are engrained in their beings - in their hearts and souls - but are not readily accessible as memories in their physical brains. Now, by "sensitives" I realize I am using an old term, one used by the Spiritualist movement many years ago. This does not add or detract from its usage, I am merely reminding you that this term has been used before. I find that, as I channel through to Diane, there is no other word in her repertoire of English which can be used in this concept. If we said that psychics have memories which are engrained in their hearts and souls, the earthly concept conjures up "official psychics" - professionals. Again, neither a negative or positive in itself but not useful for our concept.

Star people certainly are among the group of sensitives on Earth who have these strong feelings/memories but there are many others, also, not deeply involved in space contact or star guardian "research" but still with memories. For example, the man who has always been fascinated beyond logical bounds with Ireland. He saves money to visit it, he finds a special place and the only explanation is that he lived a "haunting" past life in this place. This man is "normal" in other aspects, does not feel alienated or that he has a special mission. This man fits the status quo in most ways. I do not wish to belabor explaining why I wish to use the word "sensitives" in this transmission, but I simply find it the only accurate description.

Certainly, any student of metaphysics is a sensitive. All star people are sensitives or they would not fit the "star" description.

Now, to further complicate matters, you do have a link - open and natural – to your special one. Your star guardian is also certainly a "sensitive." Most universal beings are. Mundane humankind has managed to block spiritual conduits, partially with the static of mundane life which does not transcend at all, and partially with the prejudices against being "sensitive" or "psychic" which traditional Christianity has instilled. I hasten to add that Christianity is not the only offender here, nor is it an offender at all in its pure form. Many Earth religions teach their people to be blind followers of dogma and to be afraid of reaching out for themselves.

Assume you are a sensitive who picks up past and future memories which your heart and soul remember, but which are missing from your physical brain that has been with you only in this lifetime (and by "heart" we obviously mean the spiritual heart; again, English is lacking some words!). You are also a sensitive who picks up the star guardian. You do so even though sometimes these energies may seem scrambled in with your own. And, we also add that one cannot truly define what the sub/supra consciousness is as it relates to the physical brain. The sub/supra consciousness, we have found, is the bridge to the soul from the physical brain which houses the conscious mind.

It all becomes very confusing, and this is our point. We understand why it is tempting to try to find exact answers to memories of the heart and soul - you may not be able to "unblend" the blend which has occurred throughout the ages. The unique energy which is you has been touched - loved, hated, and all emotions in between - by other energies (other individuals). In this way, even they are blended into your being, for their love, for instance, has made a difference in some pathway you have taken along the line. Certainly your star guardian/cosmic soulmate has made this difference many times and has blended well with you.

In a recent transmission, we mentioned that the star guardians would be letting our Star People know about other aspect(s) we have lived, some not as "exalted" as our current status (for we have had no free passes up the ladder; we have learned through long, hard lessons just as all souls). How can this incoming information be separated from what you might interpret as your own past life experience? Ah, there is that question again of unblending an age-old blend. It is difficult, and sometimes we feel it is not necessary. Other times, it is necessary if a particular lesson must be realized by one soul alone.

Our star people sometimes remind us of children searching for their hidden Christmas presents. If the children stopped to think, perhaps they would not want to know what the present is before Christmas morning; they also might realize that scouting out the hiding place was not the object of Christmas giving, and this scouting out is bothersome to their parents. Now, once again, I am not aiming to be patronizing or condescending in my analogies nor do I mean that our star people are ever bothersome to us! I simply mean that to find the specific present (past life or specific source of a transmission or memory) before the time it is to be made known naturally, through events of the cosmos, may not be the most important part of your star path. Yet, it is tempting. The world trains one to find answers to all questions. Mundane earth does not teach the child to treasure the question.

Sensitives can feel the currents of the Cosmos. This perhaps further complicates matters in deciding exactly where certain memories/feelings are coming from, but remember that regardless of which alternate path is taken, the star path is continued upon, as long as you are of goodness > as long as you remain a "sensitive," as long as you care about the future of planet Earth and her lifeforms - and act in some way to manifest this caring.

May the healing light of goodness surround you, always,

Tibus

TIBUS CHANNELS REGARDING UNCONDITIONAL LOVE

This is Tibus. I come to you in love and light.

Love is indeed the greatest of vibrations, frequencies! Man has had little trouble in immortalizing "love" as long as it is ego based. Man loves woman. Woman loves man. There is parental love, etc. These forms of love are very beautiful (though of course humankind manages to get physical biology mixed up with LOVE, particularly in his young years. If these two can accompany each other, there is indeed a beautiful relationship formed). Man's version of LOVE is at exactly the same stage as his religion. He "channels" love through very narrow tunnels. There is conditional love, but very little UNCONDITIONAL LOVE. There is ego-centered religion, but very little tuning into the beautiful and loving Divine Energy, feeling The Flow in the magnificent never-ending Cycle.

I wish to digress a moment to say that you must not fear that your "ego" becomes too big over our spoken truths to you...and about your beautiful awareness. Your "ego" is an UNCONDITIONAL LOVE. It is not a mundane ego. It is rather a feeling of BEING, of purity, of goodness, of LIFE. It is well and good to be reminded of these lovely qualities within yourself. It is well and good to revel in them for you know them to be universal in nature. Your center is not within mundane SELF, but, rather toward the HIGHER SELF which extends lovingly toward infinity. Allow yourself to be washed in the knowledge that you have indeed reached much wisdom and beauty. Yes, of course, there is still a ways to go, as is true for all of us!

Jesus/Sananda often spoke in parables and analogies so that humankind could comprehend the UNCONDITIONAL LOVE of which he spoke. He used these methods, as we Space Brothers often do, to attempt to make man realize that ego-base is pitifully wanting in new qualities; that through symbolism, mankind might realize himself a child of the stars and the universe. Alas, man just does not seem to "get it."

Small advancement has been made. We must teach /reach humankind to think in parables, symbols, analogies - for starters. In this way, love will advance to UNCONDITIONAL LOVE, and ego-base will advance to cosmic awareness. Also, the Whole Mind/Soul concept says this also. It is another way of saying that man must truly revolutionize his concept of his dimension, his universe, and his mind.

Yes, the whole "experiment" of humankind on planet Earth is to set up this level of consciousness. Our craft, which were spotted in Earth skies, are to be symbols as well as physical objects. Our messages hold many symbols for humankind as well as specific truths (often, specific dates are given for mass landings of our craft because a channel goes amok in translating our transmissions within his or her mind - from symbolism into practical detail, like an Earth date). Often also, our channels run amok when they take an ego trip about being a "chosen one," totally missing the symbolism, which is the hard part of the message to get across in the first place! Oh, we have no trouble in getting a man to spot a "UFO" in the sky. However, we have great trouble in transmitting to the same man what the parable is, what the analogy is, what the symbolic message is for his mind/soul and for his entire race.

This first and foremost level is, as we have indeed realized, UNCONDITIONAL LOVE and a lessening of ego-base, to a far greater degree than humankind has in the latter part of the Twentieth Century. We are, first and foremost, ambassadors of this love to planet Earth. This is our cosmic mission.

The second Level is that we are physical beings (are not all energies physical within their home dimension?) who travel the stars, who are composed of many different races from many planets, many dimensions, many timeframes. The term "alien" has been used so much in Earth movies, etc., that we hesitate to use it at all.

THE REAL LIFE UFO TRANSFORMATION OF DIANE TESSMAN

And yet, if we do not, humankind will never be able to comprehend his encounters, meetings and ultimate blending with us. If we do not give man a "conditional" and ego-based" term ("alien"), he can never begin to get the full, Whole Mind, picture, which is not "alien" at all. Eventually humans must become of UNCONDITIONAL LOVE, of universal wisdom, of cosmic citizenship.

It is a vicious circle which we travel with humans: If we give them a term they understand, they "tag" it, build a prejudice against it, or at least a very mundane base for it, never touching on the symbolism involved, never even daring to guess the greater significance than that related to their small world/ ego. If we don't give them the "term" or concept at all it goes almost totally without "manifestation" on the Earth level.

A moment ago, I spoke to you of the two levels we work on. On the more important level, yes, certainly, all forms of life are fashioned in God's image...for God gives life...God is. Life is sacred, be it humanoid or vastly different from human. Life is sacred, whether it exists in a three dimensional reality or a more "alien" one.

On our second "priority" (level), I would like to give you the interesting fact that humanoid life is spread throughout this galaxy and throughout many dimensions. Humans, of course, were not the first human-like beings. Ages ago, many humanoids were seeded on various hospitable planets. Of course, this fits into the larger scheme (our Level One priority which perhaps should be called the spiritual level, while Level Two is the scientific level.). Though there are delightful diversities and billions of variations throughout this galaxy (we will not even begin to touch on others!), the "image of man" is a familiar one across the universe. Also, the Divine Energy which pulses through humans does form itself into a physical reality which pleases it - which manifests it beautifully. Humankind has much more to be proud of than he dares imagine (not in egotistical terms but in unconditional terms).

My mission is partially to tell humankind (and particularly our star people) that rather than feeling shame at being human, we must find a new pride, one which I would like to call unconditional pride (please interchange this term with unconditional joy). It is not ego-based. It is an essential with unconditional love.

If the child does not like/love himself, there are serious problems. He must not feel that all those he meets are superior to him or he will eventually act badly.

He must realize his equality and have pride in this fact - but unconditionally , without the typical egotism entering (that is a false pride).

Finally, I would like again to stress the importance of SYMBOLS. This is a term which has been stressed so much in philosophy, and even in the occult, that one grows numb to it.

However, as in the case of Tarot cards, in the Jungian psychology findings, even the night hawks and sentient coyotes, symbols are given. We will be finding great pleasure and joy in giving you many amazing symbols in the time ahead. We realize, my friend, that you have dealt with these in wonder and joy for many years, but in the troubled times ahead, the symbols will increase in intensity and quantity.

May the healing light of goodness surround you always,

Tibus

13

MESSAGES FROM TIBUS

PART THREE

CHANNELING ON PROPHECY

Author's Update: I like our approach on this "List of Questions" format. I plan to use it soon again. Thank you, Tibus and Diane of 1987 for the reminder!

This is Tibus. I come to you in love and light.

Questions to be asked in this transmission:

1. What is meant by the expression, "the gift of prophecy?"

What is the difference between prophecy and precognition?

2. Have only a few individuals throughout human history been blessed with the gift of prophecy?

Can anyone develop a talent for prophecy?

3. Why should you work on developing prophetic abilities?

Does your star guardian (spirit guide) need your help - your gift of prophecy in order to guide planet Earth on a loving, peaceful path? How can you possibly help from the Earth plane?

4. Isn't our higher guidance omnipotent?

Can't they change things from "on high" if they wish?

Why is your gift of prophecy so important?

5. Can you be a pivotal force in stopping global nuclear war?

THE REAL LIFE UFO TRANSFORMATION OF DIANE TESSMAN

Can the power of your mind and soul make a better world for people everywhere as well as for yourself?

In perceiving the question and possible answer to #1 of this transmission, we refer to the Earth studies of psychology and sociology.

As you know, the study of psychology refers to the study of one's individual emotional and mental characteristics. Incidentally, psychology is not a study which belongs to Earth alone, because throughout the universe with all its billions of sentient lifeforms (beings) - each and every one has a unique psychology. The Creator Spirit is indeed wondrous and diverse!

Now let us consider sociology. This is the study of a race of lifeforms such as the human race and its many subdivisions such as various cultures and tribal units called countries.

Psychology is to the gift of precognition as sociology is to the gift of prophecy.

In other words, if you have the gift of predicting the future of an individual, you are blessed with precognition.

If you have the gift of predicting the future of an entire race, you are blessed with the gift of prophecy.

The gift of prophecy involves the ability to step outside a planet's historical flow and to perceive with acute vision exactly where that planet is going if it remains on its current path.

Each and every planet has a historical flow. The flow of human events on planet earth is a pageant which flows along a timeline (a time continuum) which is capable of being perceived when one steps out of it. One may do this by removing his or her unique mind/soul from this timeline and looking at it from "on high," as if in a starship.

For instance, when we perceive Earth from "on high" at its present intersect point on the time continuum, we see that this magnificent planet is headed for global destruction. If you also know this, analyze your knowledge: Is it based primarily on a logical conclusion (yes, everyone knows the facts about nuclear proliferation and the polluting and contaminating forces at work presently on Earth)? Or is your knowledge based on a feeling?

In other words, though you factually know that planet Earth is in trouble, does your knowledge of its possible destruction come from your logic circuits or from your heart? If the knowledge comes from your heart (and mind/soul), then yours is the gift of prophecy; and the intelligence which your logic circuits contribute tell you this as well. Yours is a twofold insight!

Earth is on a collision course. Is this course irreversible?

Is prophecy a truth which is a foregone conclusion? If this is true, we might think of prophecy as a curse rather than a gift.

However, do not despair because the collision course is reversible. That which the prophet perceives is a truth which is not a finished reality. There are always alternate paths to be taken.

And how can planet Earth know that there are indeed alternate timelines? This world can and will know through your gift of prophecy!

The gift which forecasts destruction is indeed a gift - not a curse - simply because it is a tool. It is the catalyst by which alternate timelines of freedom, peace, and love can be found.

Now, if you have prophetic insight such as Jesus, Nostradamus, Mohammed, The Buddha, and many others have possessed throughout human history, and you do not use it to influence humans away from the collision course, then it is of no good to you or anyone else. Prophecy is a gift which must be used, which must speak out and be heard (or scream out, if necessary), it must influence others with all the power which any individual can put behind it! Consider the great souls mentioned in this paragraph: Did not they use their gifts of prophecy in order to guide the human race away from bigotry, greed, and destruction?

All human beings - all sentient lifeforms everywhere in the universe - have the potential for the gift of prophecy. Some never think about this gift - or feel it - and so it does not develop. Others may suspect it is there within themselves - a direct conduit to the Creator Spirit - but they do not take time and energy to develop it. Still others may be humble, feeling that they have a mystical knowledge of Earth's historical flow within themselves but that it is up to the "great prophets" to do the big time prophecy work.

The truth is...the Creator Spirit which dwells in all humans pleads with all humans to use their gift of prophecy so as to guide the lovely blue/green planet into a free, peaceful, creative future reality. The great prophets were great because they stood behind their prophecies, telling others about them. They made this a fulltime mission. Though modern day demands prohibit you from working twenty-four hours a day on altering earth's collision course, still it is a universal responsibility to do all you can in guiding Earth toward a positive future. If there is not a positive future, there is nothing.

In order to develop your gift of prophecy, you must step outside Earth's historical flow but you do so from inside Earth's historical flow. You are a part of a timeline. To develop your gift of prophecy, you float above this timeline from which you spring - and you see the entire path of Earth throughout the ages in perspective.

You see the forest instead of the trees, but your take-off point is from within the trees.

If you understand this concept, then you will receive the question and possible answer to #3 and ultimately #4 at the beginning of this transmission.

Consider yourself and your link to your spirit guide (and we reaffirm that all beings have these loving, wise guides): You are a being who wishes freedom, peace, love, and creativity for Earth who is of Twentieth Century Earth.

Oh, it is true that your mind/soul may well have origins and connections to other worlds and to the higher dimensions. However, your physical body is that of a Twentieth Century human and in many ways, your daily life is that of a being who lives in the Twentieth Century historical flow.

As a being from outside the Twentieth Century Earth flow, your spirit guide (star guardian) attempts to contact, guide, and help Earth - and particularly to help you to a path of freedom, peace, and universal brotherhood. However, your star guardian cannot openly interfere with Earth's history because each planet must determine its own destiny from inside its reality base (timeline). Each planet has its own karma and continues to make its own karma.

You are within this planet's reality base. You can help determine the destiny from inside. You are a part of Earth's karma, even though you are not entirely of Earth. You are living a lifetime as a human and therefore you have a legitimate right to influence her reality base in as active a way as you can!

In this way, your star guardian needs your help. You will work from inside to help earth away from her collision course, into a bright New Age while the guides in other dimensions work from outside with gentle protection and subtle help. You are to be the positive factor personified within Earth's present reality base. Without your work, an all-important element would be missing and the collision course will indeed flow onward to its tragic end.

You must never forget that God Consciousness dwells within you. You are not an island, either on Earth or in the universe.

Your mind/soul springs from the cosmic wellspring of eternal energy - the Creator Spirit. You have also experienced life on Earth. Considering both of t hese glorious facts, you cannot simply stand by and wait for other individuals to save earth from its collision course. You are vital.

In perceiving the words in this transmission, you are exercising the muscles of prophecy. In perceiving yourself as a human standing among the trees and as a being who looks down on the forest from "on high," you are well on your way to full use of the gift of prophecy which you possess.

Feel the throb of the historical flow around you. Immerse yourself in the drama of the intersect point on the timeline on which you now stand. Be a part of the reality base around you. Now...!

Rise above this reality base in a star craft which travels the starry seas. Look down on the planet below you and perceive the flow of history which is planet Earth. Notice that the intersect point is one in billions of points in time and that this one point can be a veering off place for a whole new timeline.

At any point on the continuum, you may change the flow. The timeline need not head straight into oppression, misery, or total destruction.

This is the true gift of prophecy. You now have the knowledge not only of the future but you are aware that in perceiving the future, you can change it!

Use your gift of prophecy because of all the spiritual/psychic gifts such as precognition, healing, psychokinesis, telepathy, and others, prophecy is the one to be used the most, for the welfare of the most lifeforms - and ultimately for your welfare as a citizen of Earth and of the Universe.

May the healing light of goodness surround you, always,

Tibus

CHANNELING ON CHANNELING

This is Tibus. I come to you in love and light.

Questions to be asked in this transmission:

1. What is the definition of channeling?

THE REAL LIFE UFO TRANSFORMATION OF DIANE TESSMAN

What is the difference between channeling and mediumship, a skill which psychic spiritualists have presented to humankind for years?

2. What are the indications that a person is making contact with other realms of existence?

How can a person tell when telepathic contact is being sought from other realms?

What is the one thing to remember when either seeking contact or allowing outside contact to enter your mind/soul frequency?

3. How does one turn this contact into channeling or mediumship which will give messages of help and inspiration to other people as well as being positively useful to yourself?

4. What are some suggestions for enhancing/inviting contact with higher dimensions?

In perceiving the question and possible answer to #1, we first look into the phenomenon of thought itself.

The human brain functions much as a sophisticated computer, storing information and experience. But what of the nuances of emotion, intuition, inspiration, and revelation? Was it the brain of Beethoven which wrote the immortally beautiful music or was his music reflective of the spirit and the mind? Was not the brain of Beethoven designed like all other brains? Indeed, it was something beyond the computer/brain which created his genius and his music.

The brain of Einstein has been examined and it has been found that his brain in itself was like all other brains. There were not unusual convolutions or patterns of grey matter in this genius' brain. Yet, something in this man set him aside from the rest of humanity, put him light years ahead of the rest of his species. That something is intangible; it cannot be dissected as the brain can be.

Once you internalize this premise, we can consider the question of channeling. First we consider how real is the spirit and the mind but how very hard to "catch," to define, to dissect. One's spirit - the mind/soul -lives in a physical vessel which is the human body, for a period of years, then passes on to other worlds, other lives. When a person channels messages, he or she is allowing his own mind/soul to take a rest while another mind/soul temporarily uses the brain to give a message. The brain (the physical body) of one inhabiting the mundane dimension (daily world), must be used by this visiting mind/soul because it is the only way to interact in the Earth dimension. Unless a physical body which is native to the mundane dimension is used, the visiting mind/soul remains in its home dimension.

When an individual channels a mind/soul from another dimension or another planet, that individual is willingly allowing the physical body and brain to be host to the other consciousness. This consciousness can then transmit knowledge and information which it (he or she) possesses about Twentieth Century earth. The visiting consciousness can give warnings, wisdom, and help. It can do this because it is of a higher consciousness frequency.

As a matter of fact, one can easily tell if one is in contact with a higher plane instead of a lower one, simply by the nature and quality of the information. If the information is petty, hateful, of base sexual nature, or totally egotistical, then it is of a lower world. If the information is encouraging, speaks of peace on Earth, good will toward men, tells of universal love and brotherhood, and tells one about the wonder of the positive way of being, then it is of a higher level.

Now, all the information which has just been given may also apply to the skill of mediumship. Spiritualists and psychics have for years been able to go into trances and give messages from the spirit world, speaking in a different voice than usual, with a difference cadence or tone. Often these mediums can give messages directly from a deceased relative or loved one. Sometimes they can give messages from famous people who have passed to other realms.

Channeling, however, deals with the sharing of the physical body (brain) with a visiting mind/soul who has not necessarily passed from the earth plane. Channeling usually deals with sharing consciousness with a being of a higher plane - from a different planet or time - who is therefore an alien. He or she has not died on mundane Earth and is thus not passing messages back to the earthly plane from the spirit world. The mind/soul who channels, therefore, usually identifies him or herself as from space or from another planet.

The brain of the medium or channel is the common ground between the two lifeforms. The brain of the medium is also the common ground between the human psychic and the spirit world energy. A gifted medium or channel knows how to allow his or her own mind/spirit to become calm, peaceful, and low key so that the visiting consciousness can transmit the message.

Yes, the frequencies of the two lifeforms involved must be similar. A channel picks up the mind/soul waves (frequency) of a space or dimensional being because these waves are adaptable and similar to his or her own waves. Some channels have the ability to pick up many frequencies while others pick up one or two. However, often the channels who consistently pick up the same one or two frequencies do so at a greater accuracy and on a more regular schedule.

Whether the gifted person is a channel or a medium, we may say that he or she shares consciousness with another mind/soul for a while. Sometimes this is a short while, as in the case of the trance medium who cannot sustain the contact for hours. Other times, as in the case of some space contacts, the consciousness-sharing goes on continuously but is formally activated if a formal channeling is requested.

Humankind is ignorant at this point in time in that it accepts the fallacy that the human brain can house only one consciousness. And this has nothing to do with mental illness (schizophrenia). Humankind is foolish to assign this negative concept automatically. He limits his cosmic horizons to a tragic degree!

In perceiving the question and possible answer to #2, we first remind you of the greatest rule: Be of goodness. Be of good intent. Once surrounded with this light, once connected to this God Consciousness - then all contacts and explorations can only broaden the horizon and bring unconditional love!

Many people do not realize that, indeed, contact is being made because they fail to identify the beginnings of contact within their own thoughts. Remember, in contact and subsequent channeling, another mind/soul drifts into your head. It drifts gently, peacefully, and lovingly. It does not take over at will but waits for your "ok." It is sensitive and of goodness. Therefore, you may fail to know it is there!

However, if you are finely tuned and intuitive, you will suddenly suspect that the thought patterns which are coming to you so very beautifully are not quite your familiar thought patterns.

Now, we hasten to explain that you are also capable of beautiful universal thoughts and inspiration. But just as you can discern between Beethoven and another genius like John Lennon, so you can discern the channeled information from your own thought. Remember, another being is linked to you, is sharing consciousness with you. At first it is subtle so as not to scare you or force you into contact (even though you may have requested it).

It is a sign that you are sharing consciousness with a being of goodness in that the initial contact is so gentle, peaceful, and loving as to be hard to differentiate from your own familiar thought process.

THE REAL LIFE UFO TRANSFORMATION OF DIANE TESSMAN

Remember, you cannot contact or channel a being who is too radically different in mind/soul wave from your own (this is another reason we say, "Be of goodness."). However, this also makes it hard at first to discern.

Contact is also being sought from higher realms. In other words, they are reaching out to you as you are reaching out to them. You can tell that contact is urgently desired when you have a great and illogical need to explore the unknown, to gain universal knowledge - and also when your life seems suddenly manipulated so as you will indeed have time and opportunity for more meditation, study, and possible contact.

First comes an inkling of contact as you learn to realize that there is a sharing of consciousness at times within your head. The consciousness will be beautiful and loving. Channeling is a gift but also a learned skill. Do not expect to channel at first but only to discern a shared consciousness. However, everyone has the ability to channel! Most people do not become channels just as most people do not become famous pianists; however, everyone can play the piano with a bit of effort.

In perceiving the question and possible answer to #3, please meditate upon the meaning of the word "channel." Water runs in channels and so does a stream of consciousness. Mind/soul waves run in channels (these may also be called frequencies).

The "stuff" which makes Beethoven's music great is energy. Energy (the spiritual stream of consciousness) runs in channels - in eddies, ebb tides, swells, and currents. It is much like restless water.

On first contact, the water hardly touches you. It washes into your mind in gentle, tiny, loving streamlets. This is the time to be sure you are of good intent and that the visiting stream of consciousness is therefore of good intent, giving loving, positive input.

If you wish, you may experience this tiny stream of consciousness again during meditation. Once contact is made, it is almost always accessible again. The higher consciousness wants you to try contact again but it is up to you.

Gradually you will begin to tune into the frequency, to allow the stream of consciousness to wash over you whenever you wish. It is a beautiful, unparalleled experience and one which wise, mystical people have spoken of and sought after for ages. It is deeply and profoundly a cosmic experience and a time of growth and enlightenment for your mind/soul. It is a time of teaching. It is also wonderful for the higher consciousness' mind/soul because he or she is very happy to be able to make contact, to help, and to inspire.

If you keep at this contact, if you allow the waters to wash over you often, the messages will become more clear, more lucid, and more helpful.

At this point, whether actual channeling occurs depends partially on the compatibility of the human and the other consciousness. Occasionally the two are totally compatible and are in fact soulmates. Other times, the contact with the human has been established since childhood and worked on very actively by other consciousnesses as well, for many years. In these cases, channeling would almost certainly be the result eventually.

Basically one must remember that an open, broad, beautiful channel of flowing water was first started as a tiny streamlet. To channel again and again is to constantly widen the channel. Remember, all things are possible- and all lifeforms have the ability to reach higher levels of being!

In perceiving the question and possible answer to #4, we first must understand that any dimension is made up of seemingly physical features which the mind/soul creates and perceives around itself.

Therefore, if you wish contact with higher realms or if you are diligently working on attempting to develop the ability to channel, you must create a consistent atmosphere for yourself each time to seek contact. This atmosphere must be reflective of the higher dimension - the physical world of that higher dimension - which you wish to contact.

First, have objects which represent to you objects in the higher dimension (or on the other planet if your consciousness prefers this concept). Throughout the ages, psychics, mystics, and channels have found that rocks, crystals, sea shells, pine cones - natural objects - best make the transition from one dimension to another. In other words, if you possess a shiny, lovely multicolored rock which you always rub and hold when you meditate, then this rock will go with you (and manifest!) in the higher dimensional frequency to which you will be going during your meditative session. This special rock will represent your journey, will enhance it, and make it easier each time for you to go. It is highly recommended that you have special rocks, crystals, or other natural objects. It is surprising how much easier these items of meditation make your search for contact. They become objects of both dimensions. They become teleports. They are a reality base, a physical perception, in both worlds, for both minds. And they are a safety rope because they will give you a solid physical reality as your mind begins to join the ebb and flow of the cosmic energy.

To create an atmosphere of a higher dimension, incense or some mystical, lovely fragrance is urged. Find a fragrance which stimulates your mind/soul and use it every time. If there is particular music which puts you in a distant, mystical mood, play it for your meditation and contact session as well.

Next, find the time of the day or night and the place which best represents an environment in which both consciousnesses will be at ease. The higher realms know and love nature (which is cosmic energy manifested in Earth's atmosphere). Nature is always a good place to be. However, if you are more at ease in the quiet, secure solitude of your own living room in the evening, then make this "headquarters" for both your mind/soul and that of the higher mind/soul - make this their common ground, their intersect point. Candles are very helpful to some people, especially if they have chosen a private, indoor location for their contact sessions.

All in all, remember that you are creating an atmosphere where both you and your higher contact will feel at home. You would not, for instance, find it easy to channel in a room full of Twentieth Century people chattering about the stock market or in the middle of a street filled with Twentieth Century autos!

Once you begin to find the key for allowing the water to wash over you - channels from higher consciousness levels will surely open to you because they wish this contact as much as you do. To be a conduit for The Light is a noble experience!

May the healing light of goodness surround you, always,

Tibus

SELF HELP CHANNELING

This is Tibus. I come to you in love and light.

Questions to be asked in this transmission:

1. Does the world in which you live exist in the mind of humankind only? Why is everyone in the world a victim of the money system?

Why is materialism so important in this world?

How can materialism be put into perspective and conquered in your personal life?

2. "Humankind may well be but a dream of God's sleeping mind..." What is meant by this concept?

Do humans create "dream people" in their sleep?

3. What part of the world around us is a part of God's Mind?

Are we hopelessly surrounded by humankind's creations alone?

4. "War begins in the minds of human beings. Since this is so, the minds of human beings must also be capable of ending war."

What does this wise statement ultimately tell us about humankind's mind and its connection to God's Mind?

5. What is God Consciousness? Where is God Consciousness? Can it transcend the daily world?

In perceiving the question and the possible answer to #1, we must use our gifts of prophecy and rise above the Earth timeline to a period when humankind first emerged on this beautiful blue/green planet.

We can see that, in the beginning, there was no money system, no complex society, no materialism.

Now, of course a race cannot stand still. It is a responsibility before God for a cosmic being to use intelligence, intuition, abilities to evolve. Humankind certainly could not remain in the primitive stage. However, many paths could have been taken by the human race. The path it has chosen to travel is one which is crippled by the "money system," a materialism of staggering proportions.

It is humankind's responsibility to perceive the damage this system causes to so many fellow human beings. It is humanity's obligation to stand back and examine the society he has created and then strive to correct it in places where it is negative and damaging. A few individuals do this; thus you are reading these transmitted words. However, the human race as a whole strives only to reinforce its materialistic ways. One man "lords over" another simply because he has collected more money, often through negative means. And so, often the decent individual becomes more of a victim of the money system than does the more greedy, aggressive individual. The entire system becomes inverted, off-center, and out-of-balance.

Those who are sensitive to cosmic energy are also sensitive to the "bad vibes" of the negative money system with its accompanying materialism. These gentle people (like yourself) become very frustrated and angry over the injustice of it all and don't seem to play the game as well as other people do who do not feel this resentment toward it.

However, those who lose their humanity to the materialistic system are the ones who get hurt the most, though they may have collected a huge mass of the "green stuff." Thus, all are hurt by this dominating, artificial system.

Many good luck charms are sold as a "magic" way of overcoming the money system. Sometimes these charms do have power but this is because of the power of your own mind/soul. If you want out of the money system's viciousness badly enough, you can make a charm work. However, the power comes from within you. You can overcome, whether you use meditative aids/ tools or whether you do it entirely with the strength of your being.

A first step to escaping from the grasp of materialism and money problems is to do exactly what you are doing: Look at it in perspective! Become fully aware that the system is not God. It is an artificial system which humankind has imposed on itself. This realization in itself breaks a part of the hold the money system has on you!

Everything in the world which is artificial (man-made) exists only in the mind of Man. For instance, if a man thinks up a concept for a shoe store and then acts on his mind's thought, he creates a shoe store within his society. The minds of other men perceive this shoe store, make it a thriving business by patronizing it, and it continues to exist in the mundane world.

Materialism is important because humankind makes it important. Humanity is a victim of its own artificial system. While no one with a physical body can escape the materialistic system completely unless he or she goes to live on top of Mt. Everest, a person can become less of a slave to money by not allowing money to dominate life. One should resist worrying about it constantly or obsessively. If you do refuse to be its slave, you will find that your mind can begin to overcome the money system. In other words, a first step toward solving money worries is to refuse to participate in the stress and game playing which the materialistic system forces upon one. It takes a bit of mind power, but you do have a powerful mind/soul - powerful enough to overcome this man-made "god."

In perceiving the question and possible answer to #2 and #3, we first must realize that the world around us is full of objects and forces which are not creations of humankind's mind but creations of God's Mind.

THE REAL LIFE UFO TRANSFORMATION OF DIANE TESSMAN

You have simply to look at nature to realize that God's Mind has created a very mystical and beautiful world all around you.

Look out your window: You see Man's Mind at work - and you see God's Mind at work. These two compose reality.

Now, we know that God's Consciousness is in each and every lifeform as well as being everywhere in the universe. When we look at art or listen to music, we are enjoying a human-made reality but one which is based on the God Consciousness within each man (or woman). This of course is true of many wonderful things in life, right down to a birthday cake which is human- made but which is a universal joy and a way of expressing love - which is certainly reflective of God Consciousness. We must remember not to credit a distant God who "sits on a gold throne" but rather to know that God is within each and every piece of life, everywhere - including ourselves!

Here is the key: the universal God Consciousness within you is the part which can save you from being a victim of the artificial world around you which seems to worship money and materialism.

If we truly look, if we truly perceive, we will know that we are not surrounded by human creations alone. Our world is what we perceive it to be. If we feel buried by the materialistic world, then we are buried by it. If we feel we are a part of the universe, if we let our spiritual self run free, then we can rise above the materialistic world. We can put the often ridiculous materialistic world "in its place."

At this point, we will ask: Does God dream? Does the Creator Spirit dream? Does the Life-force create thought-forms just as you do in your dreams - the dreams you have which seem very real? These dreams of yours have details in them; they are colorful, complex, and meaningful.

We may consider the fact that, since all life has a spark of the God Force within, perhaps it is that same spark which is a part of the Creator's dream. It is that spark which is us, which is our eternal spirit. We are detailed, colorful, complex and meaningful and we are of God's Mind (God's Consciousness).

A skeptic might say, "Perhaps God is a dream in the mind of humanity..." To this we say, consider the truth that the two minds/souls (that of God and of Man) are so entwined, so linked - that this statement as well may also be true. How can anyone separate humankind from the universe? How can anyone state that cosmic energy is a one-way street?

THE REAL LIFE UFO TRANSFORMATION OF DIANE TESSMAN

What an individual on Earth must do is align himself or herself more with the universal energy than with the materialistic world. What the individual on Earth must do is to call on the God Consciousness within himself more than the force of the money system, which should be viewed as a "demon" of sorts.

We do not transmit that you can totally forget about the money system while being evicted from your house! However, if you place the thrust of your being into the God-created part of the world around you, then you stop putting unnecessary energy into the human-made part of Reality.

As a student of metaphysics, you know that the more energy you put into an endeavor, the more active it becomes. There are many misconceptions about metaphysics; one is that the power of the occult mind can cause bad luck or a "hex" to be put on a person. The mundane world seldom realizes the positive side of this axiom: To concentrate one's mind powers on helping another person can be most helpful to that person! At any rate, we know that the more mind-energy put into a subject, the more powerful that subject becomes. Now, think of the mind-power you have put into the money system (the money "demon"). People give it more and more power all the time.

Refuse to do this, except where absolutely necessary. You will find as time passes that it becomes less of a necessary problem because you are no longer giving it the energy of worry. And so, the times when it is absolutely necessary to concentrate on it become less frequent, too.

Yes, you are surrounded by humanity's creations and you are flooded by the worries the money system heaps upon you. However, you are also surrounded by God's creations - the most precious of which is within you. This is where you should put the energy of your mind/soul. It will free you from the other system, the other reality. It can even help those mundane problems ease up and eventually be overcome. Stop giving your mundane problems more strength over you. Often they have you wrapped around their little fingers!

We have transmitted information on the gift of prophecy which is within you. It is this gift more than any other which can help you find the God Consciousness part of your mind/soul, the part which can help you overcome the materialistic system. You must gain perspective! You must gain perspective on who you are as a cosmic citizen. You must gain perspective on your world, where it has been, where it is now, where it is going. Rise above the mundane flow and see the full universal picture.

"War begins in the minds of human beings. Since this is so, the minds of human beings must also be capable of ending war."

We of the higher realms, those slightly above you on the Awareness Mountain, can guide you as we are attempting to now, we will do this as much as we can - as much as humankind will possibly listen to us. However, the key is contained in the above quote. Your mind/soul as a being who is in human form at this time - is the one who can and must create a brighter Reality.

It is very important to explore the many aspects of yourself which compose the Whole Self. This includes past lives (parallel aspects of your Whole Self), it includes exploring your gifts of precognition, intuition, and prophecy. This includes exploring the other cosmic beings who are there for you at any time, such as guardian angels and star guardians. There is so much involved in the individual being which you can use these various aspects, experiences, gifts-are all a part of the God Spark within you. Sadly, they often go neglected because the human-made part of your reality dominates.

Never forget that blessed nature is always there for you, as a magnificent manifestation of God's mind and soul. You are also a part of that same magnificent nature.

The power of God, the Creator Spirit, is also your power. God Consciousness is inside as well as outside.

May the healing light of goodness surround you, always,

Tibus

14

ALTERNATE DIMENSIONS
TIBUS CHANNELS REGARDING ALTERNATE DIMENSIONS

On one thing scientists and theologians agree: Alternate dimensions do exist!

Star people know this also but for us, it is as if we approach the truth from the inside, going outward. We know there are other dimensions not because of scientific theory (though we feel gratified that it supports our feelings), and not even because of a religious belief (though we are equally glad that religion in its pure form fits in beautifully with our knowledge).

Our knowledge of the existence of other dimensions can best be described as homing instinct. We know alternate dimensions are "out there" because we somehow belong in one of them. For some crazy reason (at least "crazy" until we figure out our star mission), we are simply in the wrong place!

Ordinary people have great difficulty in understanding this fact. They have no concept of this feeling of displacement - this lifelong feeling of displacement - because they are not displaced! Of course everyone hopes they will "go to heaven," as religions have taught them. However, we star people know that this is much more than reaching for heaven, or hoping to go to a better place upon death of the physical body. This is a solid, constant longing for Home...for a different mind frequency, a different world, a different time.

We know from our inner knowledge that this dimension for which we yearn is a higher dimension in terms of sensitivity, decency and gentleness because so many of the practices in the mundane dimension are cruel, barbaric, and downright incomprehensible to us. This is the problem we have had with this place since early childhood!

Star people often ask me how they can convince others of this higher dimension connection we feel. Many people tell us that any connection or feeling of communication with an alien dimension is a negative in itself. If this is so, then the human race is stagnant...and as we know, stagnation is the only true death for the essence (soul). Sadly, it is virtually impossible to have others feel what we feel, know what we know. We can appeal to their intelligence and sensitivity in explaining the Home Dimension's guidance toward peaceful ways, towards unconditional love and joy, but the truth often manifests itself that we are alien here and that they simply cannot and will not understand. What we must do above all is to keep in contact with our inner guidance which WE KNOW TO BE OF GOODNESS! We must keep the close contact with SELF who has always vibrated on a more refined and gentle frequency than the world in which it finds itself. Once we do this, more communication with the Home Dimension opens. Trust yourself, Star Child!

While scientists tell us that they are discovering, through quantum physics, that there are an infinite number of intersecting dimensions at any one point in Space/Time and that MIND seems to be the key to traversing these adjacent worlds...and while ministers tell us that there are indeed higher realms which have worked with the human race and which have sent saviors and prophets...while all of this is going on around us, we star people nod knowingly, often with tears in our eyes and sigh, "I know that already! I've always known that. But how do I get home?" For us, a "higher realm" is not an abstract. We look for the home frequency just as someone else might say, "Now where did I park the car?"

"Where did I lose myself from the home dimension? Did I truly volunteer for this lifetime? How big a fool can I be? How do I get back?"

While it is true that we do have missions here and that we did volunteer, it is also our obligation to self to ask these questions and to try to return home. When the time to return home does arrive, and we have not begun these pathways toward the home dimension, we will have difficulty. In other words, when we do find the path home, it will be the time for returning home. We create the path home as much as our co-workers on the home side create the path.

An analogy: If someone is trapped in a cave-in, he or she must scramble toward the rescuers digging away on the other side. He or she must dig the rocks on the inside of the cave-in as the rescuers dig from the outside. It may be that there is only a tiny opening to squeeze through at the proper moment before another cave-in occurs. And so the trapped person must be at the opening, not resting on the other side of the cavern! In this same way, we must always remember that this is a dual mission. We work from this side to create conduits into the home frequency just as much as our co-workers work at it from their side. We agreed to this before the mission began. This is a vital part of the entire mission: To create the energy vortex/pathway home. If we do not try, no one on Earth has a chance. On a more selfish basis, we certainly shall never see home again.

We can do it. We can do it individually. We can do it collectively. In this way, we can create home itself...for it is otherwise not reachable and therefore might as well be non-existent. When Tibus and others of The Federation tell us that we are equals, not inferiors, they mean that we therefore have the responsibility to tunnel out from our earthly existence. Together, we and they can work miracles but it takes both sides! We cannot stand by, awaiting doomsday, sitting on the opposite side of the cavern criticizing the mundane world. We must be at the opening/doorway and we must help create that doorway as well!

TRANSMISSION #1

This is Tibus. I come to you in Love and Light.

What is an energy vortex?

Quite simply, it is a place where several kinds (frequencies) of energy come together to form a focal point - an intersection of energies.

What is a dimension?

Quite simply, it is a "place" wherein one frequency is dominant. Within the bounds of a dimension, most minds respond only to this dominant energy.

An energy vortex is therefore as if oil were dropped into a whirlpool of water. You may see a swirl (energy charge) of the non-dominant energy of a given dimension; you may feel a doorway opening into the home frequency from time to time.

This "wash-over" may happen either because you are near a natural energy vortex such as Mother Earth offers in various places at various times, or you may have psychically/ telepathically created this wash-over of dimensional energies through your own meditation and/or mind power.

Here we must clarify what we mean by "power" because this word often has a negative connotation, especially to star people who have seen how power in the earthly sense can corrupt and do harm.

THE REAL LIFE UFO TRANSFORMATION OF DIANE TESSMAN

To us in The Federation, power is merely energy, pure in itself. To have life is to have power. This is as it should be. Life takes many forms (and thus we refer to "lifeforms"), but it is life itself which chooses to manifest in these various ways. This life takes its power from the God Force and - just as you form dreams at night - life forms itself into various manifested realities. Yet there are an infinite variety of life forms throughout the universe and in this fact, we rejoice!

On mundane Earth, there is much misuse of power. It is interpreted almost totally in the egocentric, non-spiritual sense of power (political power, military power). Our star people by nature do not misuse this power nearly as much as mundaners do. This is precisely the reason our star people are not big financial successes, in most cases. We need not dwell on power used negatively!

I wish to remind you at this time that we have spoken of frequency wash-overs. You have all experienced this phenomenon when feeling the very simple yet eloquent connection to the Home Side. You have felt a wash-over of dimensional energies when you feel close to - or feel communication with – the Special One. Also, of course, the viewing of visions, the experiencing of miraculous yet unexplainable feelings, healings, and memories represents a dimensional wash-over. Yes, your Special One and co-workers on the Home Side help...but you have been equally involved in this creation of a vortex (and use of it). Please remember that if your mind and essence (soul) is not participating, Home cannot be interacted with or reached at all!

We have established that you have all experienced wash-overs. These might be called "baby" vortexes for the principle is the same, though the amount of power involved is less (than to actually create a working dimensional vortex/door).

Remembering the oil swirl on water and the definition of a vortex, consider that these vortexes can lead to other places. One may follow either the dominant water, or one may follow the oil swirl to its source. If two (or more) frequencies intersect and one is sensitive to the alien frequency, one may follow it. We hasten to add that this is not as easy as it sounds (as sad as this may seem to a Star Person trying to return Home, it is a fortunate thing that dimensional slippage/"slide zones" is not a common phenomenon in the universe!). We also add that obviously it is much easier to follow the alien frequency intersecting with the dominant frequency/Nature's energies are helping you.

In other words, if you create a dimensional door psychically, this is a much more difficult door to go through than one already established in Nature, which can supplement your own psychic energies. Both together are stronger than one, so we of The Federation also turn to natural energy gates (doors) both on Earth and throughout the galaxy for help in dimensional travel.

Another important aspect is that one can only pass through a dimensional door if doorways are open on both sides of the corridor. In other words, visualize an energy vortex as you would visualize a hallway with doors at both ends. If you are standing at one end of a hallway looking through an open door, what will you see? First, you will see the hallway itself - and the door at the opposite end of the corridor.

If the door is closed and there is no way to unlock that door, it would be impossible to proceed down the hall. On the other hand, if you look down the corridor and see that the far door is open, then it is time to pursue your explorations.

And so, the first skill which one must acquire is to know when the energies are right, not partially right or at half-strength. As you all know, beloved, some days - and particularly some nights - are (simply put) more psychic than others. Sometimes the energies wash in of their own accord, and other times, no matter how hard you try, it just doesn't "get off the ground." Do not feel frustrated by this or feel that you alone in this problem. Other Star People experience it all the time. We experience it as well.

The second important skill to acquire is that of sensing where the energies are washing in from (what frequencies are intersecting with the mundane one). If you are a person of basic goodness, this problem is 99% solved. In other words, the Home Energies zero in on you as well as vice versa. You are spiritually protected. And so, if you are meditating on the Home Dimension and the energies are high, the Home Frequency will be seen, felt, and experienced...and if there is a vortex open on both ends, then the path indeed leads Home.

For example, if you were using psychic energy - as Star people never do - to "get" another person (this being in the stereotyped sense of casting a curse or making bad luck for another person), then obviously as energies open up, you would not find Home but rather a lower dimension. Remember, you are tunneling out from your side as well. You are creating...and so the dimension you reach is what you create. Yes, Home exists on its own..but in searching for it, you make your own path. And yes, we help. But if you insist in saying you wish to go to a beautiful mountaintop when in fact you keep walking around in circles in a factory area of a big metropolis, your Special One and other guides cannot, by universal law force you to head for the mountaintop. We can advise, indicate, nudge... To put the concept of this paragraph in a nutshell, be of goodness!

Dimensional doorways and vortexes are like roads and streets on planet Earth. There are thousands of them and not all of them will get you where you want togo, either for a meditative experience or an actual trip back Home.

Please interiorize this statement: Your own intuition must lead the way. Trust your instincts! You are a unique and special essence within the universe. You are one of a select group of Light Workers who sacrificed a lot to help planet Earth at this focal point.

The Star Person's intuitive gifts are highly developed. Think for a moment: You can tell when an energy "hot spot" is nearby, correct? Even if you do not know how to use it, you can tell when psychic energies are high. Using that same intuition, you must tell the difference between a Homeward bound energy vortex and a negative one - or one which is simply o.k. but does not lead Home (in scientific terms, we mean a parallel dimension to the mundane one which is not of exceptionally high energies). An example of an energy vortex which is not negative but which does not lead to a higher dimension would be that of a cemetery on Halloween. The celebration of Halloween creates strong energies and cemeteries certainly hold psychic energies, anyway, but one would be less likely to have a transcendingly positive experience there than, for instance, at a high energy spot along the seashore at sunrise.

Of course there is also a door which opens into the spirit world and this door is one psychics have used for ages. There is a close, loving connection which The Space Intelligences (Federation) and the Earth Spirit World share, and it is not uncommon or dangerous to feel this connection when seeking the Home Frequency.

For example, Diane was visiting the new home of a friend. This home has much energy...and can indeed be helpful in contacting the Home Frequency. During a psychic/meditative session with her friend, Diane encountered a small ghost. The spirit-child could be seen visibly, standing in friendliness and curiosity, attracted by the psychic energies. It was learned that the child, a girl named Millie, had died in a neighboring swimming pool.

This is an example of another dimension being reached while in search of the home frequency. It was not a negative encounter, energy, or dimension. However, it was not the place being sought. Intuition/psychic sense and inner guidance told Diane that this was not a dimension to which to make a permanent pathway.

How can you use the power of an energy vortex for seeing into/visiting the Home Dimension and for ultimately finding the permanent pathway/ frequency back?

Remember, the energy which emanates from a Home vortex will attract you, because its energy is your energy. If raw, natural energies are used (for instance, the psychic feelings one has during a wild storm), remember that you can turn them into the Home Frequency through the very goodness and "star quality" of your personal energy. When you are on the pathway to returning Home, the wonderful feelings are indeed intuitively and soulfully evident. How can you miss them! And before the final pathway is made, you may draw energy from the Home Frequency for survival on earth, so it is a two-way street. You draw strength and power from the Home Energy, thus increasing your energy flow, thus giving you strength to get a few steps closer to Home.

You therefore find it easier to move the rocks blocking your pathway out of the cavern from inside as well as waiting for co-workers to help from the outside.

This is indeed a cycle...a sustaining and beautiful cycle. You can always reach the Home Frequency at least this much! In other words, you may not be able to immediately return Home, you may not be able to feel verbal communication from the Star Guardian - or at least, not all the time - but this wonderful, revitalizing Home frequency is always within reach. It does not require extreme psychic ability or spectacular channeling gifts. It is always there to help get you through the day.

Dimensional doorways and their thresholds (energy vortexes) are on Earth and in the cosmos for you to use. They are pure creative, cosmic energies which await only the goodness of your star essence.

TRANSMISSION #2

This is Tibus. I come to you in love and light.

As I have transmitted before, star people have many specific home world sources (frequencies). Some are of pure energy dimensions (what theologians would call the angelic higher realms); other star people are aliens in the popular sense of the word (from other planets circling other stars); and still others are of the future (human time travelers).

We are all members of the Federation (also called Space Intelligences and the Higher Realms).

Do not concern yourself as to your specific origin of consciousness because the answer will manifest itself clearly when the time is right.

These diversities are like tributaries flowing into the main river. The Home Frequency is the main river. The specific tributaries maybe embarked upon after the main frequency is tuned into.

In short, we may say that your connection - and that of your Special One - is one which traverses trillions of miles of Space/Time but which may also be reached through dimensional shortcuts (doorways). Analogy: An ant can make his way around a 33 rpm record by going around the edge to the "flip" side. An ant can also get to the other side by going through the hole in the center. The latter would be analogous to a dimensional vortex.

There are times of overlap for dimensional intersect points (which exist throughout the universe in infinite number). There are times of wash-over.

When this happens naturally, there can be numerous UFO sightings, paranormal events and/or psychic feelings in abundance.

Become skillful at sensing if a particular day (or night) is a psychically-oriented time. Some days simply are, other days simply are not. These are the days when mundane energies dominate. Become skillful at sensing if a particular geographical spot is high in psychic energy. Return often to this spot once it is found. Attune your energies to it.

There are other dimensions involved in The Federation's work which may be called "interim dimensions." When we on the Home Side live on Earth for a while, we often use these interim dimensions. Often when we appear on Earth, we take refuge in these adjacent dimensions (very similar to the mundane one). For example, when a UFO blinks out, right before the eyes of an Earth military jet, it has "hopped" a dimension...but it has not returned directly to the Home Frequency.

Another example: There are numerous reports of UFO occupants "beaming in" (or out) of visual perception. Often a star person encounters the star guardian on the street or elsewhere in public...only to have him or her vanish before one's eyes.

Hopping back to the Home Frequency in this physical way is rather like hopping a twenty foot pond. It is wiser to use the stepping stones of the interim, friendly dimensions. You will come to know of these interim dimensions as well.

However, you must always have the Home Dimension as the target, the goal. The interim dimensions are ones which you need not worry about and which you may not even realize you are visiting. One need only be of goodness in order to avoid the ones you do not want to visit.

An example of a nearly-identical dimension manifesting: Diane and a friend went in the side door of a restaurant, having left their car in a memorable spot in the parking lot. When they turned to leave the restaurant, the side door was non-existent and their car was in a decidedly different spot in the parking lot. This was a slide zone. We took advantage of the natural high energies of that day to illustrate to these star people what an "adjacent interim dimension" truly is.

All star people experience these, both of their own making, and with the help of the Home Side, in order to prepare them for more drastic dimensional changes.

It has been stated before that Earth energies sometimes converge to form a natural energy vortex. Please be aware that these vortexes often (but not always) can be found in rock formations due to natural electromagnetics.

There is much in the field of dimensional physics which will become apparent to Earth science in the future. The Federation has many scientists who study this complicated and illuminating subject. However, there is always a quality to it which defies science. It is the God Force. And so, mastery of dimensional doorways unifies science and spirituality by its very nature.

TRANSMISSION #3

This is Tibus. I come to you in love and light.

All planets have natural dimensional doorways. There are those "star gates" which exist in the void and blackness which is space...and Earth science is presently beginning to suspect these exist through their research into black holes and white holes. And so we see that dimensional doorways are universal phenomena. Most of the vortexes fluctuate and change location or close up entirely at times. This is the norm. A few remain as infinite phenomena and are memorials to the pure Creator Force.

THE REAL LIFE UFO TRANSFORMATION OF DIANE TESSMAN

Before his death, Einstein worked many years on a unified theory which would combine gravity force with space/time energies. Electromagnetics play an important role in this theory, which the human race will soon unravel, (though slightly different than Einstein envisioned) and use. Once this theory becomes apparent to a race of people on a given planet, dimensional travel is theirs to command. As it is now, there are puzzles (such as the disappearances in Bermuda Triangle) but no comprehension. It might be added here that it is not wise to travel into a strong natural vortex anymore than to walk off a cliff if one is not intelligently, spiritually, knowingly using this vortex! Do not go blindly into, for instance, the Bermuda Triangle! However, its intersecting frequencies certainly are helpful to those who know how to use them.

The most startling quality about the culmination of the work which was begun as the Unified Field Theory is that humankind will find himself "touching the face of God" as he explores this scientific revelation. Science and Spirituality, Logic and Religion will become forever and irrevocably melded together. This is the reason why we try to guide the human race, at this time in particular, toward higher spiritual insights (and this is the specific reason for many missions!). The Change Point (indeed, a dimensional change point) should also be called "The Choice Point" for at that time, the human race must choose a higher spiritual plane - or perish.

The natural dimensional doorways of which we have spoken are more active at some times than at others. Why is this so? Our scientists and spiritualists cannot even tell you exactly. We may say, quite honestly, these fluctuations are God's will.

Usually, dimensional passageways are in harmony. When one is open, most are open. When they are open, the entire earth (and the rest of the galaxy, in all dimensional aspects), is bathed in radiant energy - good, positive energy which emanates from the God Force. An example of this is the Healing days held by many New Age groups which unite those of higher consciousness all around Earth at the same hour.

This energy of which we speak can of course be used for spiritual growth, for more enlightened astral travel, for increased powers of concentration. These primal creative energies are like an underground spring - a spring which brings life to the desert and feeds the immortal soul of life everywhere. This is the Life Force.

To use this energy when it is at its highest, find a place on planet Earth (since your mission is there at this time), which feels positive and powerful to you.

THE REAL LIFE UFO TRANSFORMATION OF DIANE TESSMAN

Sometimes this can be a private spot in your backyard or you may wish to actively search for one in the forest, near a lake or river, in the desert, or the mountains.

Take a place where you can feel the power. Just as some people are more sensitive to temperature changes while others are more sensitive to barometer changes, so some dimensional doorway's energies are more suited to you than others are. In short, find a place which makes you feel like the Home Dimension will make you feel

Once you have found that spot, you may rest assured that you are very close to an energy vortex (trust yourself!) and that your soul is indeed absorbing some of the magnificent energy which gave you Life in the first place!

Because your soul springs from the Home Dimension, it is essential that your soul always stay in contact with it (and the way described above is the simplest and yet most effective). This is one reason why energies vortexes exist...because you have never forgotten Home. Just as Earth provides air, light, and water for her children, the Home Dimension provides unique energy and soul nourishment, always. This is why you are "different." You continue to draw strength and power from this energy, just as you replenish it and keep it alive in your heart, despite adversities on mundane Earth. The Home Energy is the type of energy which your body and soul can store just as a battery stores energy for future use.

As you know, dimensional passageways are used by us of The Federation as well as by other beings. There is no reason why these passageways are one-way streets only. There is nothing in your human physiological structure which makes you non-qualified as a dimensional traveler. After all, you have traveled from the Home Dimension to Earth already!

We Star Guardians use vortexes for travel constantly. The immortal soul is not damaged by energy corridors but rather, is enhanced by them.

Many vortexes appear in places which are not easy for you to reach. I have mentioned before the "star gates" in the blackness of Space/Time. Also, vortexes appear high off the ground (though within Earth's atmosphere). This is why so many planes disappear in the Bermuda Triangle. The scientific proof of this doorway is difficult to find because often the actual vortex is high in the air...and also, it fluctuates in exact location. However, the U.S. government does have proof of this and other dimensional doorways...do not let them tell you otherwise.

THE REAL LIFE UFO TRANSFORMATION OF DIANE TESSMAN

Often natural vortexes appear on top of desert rocks or mountain peaks because of electromagnetics. The ultimate "mountaintop" is The Great Pyramid. Its geometric perfection offers an excellent "door opener" but also nature's rocks and mountains, though not perfectly geometrical, offer the enhanced power key of Mother Nature's raw energies. Large trees can also draw this energy and so the magnificent forest offers passageways to the Home Frequency.

With practice, you can draw vortex energies of a place to you and you may begin to do this at will, almost every time you visit the place. The first step is to reach out with your intuitive/psychic abilities to ascertain that a vortex is near. Now, narrow it down to the exact location of that special area which you have chosen (and which has chosen you). This process may take several visits to this spot, at different times of day or night.

If your intuition tells you that the vortex is hovering 1000 feet above the ground, you should - with the power of your mind - use your best energy to draw the vortex closer to you. Think of the energy vortex as being sentient, because in many ways it is a sentient entity (though very alien in nature from what Earth thinks of as a conscious energy). A vortex is sensitive to an energy which is similar to itself in some respects and so your "star energy" can draw the vortex closer. Although this is not an accurate concept in many respects, we often think of a vortex as an "energy animal" with which contact can be made and nourished. Many times we have found that vortexes seem to follow certain people throughout their lives, and this is a beautiful blessing as long as the person is of basic goodness. Some star people have weird occurrences all their lives - everything from UFO sightings to actual face-to-face meetings with their Home Guides.

If you wish a vortex to follow you, you must be ready for slide zones and other silly happenings such as Diane and her friend encountered when the side door of the restaurant had simply vanished when they turned to leave, and their car had moved in the parking lot. A sense of humor is helpful as energies careen and manifest in sometimes odd ways. THESE WILL NOT HARM YOU. However, if the unknown frightens you, then you are not ready for interactions of this nature. By your star nature, the unknown is more your friend than is the mundane dimension and 99% of star people know and feel this to be the truth. BE OF GOODNESS. You can only open the doors which you wish to open, for your hand (your mind/soul) is doing the opening!

Visualize yourself lying in nature, in full harmony and balance - you are a part of nature. You are lying near or on the spot which you have felt intuitively/psychically to be your energy vortex. When you are in this spot, you feel almost Home. Now concentrate on drawing a vortex to you (this is an intersect point with the Home Frequency). Remember the visual analogy of the oil and water. Attract the oil as a magnet would, so that it swirls toward you.

During this meditation, forget that time exists. Of course you must also forget, for the moment, the humdrum hassles and worries. But far above that, simply forget that there is a date, or a clock. Do not be discouraged if you cannot draw the vortex to you in your first several meditative sessions. Remember, this vortex energy is like a wild animal in some ways. Those in human bodies, even star people, can be so impatient!

At first you may only receive a glimpse of Home. Visions. Insights. Memories. Flashes. Then, contact! All of these will happen. The permanent path Home is now at least within sight, feeling, memory, and hope.

This "letting go" in a natural vortex setting promises to be a wonderful and enlightening experience. It also allows the vortex to "know" that you are friendly, that you have a positive mind/soul that you are a kindred energy, and that may work with you. One must attempt contact, must lower walls and blocks, before working with dimensional energies can be accomplished. The psychological survival walls which you have put up in the mundane dimension (and which are necessary there), must be lowered. This may take some time but it is necessary before a vortex can be attracted.

We realize what a frustrating experience it is: you have learned survival techniques, qualities which help you survive against the cruelties of the mundane frequency...then you are asked to lower psychological defense mechanisms in order to communicate with the Home Side and in order for you to use dimensional doorways.

TRANSMISSION #4

Time travel is a much simplified concept on mundane Earth. It is possible to travel to Earth's past; it is possible to travel to Earth, 1988, from elsewhere/elsewhen in time. As metaphysics has taught for ages, and as science is now beginning to realize, there is no "time."

THE REAL LIFE UFO TRANSFORMATION OF DIANE TESSMAN

Science tells Earth that time seems to be consecutive moments as opposed to a steady and ever fluctuating stream. These moments maybe "hopped" just as one skips stones in a creek.

Alternate timelines play an important part in time/ dimensional travel. An obvious example of an alternate timeline is one in which President Kennedy of the United States was not assassinated. Twenty years later, how much different that country - and the world - would have been! And yet, how very similar as well! In an alternate timeline, Kennedy lives still.

In another dimensional plane, the dinosaur flourishes; yet, it flourishes side by side with the alternate "modern" timeline in which Kennedy lives, and so on.

You can begin to grasp the complexity! We are dealing here with past/ future time travel and also alternate travel to the past/future. You can visit the ; past as you remember it...you can be in Dallas on the day Kennedy died. Or you can travel to the past where his motorcade was not mysteriously attacked on that fateful day.

We now give you two documented examples of this for your consideration:

In the 1960s, on Earth, a pilot decided he needed to make an emergency landing at a little-used airfield. One of his engines was running hot. As he approached this airfield, he saw World War II planes in active condition and men scurrying around on the ground dressed in typical WWII vintage attire. According to the pilot's knowledge of this field, it should have been deserted. The pilot established radio contact with the field only to discover that it was indeed 1944! Had he flown through a dimensional door? He did not land because his fear was great. We offer the additional insight that his fear over his hot engine may have dropped his psychological shields sufficiently so as to make his psychic mind responsive to dimensional energies as he flew through them. Keep in mind that "the fear factor" is at times helpful in lowering barriers psychically; thus in childhood on a dark Halloween night, you feel certain you have actually experienced "the beyond." By "fear", we do not mean the horrible kind of fear you feel when you suspect there is an intruder in your home. We mean instead the exciting/adrenalin-pumping feeling of being in the forest at night or seeing a UFO close-up! Incidentally, this World War II airfield case was investigated thoroughly and it was certain that no practical joke had been played upon the pilot, who did make it to another airstrip in his own timeframe safely.

Another example of an alternate timeline:

THE REAL LIFE UFO TRANSFORMATION OF DIANE TESSMAN

Two women happily visited an old castle, taking particular note of a small chapel area. They noted that the other visitors were all dressed "in costume," as people had dressed hundreds of years before. The women left the castle, having had an enjoyable tour. When they returned the next day, the tiny chapel was nowhere to be found and other visitors were in modern dress. Upon careful examination of old blueprints, the women found that the chapel was to have been built, but never had been! These women, who were very psychic and New Age oriented people in the first place, had created a vortex through their fascination with the place, and temporarily stepped through it.

This represents not only time travel but travel to an alternate dimension as well...the alternate past. Remember, in the women's mundane dimension, the chapel had never been built.

And so, we of The Federation give the human race warnings about the upcoming nuclear and natural disasters...but we also transmit that this holocaust can be prevented. Yes, in some timelines/dimensions, Earth does destroy herself. You may enter into a dimension in which this does not occur...an alternate reality. This is part of the mission of the star person - the Light Worker - to create these alternate realities. The Home Energies will help you, just as we Star Guides help humanity (and just as you help humanity).

All past and future dimensions exist side by side with the one in which you now sit, reading this transmission. The future is a conglomeration of unfulfilled prophesies and fulfilled prophesies - a road map with many variations possible for you. Your mind/soul may embark on any number of different life paths in any number of alternate realities. This is why we encourage you never to sit and wait for "doomsday." Doomsday need not come in your reality.

The future is always in question, is always The Question. And yet, it exists, for I am a part of it. It has an infinite number of alternate paths to be considered. As you know, even small decisions made during the day determine the future in major and minor ways. You are all aware of the reality one creates when one makes the decision to marry one person instead of another.

Consider this: Suppose you were planning a trip to the snow-covered mountains but you were told by a trustworthy psychic that an avalanche would occur while you were there. This affords you the chance to engineer your own reality, because if you are injured or die in the avalanche, the timeline will be without your possibly valuable contributions. The human race will not benefit from your contribution. Just as there are changing alternatives for the individual, so there are changing alternatives for the human race as a whole. In this way, new dimensions are traveled by the second, by the hour.

The question also occurs here: In the avalanche, were you "supposed" to (fie? Did you somehow cheat Death and destiny? Or, if you did die in the avalanche, did you die "before your time?" Both of these questions are examples of "one dimensional thinking." The human race must broaden its perception, must raise awareness and realize that, (1) there is no death for the soul; (2) life itself is much more flexible than perceived.

The concept of "cheating death" is an absurd one as is "dying before one's time." Both realities are valid. Both exist. Therefore, we must always go forth with the star mission/purpose (growing and developing spiritually and helping Earth) because all alternatives are reality and are aspects of the Whole.

Here we see that to speak scientifically of dimensional travel and alternatives is also to speak of spirituality and the immortal soul. As we have told you, these two fields are not segregated as humankind has assumed and believed. They are instead inextricably bound; they are one and the same.

Remember that a "seer" or prophet can step outside the flow of history, outside the timeline. When this occurs, his or her mind/soul is dimensional traveling. A great prophet exists not only inside the timeline and outside the timeline, but simultaneously on all dimensional levels. Jesus is such a prophet.

Past, present, future— and all alternatives of each— are all tied together in a pattern so complex that only the God-mind (Whole-mind) can begin to comprehend. We of The Federation have more of an overview than those who live on Earth. We can and do hop these dimensions, just as humankind will one day...and just as our Light Workers (star people) have always done, whether in conscious recollection or not.

The past is a dimension easier to perceive. If you are in total harmony with the energy vortex, it is possible to travel back in time. However, that is not where Home lies.

The Eternal Now is, of course, always with you, with your mind/soul. The present, however, in terms of history, is non-existent just as "tick-tock time" is non-existent. There is always the micro-second into the past or the microsecond into the future.

THE REAL LIFE UFO TRANSFORMATION OF DIANE TESSMAN

What is the future? You are the future!

All choices are possible at this micro-second for planet Earth. Your star purpose, as your soul remembers so keenly, is to help the mundane dimension you inhabit during your human lifetime...choose the good path, the peaceful path, the free path, the universal path. And then you will find Home, leading humanity there.

TRANSMISSION #5

The large governments on Earth are working on ways to use dimensional doors, because they have already found the rudimentary scientific secrets of such phenomena.

The tragic thing is, they do not have the spiritual goodness of which we have spoken so often...to be dealing with these phenomena. Great forces are opened up which may be used much as "The Force" in the Earth movie STAR WARS. The Force can be used for goodness. The Force can be used for progressing evil. It is a neutral force. It becomes the God-force when it is used for the positive. One manifests the beautiful God-force by practicing goodness and being of goodness. Of course there is God! The point is: Do Earth governments know this?

There are many paranoid and "spooky" stories in the paranormal and UFO research fields about frightening occurrences which star people or UFO contactees experience. The "enemy" in this case is not true aliens from other dimensions or planets but rather the Earth governments who often pose as "paranormal bogeymen" or simply harass those in contact with the beyond in mundane ways. Thus we have the infamous "men in black" accounts prevalent especially in the 1950s.

As a star person, you must keep a low profile where Earth governments are concerned. We are not always able to protect you from government harassment because we cannot interfere directly in this timeline's flow. If lower psychic forces intercede as occasionally happens, we are more within our "rights" to protect you.

More and more, the so-called super-powers of Earth are discovering that the secret to unlocking great energies doesn't lie in the development of nuclear power or orbiting laser satellites. Instead, they are finding that the secret to great power lies in the minds of individuals like yourself who are keyed into other frequencies. Psychic ability coupled with new technology will give these super-powers awesome capabilities which we can only hope that we of The Federation will not have to overtly stop. It is our dearest law that we not interfere with the natural evolutionary path of a planet. However, if our worlds as well are threatened...if it threatens the future and also the future of other worlds...we will physically stand at our star people's sides to help avoid catastrophe.

Keep your secrets close to your heart, star person. Again, trust your instincts. Do not feel you must broadcast to the world because yours is a much deeper and more subtle mission than shallow "missionary" work. Your task is literally to change the frequency of a dimension!

TRANSMISSION #6

We have attempted to guide you clearly and specifically as to how to use a natural vortex which you can find, if you only look. Remember, choose the natural energy flow which feels friendliest to you...and be patient as your two sentient energies merge. Remember also that there are some points in time (a particular day or night or part of a particular day or night), which has higher psychic energies for you personally than usual. And so, you must feel the time and place within yourself (by "psychic", we refer to all which has been spoken of in these transmissions).

On occasion, one can create a dimensional door within his or her own home or property. These are temporary doors, forced open through sheer power of mind, plus natural energies of the day or night.

Star child, as you begin the creation of the intersect point which will lead you to the Home Frequency, cleanse yourself in the light of God and goodness as you meditate. Do so on a night (or day) when you feel totally close to Home (do not attempt this when you are angry, hurt, frustrated, or low on energy).

After the cleansing, visualize yourself on a stellar path, strewn with sparkling stars. You may walk along this path and the stars will be as flowers all around you...glistening diamonds in the blackness of space.

You begin to relax, your breathing becomes slower. All the cares of the days are forgotten. Your mind/soul are floating, totally at peace, completely safe and secure.

Ahead on the shimmering star path, you perceive that there are ten stars. You begin your journey at the tenth star which is an electric white/blue color, the size of a large sunflower at the side of your path. You can feel the beauty and the consciousness within this star.

Now continue on to the ninth star. It is delicate and tiny, much like a violet. It is deep purple. You know it well and love it dearly. You feel a release of tension, a release from worldly cares...and the Home Energy encompasses you.

The eighth star is emerald green. It is as a wild flower in a fragrant forest It is a healing star, a Home star. Allow it to help you, healing the hurts and injuries which the human lifetime has brought you.

The seventh star is yellow and you know this one as Sol, home star of planet Earth. Sol is highly sentient in itself, giving warmth and light to all who seek. Let go of the frustrations you have felt while under Sols light on planet Earth. All is forgiven. Remember that Jesus also forgave his earthly brethren.

The sixth star is rose pink/white. This is the star of joy, the unconditional love one feels while traveling the path Home. Revel in its beauty now.

The fourth star is the color of warm orange. It is the star of friendship. Remember friends and companions, your comrades on Earth who are also Light Workers. There are also those beings whom you cannot see with human eyes but whose presence you have always felt. They are your spiritual family and your own Special One (star guardian). Let the love flow!

Walk on along the star path. The third star is pure, sparkling red. This is the color of life, of energy, of passionate love on an unconditional basis. Feel re-energized as you pass it because the love you have sent out is returning to give you new life.

The second star is gold. It is intense and magnificent. It is the Question and the Answer rolled into one celestial flower.

The first star on this path is of purest energy, glowing with all the colors combined in swirling patterns. It is the God-force and in order to comprehend it consciously, we see all the colors turning into a massive white glow as they swirl. This is an energy intersect point where the love of all dimensions, all worlds, all galaxies, all times...converge. Your mind/soul communicates with this love and power and become one with it.

You should work with this star path as often as you wish, in meditation and contact sessions when you wish to reach the Home Frequency, Even though you will not transcend Home to stay at this moment, you will know the path well in your mind/soul when the time comes that you must find the way Home.

If you wish a more physical energy vortex to be created, you may use this star path we have given you as a beginning.

After you have reached the place at the end of the path, remain in this deep state of concentration. Now, through creative visualization, create a doorway/vortex in your backyard (or wherever there is privacy). Or, you may even enhance the energies of the natural special place away from your house by solidifying it as a solid, positive vortex in meditative visualization, and then physically travel to that special place once again.

Whether you are concentrating on your own property or that special place some distance away, tell yourself as you do meditative creative visualization that you are now projecting each step of the way to this vortex so as when you get to it, it will indeed be the actual solid vortex you have felt it to be potentially. In other words, when you are through meditating, you visualize how the sun will feel on your face as you physically head for the special place (or if you prefer to do this at night, you will project how the cool night air will feel on your face and how the stars will be out. Look up at the stars and know that they are as real as the star path you are creating for yourself, and vice versa).

Again, we urge you to try this creative visualization when the time is right for you and when energies are positive and high.

All that you have ever read, studied, known, felt about Mind over Matter, about metaphysics, about your own "star" nature, about being different in a mundane world, about feeling in contact with higher intelligence, about your belief in God....all is in play now! You know the vortex will be in the particular spot in which you have placed it.

The yard is dark and so you gaze toward the far corner to catch a glimpse of the light...There it is, the door!

Star person, in this way, you can - temporarily - create a passageway Home to be used for communication, experiencing, healing.

When the time is right, the passageway will be open for you. The time is sooner than you might dream. You must at least know this path well. You know not to be impatient in finding it. One does not run a race in world record time on his or her first race. Remember that all must be in harmony and that time must be cosmically right...your mind/soul must be at full force as must be the natural energies at that intersect point in Space/Time.

Remember also that you are not alone. Remember the analogy to the trapped individual within the cave. There are those rescue workers who help from beyond, as well. But there must be an effort on your part or the path will remain a secret to you.

TRANSMISSION #7

This is Tibus. I come to you once again in love and light.

This and other transmissions about dimensions are a part of the "digging out" which we on the Homeside are doing as you struggle your way out from your dimension. This is not the only help which you are receiving. We are helping each and every Light Worker in ways which may not be readily evident. And our contact grows stronger and more active each day.

We have told you that the path Homeward blends science and spirituality. It is The Whole. It is the River.

Einstein, the scientist who moved Earth along on her destiny's path, was also a mystic. The Earth scientific community took his theories in their typical absolutist manner and created a set order and dogma out of them. Einstein offered them only as stepping stones along the path. He felt, at his point in time, than nothing could travel faster than the speed of light. His belief was essentially correct but it is also irrelevant (something he later realized but the scientists who started preaching his works as dogma had already closed their minds, until recently).

I will explain why I have called Einstein's work irrelevant: Humankind will not travel faster than light but will instead travel through light (as we of The Federation do now).

All matter is composed of molecules (sub-atomic particles) moving at different speeds. There is always space between these molecules. If you know beyond a shadow of a doubt, that you can get up and walk through the wall, you can do so! However, your mind/soul is conditioned to have at least a shred of doubt because it has had to survive in the mundane world. This is not your fault!

Hyperlight speed gives our star ships the ability to move between molecules, between light and time itself. Again, I remind you, you may float down the river on a boat, participating in its movement or you may hop the stones of the river, moving not against it but rather bouncing over its space, not subject to the laws of its motion, momentum, or flow.

If you travel through the sub-atomic particles which make up light itself (remember the space between these particles which is already an established scientific fact), then you are traveling faster than a beam of light through which those particles pass. Consider spacial displacement: When you travel through water, the water's molecules are parted and you pass through.

Do not be afraid to consider these "future science" concepts. Do not feel that "perhaps your brain can't comprehend."

It can, it will, it must...for you will be traveling through light in the future, within the lifetime you now live!

Mysticism, psychic pursuits (when of goodness), spirituality, meditation...all of these are shortcuts to the science of which I now speak. The mind/ soul need not fully understand every equation or every theory in order to be, and to do! It is well and good to understand scientifically what is happening and someday soon, the human race will begin to do this. It will begin to do this, thanks to our Light Workers' (star people's) completed mission.

Never make the mistake of excluding science for spirituality, or vice versa. Go with the path which is right for you but never be intolerant of those who stress the other end of the spectrum. In other words, some people are UFO, parapsychology, "Let's-build-a-starship" oriented (science oriented). Other people are purists in the religious, spiritual sense and easily make the connection from the Space Intelligences to the Higher Realms to Jesus. All is in balance! Each person's focal point of concentration is a natural "star" quality of his or her mission and must be allowed to flower as it wishes.

Power outages have been and will continue to be a major source of "inspiration" for more scientifically oriented people. This is, of course, not our only reason for causing them occasionally. At this point, be aware that electricity offers a primitive though intense source of energy which is abundant on planet Earth. It is easily located and already harnessed in millions of miles of power lines and cables, focused in transformer stations. Just as you can use a train, car, plane, bike, roller skates, your feet, etc., to go fifty miles, so various concentrations and types of energies can be used in our operations and missions. Power outages cause distractions so that other energy sources can be drawn from, in some crisis instances. Many of you have felt communication from us through electrical energy in your homes (hums, beeps, pulses, etc.). These are forerunners and beginnings to more specific communication.

When the Change Point comes, power outages will be "mandatory" due to all forms of energies being in flux.

Star person, you must know the path Home or you will be lost when the time comes that it must be taken. Know that the alternative timelines and adjacent dimensions must be areas of knowledge and familiarity, not of fear of the unknown.

Whether being re-energized in the Home Frequency or traveling the final star path homeward, you will take to dimensional traveling as the fish takes to water or the bird takes to the air.

Do not let the human fear of the unknown nor all the bogeymen of past religions frighten you. God is everywhere in the universe, not on planet Earth alone. As a matter of fact, your mission is to bring the God-force into more active play on Earth, because God's love is stronger on other worlds! You know this through the Home Energies you so familiar to you. They are more peaceful, more sensitive, more God-like. And so, forget science fiction movies on dimensional travel which ended with the hapless humans meeting ridiculous monsters or "aliens." You know what is in your heart. The God of the Solar System, the God of the galaxy, the God of the universe...responds to love. The God-force sends you a constant and never-ending radiant love/ energy. You have only to respond, to be of this love, to be in constant contact with it. It protects you in dimensional travel when you are in the unknown. You have only to love God back through loving all life - then the bogeymen will disappear from your reality. Fear feeds on itself. Do not let it in.

Dimensional travel is not new to you. You have done it to be where you are right now. You have had command of it and you will again. I promise you that you will walk through the passageway and that Home does await!

We try in many ways to prepare you. You must dig your own path out of the cavern as we work from outside. Do not despair. You are making progress. We share your impatience but that doesn't help much, in moments of frustration.

Please internalize the blending of spirituality and scientific theory. When considering dimensions, no comprehension can be attained without this blending. All consciousness works on energy frequency (mind waves) throughout the universe. The physical body may " go along" if the mind/soul is strong enough to take it along and if the mind/soul wants to be "burdened" with the physical body.

Some people hope that this physical burden will be lifted before they transcend, others wish desperately that the physical body go along at the Change Point. This is the concept of being able to pilot a starship and to actually be a starship crew member. Either alternative is possible at the Change Point. That decision is between you and God.

Love transcends time/dimension, it transcends space, it transcends all, and at this time, I give you my unconditional love, my friends.

May the healing light of God and goodness surround you, always,

Tibus

15

PERSONAL CHANNELINGS FROM TIBUS FOR ALL STAR PEOPLE

Author's Update: Fascinating how situations come back to haunt us! The concerns about extraterrestrials being cryogenically frozen by our government has arisen again recently. We first received psychic transmissions about this horrific situation in the mid-1980s when a friend and I kept tabs on a huge underground military base in Southern California wherein we intuitively and psychically felt extraterrestrials and future humans form crashed saucers, had been cryogenically frozen – alive. Today, Tibus predicts you will be hearing more on this in coming days.

The following section is a compilation of excerpts from personal readings and channelings Tibus and I have done for individual star people. Though these words were intended for individuals at the time they were channeled and written down, it is our belief that all star people can benefit from these teachings.

Each individual channeling is preceded by a "title" which gives a vague idea of what the channeling was about, as well as a date when the channeling was originally done. Sometimes, at the end of Tibus' channeling, I will include my own comments and observations in the hopes of clarification and continuity. It is our sincere hope that these words will enrich your spiritual development, enlighten your star spirit, and help to guide you along your continuing star path.

DIANE M. TESSMAN, DD, DL STARLIGHT MYSTIC CENTER

TIBUS CHANNELS REGARDING STAR GUARDIANS TAKEN CAPTIVE BY GOVERNMENT FORCES

September 1986

THE REAL LIFE UFO TRANSFORMATION OF DIANE TESSMAN

As Diane and I have often mentioned, star people such as yourself do have unique and very specialized spiritual gifts, and it is these gifts and how to use them that I would like to discuss with you during this reading.

As you know, many of our star brothers who have visited your planet have been taken captive by governmental forces around your world. Many times, these star brothers manage to "escape" on their own; other times, we are able to "rescue" them using technology which governments of your Earth does not yet understand and for which they cannot defend against. And yet, there are occasional times when our star brothers cannot be freed – and as we have often mentioned, the "fate" of these brothers is sometimes cruel.

Those who cannot be freed, and who are to be "permanently held" by governmental forces, are often placed into cryonic suspension - a means whereby all physical lifeforces of the body can be "suspended," rendering the "patient" completely helpless and at the mercy of the captors. The other thing about this type of "suspension" is that is does permit the mind-energy (or astral body) to "travel." In other words, those who are placed into suspension are physically unable to move, and all life functions (such as heartbeat, respiration, digestion, etc.,) are "suspended.*' On the other hand, the mental/spiritual activity of the mind/brain cannot be suspended - and many of our star brothers do manage to find a "freedom" of sorts in the astral realm.

There are, of course, many star people who feel this is the "destiny" of those star brothers. And yet, I transmit to you at this time that "destiny" is often a matter of choosing and not a matter of pre-destined "fate." In other words, we can and should choose our own destiny; we can and should engineer our own destiny in the best interest of all concerned. We star guides are concerned and saddened over the fact that this choice - the fundamental and irreversible choice to life- has been taken away from those who have been captured and placed into cryonic suspension.

We remind you again that the mind/soul/spirit is still active and very much alive when the body is suspended - and therefore, cryonic suspension can and does become a prison which binds the body to "life," and condemns the mind/soul/spirit to a possible eternity in prison.

As an analogy, consider your own nightly dreams. While you sleep, your mind/soul is very much active -- dreaming, often travelling on the astral plane. Your body, on the other hand, is inactive and, for that particular time, "useless." In short, even though the mind/spirit/soul is certainly more important, it is fundamentally wrong to deny to any living creature the right to live as a whole being. In short, during your nightly sleep, you have chosen to rest; but during the long, cold sleep of cryonic suspension, that choice has been removed and replaced with an order given by some politician a thousand or more miles removed from the reality of the situation.

The "good" thing is that the mind is still active - and can therefore travel the astral plane and still remain in contact with those of us still on board the starships. But the lifeforce itself has been taken away - and it is that injustice which we protest and which we encourage you to protest as well.

In almost any state in America, there are "top secret" government installations - places which specialize in weaponry, weapons research, military secrets, and so on. As a star person, you are undoubtedly "sensitive" to the energy of such places. When you travel by one of these installations, perhaps you feel chilled or otherwise "uncomfortable" with the general vibrations of the area. This is very common in installations which "house" those of our star brothers who have been taken captive and who are being held against their will. The reason you may feel "chilled" or uncomfortable is that you are sensing the psychokinetic energy which is expended from a mind trapped in suspension. In a very small way, when you are near to a place such as this, you are sharing a temporary "consciousness" with the being or beings who are inside, who are being held in suspension, and who are essentially reaching out to you for psychic help.

Of course, the most important thing is your own awareness of what you are feeling as well as what you can do about it. Primarily, we star guides urge you to always test your own spiritual sensitivity - particularly if you live near one of these installations or military bases. Believe it or not, the places which "house" captured extraterrestrials are more prevalent than you might imagine. Which is one reason the national "interest" in UFOs and other such phenomena has dropped and the governmental attitude has become one of denial. In short, many different races have visited your world - some more technologically advanced than the Ashtar Command, others less advanced. But among all of those who have visited your world, the government has always had a policy of keeping the information away from the public and thereby holding complete control over the eventual "fate" of any extraterrestrial beings who may have been taken captive and/or placed into suspension.

THE REAL LIFE UFO TRANSFORMATION OF DIANE TESSMAN

As to what you as a star person can do about it... there are many things. First of all, as we have already mentioned, sharpen your own personal awareness. The first step toward solving any problem is the awareness that it does exist. Secondly, if you live near an installation which you suspect may be involved in housing extraterrestrials, or if you have suspicions about any area, we urge you to probe that area with your mind - with your astral/ spiritual energy. If you still feel that you are on the right track, we then urge you to call out with your mind to those of our star brothers who may be being held physically captive.

Keep in mind that the thoughts/spiritual energy/mind energy of those star guides is still active - every bit as active as yours or mine, and that telepathic communication with these star guides will give you additional information in many areas. Additionally, by attempting to communicate with our captured brothers, you will, in your own way, be alleviating a small part of the terrible aloneness which comes with being placed into "sleep suspension" against one's will. Keep in mind that these captured star guides have been taken from their loved ones, too. And imagine how you would feel if you were suddenly placed into a unit where you lived forever in a land of endless dreams.

While some dreams can certainly be pleasant, others can be an eternal nightmare if the dreamer is never permitted to awaken. We hesitate to divulge this information for a variety of reasons – not the least of which is that there can be a danger to you if you are not careful and if you do not continue to employ your precious spiritual gifts. In short, so long as you protect yourself with the White Light of Truth, and so long as you call on your guardian angels and your own Special One for guidance and protection, you will be safe. But please remember, my friend, that your safety must always come first. We value you immensely, and will always protect you and those you love.

Remember also that your thought energies can reach those of us who have been unfairly imprisoned on the astral/dream plane - and that by reaching them, we are taking the first step toward freeing them. During the End Times and the Change Point, your course in this direction will become clearer, and we urge you to meditate further on this entire area of thought. In short, open your mind during meditation to the concept of eternal dreams - dreams which you might not choose to dream if you had the choice. That is the "fate" of the star guides who have been captured, and we ask your help in reaching them.

THE REAL LIFE UFO TRANSFORMATION OF DIANE TESSMAN

We ask your help in reaching these temporarily "lost" companions. Without your unique energies, without your love, your world would be in far worse condition than it is. You are the guiding light of the future - for your world, and for those of our star friends who have had the right of choice taken from them.

May the healing light of God and goodness surround you always,

Tibus

Comment: Finally, I would just like to add that star people must always remember that our star guides such as Tibus, Micha, Ashtar and others are not "invincible." In other words, we are brothers and sisters – which means, in very simplified terms, that we are "of the same flesh." We have all come to this Earth for a very important mission – and only when we can work together for the betterment of Humankind will that mission be fulfilled.

Also, please keep in mind that our simple awareness of this type of thing is vitally important. So long as we remember that we are not alone, we have taken the first step toward the stars... and home.

Primarily, it is my impression that Tibus wants us to remember our imprisoned star brothers - and by remembering them, we are increasing our own commitment to help them... just as they have helped us so often in the past, and as they continue to help us as we journey into the future.

Peace, love and light always,

D.M.T.

TIBUS CHANNELS REGARDING WORLD GOVERNMENT, CENSORSHIP & RELIGIOUS FALLACY

October 1986

In this channeling, I would like to discuss with you some of the conditions your world currently faces and what you as a star person can do to change world attitudes and trends which may not be to your liking.

Essentially, as you have undoubtedly noticed, your world is in the grips of many divergent forces at this moment. There is tension due to the expulsion of diplomats from the US, the Soviet Union, Britain, Syria and so on - and as know, these political maneuvers are often the first signs of conflict. In the past, this potential conflict, while certainly a danger to life, was not a worldwide threat. Now, however, with the continuing threat of nuclear exchange, any conflict has the potential to become the final conflict.

In addition to the nuclear threat, there is also a domestic threat which is, in many ways, equally as frightening. As you may have heard, there have been recent rulings in certain states which prohibit the teaching of certain books - among them *THE WIZARD OFOZ* and *THE DIARY OF ANNE FRANK*. These books have been deemed by a so-called "supreme court" to be "offensive to the religious beliefs" of certain individuals. Why? *THE WIZARD OF OZ* was so-banned because it allegedly portrayed witches as being good. And *THE DIARY OF ANNE FRANK* was banned because "it tolerates all religions."

Essentially, these two books - and others are certain to follow-are being made unavailable to children in certain states because a few so-called "religious" individuals cannot tolerate the concepts which differ from their own. We star guides certainly have no "say" in the matter, yet it has been our experience that censorship in the name of religion can and will lead to the eventual censorship such as exists in many foreign governments. In essence, any religion which states that all other religions are not to be tolerated should be seriously examined - not only by the individuals who subscribe to that religion, but by the law-giving bodies of your government as well.

While we realize how radical this may sound to some, we urge you to consider the matter for yourself. We believe you will agree that more wars have been fought in the name of religion, more lives have been taken in the name of religion, more "hatred" has arisen in the name of religion... than in the name of any other collective concept.

In short, when Man begins to use his "religion" as a tool for war, as a tool for suppressing the beliefs of others, then is that religion truly in the name of God or any Supreme Being? The Biblical God teaches us to "love our fellow man," and states that judgment is reserved for Him alone. And yet, with the censorship of books in Tennessee, it is wholly apparent to us star guides that Man is taking judgment unto himself.

Other allegedly "offensive" concepts which were mentioned in the trial were as follows:

THE REAL LIFE UFO TRANSFORMATION OF DIANE TESSMAN

It was found offensive to certain religions to tolerate the idea of a "world government." (In essence, this means that some religions perpetrate the concept of nations such as the US, the Soviet Union, China, South Africa, and so on. And while each of those nations certainly has a right to exist as an entity unto itself, these "religions" seem to be perpetrating the idea that they must continue to exist as entities unto themselves).

In explaining further, allow me to say this: It is only when your world becomes united that universal and spiritual unity will become possible. In other words, so long as nations exist and co-exist peacefully, there is no problem. However, when those same nations demand the right to exist separately and without cooperation with others, your world is doomed to eventual war, your people doomed to eventual annihilation from the face of the Earth - which is where the Biblical God again comes into the picture.

In essence, it is Man's wrongful interpretation of "religion" which has led to your current world condition - at least in certain areas and under certain circumstances. When Man begins seeing himself as God, and when Man begins interpreting the Bible or any other religious document wrongfully, Man then dooms himself as a species and as a planet. In other words, if one went back to the original Hebrew transcripts of the Holy Bible, Man would discover that at no point does that Word state there is only one religion, nor would he find anything denouncing a "world government." In short, Man has placed his imperfect values on the "perfect" word of God - whether that "perfect word of God" is found in the Bible, in the Koran, in the Dead Sea Scrolls or in Nature itself. And as man is, by nature, an imperfect creature, it is inevitable that Man's values will fail him and lead to destruction of all he knows.

As an analogy, the term "human error" has become quite common in this day and age - and with good reason. Humans do make errors. Nature and/or God do not. By nature, your species is non-violent - by nature, not by training or social customs. In other words, by nature, all living things retract from violence or the threat of harm. By nature, man fears death - not only the death of himself, but the death/extinction of his own species.

Therefore, it is possible to assume that only your social and political structures have made it "acceptable" to fight wars in an attempt to superimpose one set of beliefs over another - i.e., a war fought to make the world Catholic, for example, instead of Baptist, Methodist, Buddhist, and so on. By nature, man is basically an inoffensive, tolerant creature - sharing his planet with a variety of other lifeforms. But when social and political values intervene, that nature can be upset and even destroyed, leaving Man vulnerable to himself and those around him.

As a star person, we strongly urge you to consider these concepts at length, meditating on the concept of human nature and human error. In short, we ask that you look into yourself to determine where your personal beliefs lie in this area. Perhaps you have never considered that a "world government" would be offensive. It shouldn't be offensive-for it certainly represents a possibility for world peace, an end to wars, and an opportunity for all the peoples of your planet to co-exist in harmony. But remember that there are those who do find the possibility of a world government to be a terrible threat - perhaps because those individuals are simply frightened that it wouldn't be "their" government, perhaps because they have become so inundated with propaganda that they are afraid even to give it consideration.

When we speak of "world government," we must understand that we are speaking of unity and peace - neither of which has existed on your planet in its history. In short, a world government would have to be a mutually beneficial one - for Man's nature is also not to live in captivity, not to live in an oppressed state, not to be a slave or pawn of any government. And when we consider this, it becomes obvious that Man's very nature would not allow a bad world government to exist. Man's rebellious nature would be awakened, and any world government which was not mutually beneficial would certainly fail and be replaced by another... and so on... until eventual world peace became a reality.

As with anything, it is not destined to be "easy," but it is destined to be. And when such concepts are "fought" against in the name of religion, we urge the star person such as yourself to look more closely at that religion, in order to make the determination as to whether it really is a religion, or whether it is Man's wrongful interpretation of the world and even of the Word of God and/or Nature.

Additionally, on the topic of censoring books and dictating what can and cannot be taught, we ask you to consider that awareness is the key to continued existence for your world and her people. In short, if everything that someone found offensive was censored, your world would exist in total darkness, and awareness would become impossible. In other words, it is only through knowledge of other ideas and other ways different from one's own that one can grow and learn to make intelligent choices for himself. By censoring, Man only makes certain knowledge more desirable - and, like Adam and the apple, Man will inevitably misuse forbidden knowledge. Whereas, if that knowledge had never been forbidden in the first place, perhaps the temptation would never have existed to bite into the apple. And yet, if Man tries to remove the apple, if he tries to censor ideas and concepts, he is essentially shoving the apple into his own mouth and virtually tasting his own destruction. Again, awareness is vital to the survival of your world -- and when even one small book or concept is removed from availability, awareness becomes limited.

Again, we ask you to dwell on these concepts at length – on the idea of "religions vs. God/Nature." God is not a religion; neither is he a Baptist, a Catholic, a Buddhist or a Methodist. The Supreme God/Nature is all things, and therefore should represent a tolerance for all things by all people.

As you meditate further on this, I am confident you will discover your own Truth, and that you will utilize that truth to bring awareness to others. Let your Truth be a light which illuminates the darkness – and I know you will find others coming to you, asking you where this inner peace comes from. And when you tell them, when you share your awareness, you will be doing one small part of your Earthly mission - bringing awareness and light into the darkness often inhabited by those of the mundane/Earthly vibration.

May the healing light of God and goodness surround you always,

Tibus

Comment: Finally, I would just like to say that the topics of "censorship" and "world governments" are very close to both Tibus and myself - and with very good reason. There are those who feel the work we do here at the Starlight Mystic Center is wrong - because it does not teach one specific religion. For that reason, we have often received threatening letters, our mail has been "audited" on occasion, and our hearts have sometimes been close to breaking because of the intolerance and hatred in the hearts of our fellow men.

I feel very strongly that our world is on the very brink of disaster, and only through continuing to spread awareness and Light will we as star people be able to make a difference in our planet and its attitudes and, especially, its future.

D.M.T.

THE REAL LIFE UFO TRANSFORMATION OF DIANE TESSMAN

TIBUS CHANNELS REGARDING "THE HOLIDAY SEASON" AND HOW OUR SPIRITUALITY CAN SEE US THROUGH LONELINESS AND PERSONAL PROBLEMS IN OUR DAILY LIVES

November 1986

The star person such as yourself is always sensitive to changes - changes in the environment, changes within oneself, changes in the attitudes of others. And it is that kind of sensitivity which can so easily be disturbed at this time of year. As you know, the Holiday Season should be a joyous time – a time for sharing with friends and loved ones, and a time for deep personal reflections. And yet, as our world grows more crowded and the mundane society grows more aggressive, it is important to remember to take care of yourself just as much as you take care of those around you.

As we move into the end of this year, I ask you to take a few minutes each day to reflect on your accomplishments, your spiritual growth, and your goals for your own personal future. For without you, this planet would be a different place. You do make a difference, my star friend, and we encourage you to remember that, and to take those few minutes to strengthen your spiritual shields and to meditate on what you would like to accomplish in years ahead.

It is at this special time of year that we star guides again wish to thank you for your spiritual involvement with your planet, with us, and with your own Special Ones. Sometimes, we all tend to take for granted the fact that we are special - and star people are among the most unique and special of all beings. Why? Perhaps because you represent to us the future itself, Earth's survival, and the coming of the New Age of Man. Without you, my star friend, the world would be a much more empty and lonely place. And though we may not mention it often, we wanted you to know that your efforts are felt and appreciated, and that your presence is experienced among us...just as we hope our presence is experienced within you.

As Diane mentioned, your planet is entering a time of year when there will be much happiness, much rejoicing, much celebration. And yet, there will also be increased chaos - and, in some cases, increased loneliness and despair.

As you know from your own star experiences, the star path can be a lonely one - especially before one realizes that it is a star path. To explain, remember back to the time before you became aware of your star nature and your star destiny. As a child, you were undoubtedly "different," often set apart from friends and even family - mentally even if not physically. You did not understand why you didn't "fit in"; and for that reason, you were often lonely and perhaps even unhappy at times. You felt that you were not understood by your peers and your relatives, that you were never quite a "part" of what was transpiring around you.

And yet, once you discovered your star nature, you could at least understand where these feelings of alienation originated. You could logically comprehend that you were different - and that that difference was a source of joy and accomplishment rather than some incomprehensible "negative personality trait" as you may once have believed.

So, in many ways, the key to spiritual happiness and fulfillment is personal spiritual awareness. And yet, now that you have achieved that awareness of who and what you are, you have taken on a great responsibility—the responsibility of helping to "awaken" other star souls who are experiencing those same dark, despairing years that you once travelled earlier along your path.

During this Holiday Season, the spiritual energies of the world will be high. Some good, some bad. The good energies are for obvious reasons - sharing, seeing loved ones after long periods of being separated, and so on. But the "bad" energies are often less easy to define—for they are the energies of those despairing and lonely, the energies of the homeless, the energies of those who do not have the good fortune that the majority of us in the Star Network have achieved.

And so, during this time of year, we ask you to spiritually reach out to these people - not as a "mass consciousness," but as single, individual human beings in need of spiritual guidance and assistance. And we are confident that, by doing so, you will increase your own spiritual gifts ten-fold, as well as helping someone else on toward their eventual spiritual destiny.

In essence, what we are asking you to do is to select one person. To do this, I would like to ask you to meditate. Choose a time over the next three days that is a time when you will be able to spend at least an hour undisturbed. Establish your "personal solitude frequency" with music, candle light (a yellow or golden candle is excellent for this meditation); and then allow your mind to settle into its contemplative and spiritual meditative state.

Once you have achieved that state, open your mind and heart to the name of one person on the face of this Earth. The first name which comes to you is usually the name of someone who is reaching out. But, more than that, it is the name of someone who is on your own personal energy frequency - allowing the two of you to communicate in this manner more easily. It is also the name of someone who has been reaching out to you - whether they are aware of it on a conscious level or not.

After you have received the name of your spiritual brother or sister, we ask you to send a loving light to that person – the spiritual light of Truth. Remember again that you have already achieved your own awareness of your star nature and your personal destiny. But the person to whom you are communicating in your meditative state does not yet share that same peace of mind and comfort of spirit.

Again, it is your responsibility to guide others toward their destiny – and very often this can be done through meditation and a deep spiritual commitment. As your meditation continues, impart to your spiritual brother or sister that they are not alone. Encourage them to look into themselves for the answers they are seeking. And, even more, encourage them to open themselves to awareness of their own star nature. Through your spiritual, meditative bond, wrap this other lonely star person in light and love - showing them that there is a place for them, a place in your heart and in the hearts and minds of all star people everywhere.

And, most of all, ask them to communicate with you again whenever they feel the need. Encourage your newfound brother or sister to call on you for guidance and support - and be willing always to share the benefit of your own personal awareness with your new charge.

I think you will find that, in the course of a single meditation, you will develop a deep, lasting bond with another living being ~ a person somewhere who is feeling those same lonely and despairing feelings that you once experienced. And, more than that...try to remember a time when you suddenly felt and knew that someone was reaching out to you. You may never have seen or "met" this person in the physical world, yet at some point in your life, you began to "know" the truth - and in knowing, you gained the ability to seek awareness and a higher knowledge. Now, when you think about it, the positions have become "reversed." Now, you are the one reaching out to another lonely, aching star soul. You are in the role of teacher and friend. And you have made a spiritual friend who will be with you always – a brother or sister in your star mission, a supportive influence in. your daily life.

As you end your meditation, be sure to impart your own inner peace and awareness to your new friend. Assure them again and frequently, that they aren't alone, that there are others like themselves who are on your planet for a very important reason, to fulfill a vital spiritual mission. Remind them again of their own self-worth - just as you were undoubtedly reminded of your self-worth by your spiritual star brother or star sister long ago.

In doing this meditation, you are bringing the energies full circle - in that you are taking the despair, loneliness and spiritual pain of another star person and helping to channel it toward awareness, productivity, and spiritual enlightenment. You are literally creating a complex energy-chain – a chain which will reach around your planet and bring your world one step nearer to global harmony.

In addition to your meditation in this area, we also encourage you to seek your own inner harmony level often during this Holiday Season. Remember that the energies of this time of year can be chaotic just as much as they can be joyful. And since you are a high-energy being, it is natural that others will inadvertently try to "draw" on you from time to time - just as plants draw their life-sustaining energy from the sun. But, just like the sun, you must replenish your own energy as well as giving that loving energy to others.

During this time of year, we highly encourage increased meditation as well as nature walks whenever possible. By going out into the quiet parts of the world - such as a field, a lake, an ocean, for example - you can help to protect your own inner peace by "drawing" energy from nature as discussed earlier. By becoming "one" with your planetary fields - even if for a short time - you are becoming a part of the natural energy flow of your Earth, existing in harmony with your planet and all the creatures you share it with.

Finally, we ask you to simply enjoy the goodness of life during this special time of year. Think of what you are even as you think of what you have. Think of what you will do for this world even as you think of what it can/has done for you. And, most of all, think of where you are going as you continue your star mission. The stars of home await you.

May the healing light of God and goodness surround you always,

Tibus

Comment: Sometimes, it's easy to forget that we were once the ones searching, that we were the ones despairing and lonely because we didn't fit in, or just didn't feel like a "part" of this world. And even though we are still not a part of the mundane (Earthly) reality, let us give thanks for the fact that we have learned to be comfortable and happy in the awareness of what we can do, what we are here to do.

Let us give thanks for our differences, for it is those differences that set us apart from the Earthly reality, and allow us to perform our destined star tasks.

D.M.T.

TIBUS CHANNELS REGARDING CHRISTMAS, UNIVERSAL LOVE, AND THE STAR PERSON'S ABILITY TO "MANIFEST" GOALS THROUGH CREATIVE VISUALIZATION

DECEMBER 1986

As you know, this time on your Earth is indeed a very special time - a time when all living creatures can exist in harmony and peace, a time when all trials and tribulations can be temporarily laid aside in order to share the love which should exist naturally on your lovely blue and green planet.

It has been observed by your star guides such as myself that the holiday season is a time when strangers can become friends, when humanity can be seen at its best. Strangers passing one another on the street will smile, even speak a friendly "Hello"; children become vibrant, the elderly pour out their love, wondering, perhaps, if they will live to see another Christmas, another holiday season, another birthday of their children and grand-children.

It is a time of universal love and brotherhood ~ a time when even divergent languages are no longer a problem. Voices raise in song, the snow covers parts of the planet in order to protect fragile seedlings which will grow in Spring, and essentially your world renews itself both spiritually and physically.

And yet, it has also been noted that, soon after the New Year begins, this air of festivity and peace lessens; and by February, all remembrance of the holiday season is pretty much past. Perhaps not in the hearts of people, but certainly in their attitudes and actions toward one another. It seems peculiar indeed that a species (Man) capable of such love, such affection, such openness during one time of year can become almost completely opposite, showing hostility, jealousy, hatred and so on, once that season is past.

My primary reason for mentioning this is that we want you to know that this need not be. Man need not behave one way one minute and a completely opposite way the next minute. In essence, Man is basically a creature of love. He is a social animal, with obvious needs for solitude as well. Man needs the company of others of his own kind in order to achieve happiness, to have contentment. And yet, throughout the year, the majority of humanity would appear to seek to drive others like himself away, to isolate himself... perhaps to confirm to his subconscious mind that he is not worthy of companionship, even love.

And yet, you can make a difference. What would happen if every day were Christmas, or Chanukah, or Valentine's Day? Isn't it possible that many of Man's inborn aggressions would start to lessen if such were the case? And, for that reason, we urge you to live your life as if every day were a day of universal love, brotherhood, a day when all hostilities and aggressions can be laid aside in order to facilitate a more universal goal: that of harmony and peace on Earth.

We understand that you are only one person among approximately four billion. And yet, you are a very important person, for you are a part of the New Age, you are a more highly evolved spirit, a more advanced soul. And, for that reason, you are existing at all times as an example and a guide to those around you. You are, in essence, a light toward the future, for you show others through your attitudes, actions and spiritual advancement the manner in which the future must exist. It is a certainty that, if your world should continue on its present course, there will come a time when all life will be obliterated – the "good" and the "bad" alike. And so, we urge you to remember that you are different, you are unique, and you are - above all else - a soul advanced beyond your biological and social years.

We also understand that this can be, at times, a burden. And yet, when you embarked on this Earthly life, you chose to carry that weight, to shoulder the responsibility not only for yourself and your loved ones, but for your fellow man as well. We congratulate you on this advanced spiritual decision, and we want you to know that we will support you at all times. When you feel lonely or in doubt, remember to call on your own Special One for guidance, love and assistance. We are with you, my star friend, and we look forward to the day when you will be joined with us in physical reality, too.

Additionally, I would also like to remind you that star people have a very unique ability – the ability to "manifest" certain things into reality. This can be anything from a thought or a concept to a physically real and tangible object. And while that may, on the surface, seem ludicrous or even impossible, we urge you to consider that the mind is, after all, the most powerful human force on your world today.

THE REAL LIFE UFO TRANSFORMATION OF DIANE TESSMAN

Do you realize that whenever there is a thought, then that thought becomes reality in some definition? When you think of the love you have for your children or your mate or lover, you have, in essence, loved that person. By thinking it, you have activated the process whereby love becomes not only possible but inevitable. Of course, there are varying degrees to which this manifestation process functions. Mainly because there are varying degrees or sincerity within the manifestor, varying degrees of desire/need to see that thing/emotion manifested in the first place.

As another example, there are cases in your Earth history whereby theoretically "unreal" things have become real because of the desires of people like yourself. Consider space flight. As short a time ago as fifty years, the mere thought of space flight was considered not only impossible but silly. And yet, because enough people dared to dream, because enough people wanted space flight to exist, it did in fact, come into being.

This is no accident. And it can be proven with other examples as well. Consider for a moment the personage of Sherlock Holmes, James Bond, Captain Kirk, Mister Spock or any other seeming "legend" of modern Earth. Even though these characters began as fiction, there has been so much energy applied to them, so many stories written, so many people needing them that, in all likelihood, these "fictional characters" have taken on physical flesh and now exist as living beings. In essence, those people who have "dreamed" of these fictional characters have perhaps become spiritual "parents" of actual living entities.

We urge you, if you are interested in this phenomenon, to study the works of A.E. Powell - particularly in a book entitled *THE ASTRAL BODY*. We believe this work will enable you to better understand what we are referring to when we speak of manifestation and creation.

And yet, you may wonder why this is so important, what bearing or impact it can have on you or your planet. The answer is simple. When star people begin to realize that they can manifest thoughts into reality, it will become clear that the thoughts of one person such as yourself could mean the difference between destruction and survival on a global scale.

For example, if enough people want peace enough, then peace become inevitable. But on the opposite side of the scale, if enough people believe that war is unavoidable, then inevitably war will be fought.

And so, as you can see, it is a matter of mind over reality – a matter of the human mind being able to engineer its own reality through conscious direction of thoughts and desires. More and more, we see evidence that your people are "catching on." The World Moment of Peace is one such example, as are the efforts of certain conservationist groups such as Greenpeace, The Fund For Animals, and so on.

At any rate, please do meditate further on the concept of manifestation and thought-creation. We fully believe that this is one answer in your quest for harmony and peace, one answer on your spiritual path toward personal and world-wide fulfillment.

Remember also that we are with you and that you have, in a way, helped to create the atmosphere which allows us to move among you and to share universal views with the people of your planet. Through your efforts, the Earth is changing... and through your continued efforts, it will evolve and grow as your people move into the New Age.

May the healing light of God and goodness surround you always,

Tibus

Comment: I would just like to add that we are all a part of the Creator - and perhaps we should realize that, in some small fashion, we have been given the ability to create, to change, to mold reality to a more perfect union between Man and his environment. We are all, after all, a small piece of the universal soul, the Universal God-Force, the force of Creation itself. And how we use that power is up to us and those like us.

D.M.T.

TIBUS CHANNELS REGARDING THE PHENOMENA OF DÉJÀ VU, AND HOW TIME LOOPS APPLY TO THE STAR PERSON

January 1987

There are several topics I would like to discuss with you during the course of this transmission, and it is my hope that you will give serious thought and meditative awareness to some of the things I am going to tell you.

Have you ever wondered about the sensation of déjà vu? This is a phenomenon which everyone has experienced at some time in their lives, and most people tend to just brush it off or try to explain it in a mundane fashion. And yet, this sensation of "I've done this before" or "I've been here before" is one of the most profound experiences anyone could ever hope to have.

Obviously, you have been driving in a car, perhaps, or involved in a conversation with friends or acquaintances, when suddenly you know exactly what is going to happen next. You know what will be around the next corner - in precise detail. Or you know what someone else is going to say - right down to the phrasing and word inflection.

This déjà vu experience has existed since Man was advanced enough to understand that he had a mind; and aside from a few attempts by scientists to pass this experience off to "chemical activity in the brain," no one has been able to satisfactorily explain the phenomena. Essentially, it is the belief of your star guides that the déjà vu phenomena is basically proof that you have been in a particular location before, or you have had that same conversation at a previous point in your universal life.

More than just evidence to support the reincarnation theories, déjà vu is evidence to support the theories contained in quantum mechanics – theories which state that certain "segments" of history/time are circular rather than linear, and that those same segments of history/time are occurring simultaneously on a multitude of dimensional planes.

For example, if we view Time as a location rather than a linear measure of events and history, it becomes possible to understand a little more about how déjà vu and other "psychic" events occur. Consider that Time could be a physical entity existing in the space of the Universe—in which Time could be a physical place; another "world" just as the Earth, the moon, Venus, Mars and the other planets are other worlds. It is simply that the world of Time is far more complex and more difficult to see than these other physical places.

And yet, I transmit to you now that Time is no less "real" than the Earth, the moon or the stars. And for that reason, Time becomes a phenomena to be reckoned with - a force with which all living things much contend if they are to grow and evolve on the Cosmic Evolutionary Scale.

I use the example of déjà vu to highlight the fact that there are "loops" in time as well – moments when Time becomes temporarily out of synch with itself ~ just as earthquakes, volcanic eruptions and even violent storms are moments when the physical Earth becomes out of synch with itself. The sensation of déjà vu is one which star people such as yourself should explore fully - for when you begin to comprehend the nature of déjà vu more fully, it will become possible for you to more fully understand the concept of actual time travel Essentially, we star guides are as much from your future as we are from the stars – and it is our strong impression and belief that you can begin to travel the galaxy in your own lifetime - partially through a more thorough understanding of time loops.

When you experience déjà vu, what is your reaction? Do you get chills or try to pretend "it isn't happening"? Do you try to analyze it while it is happening? Or do you find it a "good" feeling? Your own reaction to this phenomenon is of great importance - for it could give you valuable "clues" as to where you are going in your own future.

If, for example, déjà vu leaves you with a feeling of uneasiness or distress, it is possible that your "temporary future" (that future which will exist if you continue on your present course) is not very good. If déjà vu leaves with you a sensation of wonder or great joy or elation, then your "temporary future" is undoubtedly "in line" with your personal Cosmic Destiny (in other words, you are undoubtedly on the right path). I mention these things mainly to illustrate the potential for you to change the future in what is usually a split second! If, for example, you experience the déjà vu phenomena and your reaction is a "negative" one, what you must realize is that this is a crossroads in time - a moment when all of collective reality is singling you out and offering you an opportunity to "change" something in your own future.

In other words, the time loop theory states that your future has many possible paths and, depending on which of those paths you choose, your future will be different. Thus, when you experience a negative reaction to the déjà vu phenomena, you should "go with it" for as long as the experience will last. Open yourself to the experience and see how far/long the sensations will last. Don *t start analyzing the moment you realize it's happening; instead, let your mind "give in" to the experience and follow it through to its conclusion.

Then, when the sensations stop and you are once again in "real time," take a good look at your life and what you are doing and where you are headed in your "temporary future." Are you satisfied in your job? Are you enjoying your family relationships? Are you satisfied with your level of spiritual growth and development? In short, what needs changing in your life?

Of course, the déjà vu experience is only one "indicator" of your temporary future, and you will need to take many factors into account before making any major decisions which will change your entire life. And yet, by examining the déjà vu sensations, it is our feeling that you will get a much clearer picture of where your life may be taking you.

Additionally, consider the time loop theory in more detail. Essentially, a loop in time is something which occurs for a variety of reasons. For example, time travelers must be very cautious to avoid getting "caught" in a time loop – i.e., time travelers must exercise caution to guard against travelling back in time and then returning to their "future" (actually their own "natural" time) before they left.

For example, consider what could happen if you travelled back in time. Let's say you started your journey at 8:00 A.M. on January 1, 1987, and that you were travelling back in time to 8:00 A.M. on January 1, 1800. When you arrive in the year 1800, you could spend weeks or even years without any real "effect" on you or on your own "natural time" (1987). But, when you are ready to return to your natural time, what would happen if you miscalculated and returned home at 7:59 A.M., January 1, 1987. Essentially, if this should occur, you would become caught in a time loop – for obviously at 7:59 A.M. on January 1, 1987, you were just preparing to depart on your journey.

Thus, the déjà vu experience could also be indicative of the fate of many time travelers– perhaps time travelers with whom you have come into contact. In other words, if you were to meet a time traveler who had become trapped in the loop, it stands to reason that you would become a part of his/ her loop. In other words, you would "feel" the loop bending back on itself when you essentially "passed yourself" on the journey forward or backwards in time. One of the great questions of time travel concerns whether or not a person could travel back in time ten years and talk to his/her former self - him/herself as he/she was ten years in the past. Obviously, if this could be done, it would enable people to avoid serious mistakes they had made on their life's journey, and would subsequently enable them to make intelligent choices based on future knowledge.

We star guides feel that further investigation and meditation on the déjà vu and time loop theory would prove very valuable to you for a variety of reasons. We encourage you to give thought and to increase your awareness on this subject; for it is my impression that this information will be important to you in the very near future.

Most of all, we encourage you to remember that Time is an entity - a physical, living thing, just as are all the other creatures of the galaxy. And, for that reason,

Time can be reckoned with, can become a friend rather than an unseen foe. And, of course, when Time becomes a friend, the knowledge to be gained and the range of possible experiences will increase geometrically.

Also, remember that your own Special One is always there to guide and help you further, and that by applying the full force of your energy toward your Special One, you will always receive the guidance you are seeking.

May the healing light of God and goodness surround you always,

Tibus

Comment: I would just like to comment that time loops are almost certainly an established fact for the star person such as yourself. Because of the nature of your earthly mission, it stands to reason that you have had contact with many time travelers– either in the physical realm or in the astral realms. So, the next time you experience the déjà vu phenomena, I encourage you to examine the reaction it produces within you, and to further examine your life and mission here, too.

If you have a positive reaction to the experience, then you are undoubtedly "on the right path." If you have a more typically "negative" reaction, perhaps you should, as Tibus suggested, examine your life's path to see what changes might be necessary to "set things straight" in your life.

D.M.T.

TIBUS CHANNELS ON THE CONCEPTS OF FREEDOM ANDIMPRISONMENT, AND OFFERS HELPFUL GUIDELINES FOR PERSONAL MEDITATION

February 1987

Inner well-being is the first step toward universal oneness - a fact which even the most spiritually and/or psychically aware individuals tend to overlook from time to time.

Very often, those of your world spend their days in search of wealth or social status, and their evenings are spent in pursuit of relationships, or attempting to recover from the pressures which have mounted and grown throughout the day. And, as the star person such as yourself can surely recognize, this "vicious circle" is difficult if not often impossible to "break." For that reason, it is essential that you remember to always turn inward for your own sense of peace and well being - that you establish a safe "home base" within your own heart and mind where you can retreat during times of turmoil or stress.

We star guides realize that the word "meditation" has come to be a vastly overused term - one which means many things to many different people. However, when we speak of meditation, we are referring to the inner searching, to the state of mind wherein the star person can find answers, and can ask questions of himself or even of his own Special One.

To clarify, meditation ideally should be a state of being as much as it is a state of mind. By this, we mean simply that, when you meditate, you should ideally be "travelling" to an inner sanctuary which exists within the soul of every living creature. This sanctuary is not one which will make itself known to you without meditation, nor is it a "place" where someone should "run" to escape worldly or personal problems. Rather, this inner sanctuary is a place of comfort and security, much like churches represent sanctuary to some, or as temples or synagogues represent sanctuary to others.

When you meditate, strive to actually "see" this inner sanctuary as a physically real place to which only you have the key. It may appear to you as a garden with beautiful flowers, very secluded and walled off from the outside world. Or it may appear as a vast expanse of the desert, open and all-encompassing for as far as the eye can see; or a seashore with warm breezes, or a forest with tall trees and filtered sun creating shadows on the ground.

However your inner sanctuary appears to you really isn't important in the long run. What is important is that you develop a strong sense of that place, allowing it to manifest and become very "real" in your mind - as real and alive as some place you have visited, for example. Thus, when you do meditate, you will always be drawn to this place, and will be able to fall immediately into a sense of "familiarity" which will deliver your mind into an instant state of peace and serenity.

I feel that these things bear mention for several reasons, not the least of which is that many people simply do not know or use the proper techniques of meditation. There is, as you know, more to meditation than simply "thinking." In fact, meditation is the art of not thinking - the ability to let your conscious mind rest and allow your subconscious (or Super Consciousness) to explore a variety of concepts and sensations which are simply not possible so long as the conscious (or Mundane/Earthly) mind is in control.

Additionally, I feel this information on meditation is going to be very valuable to you over the weeks and months ahead; for it is my impression that you are entering a period in your life which will bring about many changes. And in order to make sound decisions, you are going to need this inner sanctuary which I have described to you above. You will need a "place" to retreat to - a place where answers can be sought and discovered, a place where your soul can experience the ultimate freedom despite the pressures and mental "prisons" imposed on you by the Earthly/Mundane reality.

Which brings me to the main point of this reading – the concept of prisons or imprisonment, or the loss of personal freedom. This loss of freedom could come in any form - from a political/global situation to a more personal and less widespread phenomena.

And, what is freedom? Is it simply the ability to say and do certain things without fear of legal repercussions? Or is it the inherent right of individuals to live in a certain manner and carry on their lives as they see fit? Or, more precisely, is freedom simply the right to live?

Additionally, what is imprisonment? Is it what happens when freedom is taken away in one manner or another? Or is imprisonment something which exists solely in the mind of an individual at any given time?

For example, it is possible to walk through your Earthly society as a legally "free" individual, living your life as you see fit, doing the things you please.

And yet, are you ever really free? Can you really do those things your soul longs to do, or are you prevented from doing this by restraints and/or fears which have been placed upon you by others in your society?

At any rate, it is important to realize that freedom and imprisonment will mean something different to almost everyone. Ideally, the people of your Earth should be free to pursue their happiness in whatever unharmful manner they choose. And yet, because of government restraints and technological "impossibilities," such is not the case. For the most part, you are a "prisoner" of your world – and for that reason, a certain "freedom" has been denied to you.

I transmit to you at this time that the technology currently exists on your planet which could take men and women to the stars ~ not only to the nearest planets such as Mars, Venus or even Pluto - but to the stars themselves. And yet, this technology is withheld from the public because of governmental fears and petty jealousies. Most Earth governments don't want their people going to the stars or even having the possibility of going to the stars. For the most part, governments are designed to rule rather than to lead; and as you have discerned through your own meditations and studies, there is a vast difference between a leader and a ruler.

Also, governments are afraid of losing their authority and power should Mankind ever begin to venture forth to the stars - for how would these petty governments keep track of vast numbers of people? How would they "control" millions of people living on thousands of different worlds? And, ultimately, why is control so important to these individuals? Why must governments seek to subjugate and dictate rather than to promote creativity and support dreams?

In essence, this need to control goes back to Man's earliest days on the Earth – when it was perhaps necessary to "control" certain elements in order to insure survival. For example, in the days of the "cave man," it was perhaps necessary to control dangerous animals – and yet, to this day, we see hunters killing helpless creatures for the sake of "sport." We see fishermen slaughtering whales and dolphins because it is easier to kill rather than to utilize existing technology to prevent or even dramatically reduce the numbers of these needless killings.

In essence, Man's craving for power is a vestigial remnant of his earliest days on this planet. Many have overcome the need to kill in order to eat, becoming vegetarians. Many have overcome the desire to subjugate and control others. Many have learned that Man was put here to share his world with the animals rather than to rule or control them. And yet, for every person who has learned this valuable lesson, there are thousands more who have not. And until that lesson can be learned by a vast majority rather than a struggling minority, your Earth will remain in the control of "barbarians" - individuals who are living down to their lowest potential rather than living up to their highest possibilities.

Again, we encourage you to remember that freedom and imprisonment are as much abstract concepts as they are concrete realities. At anytime, you have the ability to retreat into your inner sanctuary of meditation. But we urge you to bring that serenity back with you when you return to the mundane/Earthy reality. In doing so, you will essentially be projecting freedom (abstract or real) to those around you. You will basically be creating a "pocket" of ultimate freedom which will eventually begin to spread. As the people of your planet learn more about their nature, and as they learn to overcome the "negative" aspects of human nature, they will begin taking giant steps toward ultimate freedom rather than allowing themselves to be content with "surface" (Earthly) freedoms.

I urge you to meditate on the concept of freedom and imprisonment over the next few weeks, and to keep a diary of the conclusions you reach through this inner searching. Be particularly aware of your "surroundings" during your meditation, and notice how those surroundings may change subtly on a daily or weekly basis. All these things are indicative of your own spiritual growth and development, and of how you are helping to shape your planet. By creating and enjoying your own ultimate freedom through meditation, you will inevitably "spread" that freedom - and the need for that freedom ~ to others. And, of course, recognizing the need for something is the first step toward realizing it in a physical and lasting way.

May the healing light of God and goodness surround you always,

Tibus

Comment: As you pursue the concepts and ideas of freedom, remember that your "ultimate freedom" as Tibus calls it is basically whatever you conceive it to be. Perhaps your ultimate freedom would be travelling to the stars. Or perhaps your ultimate freedom would be that of being able to live in a place without having the constant threat of new housing projects destroying the environment. Perhaps your ultimate freedom is gaining some spiritual ability, such as the ability to astral project, or the ability to communicate more clearly with your own Special One.

Whatever your ultimate freedom maybe, both Tibus and I encourage you to seek it always, to find it in the private sanctuary of your meditations, and to ultimately superimpose that freedom on the real world ~ thereby making it a reality which you can live as well as dream.

D.M.T.

16

THE STAR NETWORK

DIANE TESSMAN, P.P., D.L. STARLIGHT MYSTIC CENTER POST OFFICE BOX 622 POWAY, CALIFORNIA 92064

Author's Update: Please do not use the above address to reach me! I am leaving it here for reasons of nostalgia, because some of you reading this today, first contacted me there in Poway all those years ago.

Today, you can reach me at P.O. Box 352, St. Ansgar, Iowa, 50472, and we will still do a special reading for you. I offer amazing books, crystals, and gemstones for your spiritual celebration, all sent to you by Diane (me) personally.

Special readings from Tibus and Diane are life-changing in many instances, offering spiritual empowerment and advancement.

My two newsletters, THE STAR NETWORK HEARTLINE and THE CHANGE TIMES QUARTERLY are also available. Ask for a free, current sample, dianetessman0@gmail.com That is a zero in my "e" address. Or, www.earthchangepredictions.com

Love offerings to our STAR NETWORK CAT SANCTUARY are much needed and appreciated. The sanctuary is the physical manifestation of our STAR NETWORK's spiritual commitment to Gaia's beautiful, loving animals. Our sanctuary keeps going only through donations.

Check the promotional section at the close of this book for how to order our special crystals, gemstones, pendants, and more.

And so, dear friends, we all await the Transformation in our own unique ways. However, we also await the Transformation together.

THE REAL LIFE UFO TRANSFORMATION OF DIANE TESSMAN

We are being drawn closer and closer together with each passing day. The Star Network is being formed in rapid, thrilling, and spectacular fashion. "Intersect points" are lighting up on a cosmic network all over planet Earth. The Network is fast becoming completed in final preparation for the difficult times ahead.

We are all given special symbols and vital aids to help us get through the many problems we face daily as well as to assist us when The Transformation arrives.

Tibus channels to me that all we have to define the dimension around us is our mind/soul; in fact, your mind/soul has created the world around you to a very large degree! It can just as easily create a new and shining reality for Our Space Brothers knows that mind/soul is ALL and that your soul is a segment of the Great Cosmic Soul! God can be brought into your life via a Divine Energy Frequency (much like tuning into a radio station!) and many blessings can be yours. Negative luck can be reversed, there can be new thrust for your love life, new approaches with people to bring love and acceptance, and a cleansing of bad karma.

With many, people on the positive frequency of higher consciousness, Tibus assures me there is also a chance that the violence of the disasters can be much-lessened or even eliminated so that the human race will be able to move into the magnificent Transformation without the tragedy and upheaval which is prophesied.

We must also stand ready for overt contact with the advanced life, both future human and extraterrestrial. You must be able to tell other humans not to panic, not to be afraid as face to face contact is made and as The Transformation begins to take place. Because you know your own heart, mind, and soul and know your own beautiful place in the Divine Cosmos, you will stand a better chance of surviving global disasters and changes...and you can help others who do not have this Cosmic Wisdom and Divine Insight.

It is of urgent importance that we do connect, seek each other out, embrace and support each other. The preparations for the Change Point (End Times) by the Space Brothers and Higher Realms are mapped out in very specific stages. These stages are much like the ones which Dr. Sprinkle mapped at the beginning of the book: Anxiety, Analysis, Awareness, Acceptance, Acknowledgement, Assessment, and Action. We are now at the final stage, the Action Stage! We must be strong and aware now, of all times. Just as with the special symbolic power of an energized crystal, we must turn our negative energies to Divine Positive Energy. We must take action to make our own lives better as well as the life of Planet Earth better (as Jesus said, "Peace on Earth, Good Will Toward Men.")

There is a great aloneness among us and a great need to make contact, to touch, to reach out to others like ourselves. Yet, we do not know how to go about it, do not know what to do next. Many, many people have joined **THE STAR NETWORK** and have found that answer and many more! I hope you will, too!

In Ireland, the tall grass makes a great sofa.

THE REAL LIFE UFO TRANSFORMATION OF DIANE TESSMAN

Diane is thrilled to have consciously remembered more details of her second encounter at Eagle Lake, Ontario.

Chapter Ten

UFOS At Eagle Lake, My Second Encounter With Tibus

NEVER BEFORE PUBLISHED ABDUCTION EXPERIENCE

I still do not have every moment remembered, but in the past month, while living a hermit's lifestyle due to the viral pandemic, I have been able to regress myself in an atmosphere of safety, silence, and positivity. I have managed to consciously remember more about my second encounter (abduction); it is such a relief to have finally cracked it open!

I began working on this when a vivid memory came to the surface, quite by accident – or was it an accident? My daughter Gianna, who now lives in San Francisco, phoned and told me about a "virtual reality café" she would be exploring when the isolation is over. She also told me she would love to get virtual reality set up in her own apartment, but good quality virtual reality costs too much money.

I wanted to be up to date on what she was talking about, so I Googled "virtual reality" and found a site which offers brilliant star fields overhead (through virtual instrumentation) and other convincingly natural landscapes. My mind wandered, "Wouldn't it be neat to have beautiful vegetation all around in the nighttime surroundings, with the stars brilliant overhead!

Suddenly, my mind snapped to a scene which was exactly this, and I knew it was a real memory. First, I was in the lush vegetation under so many stars that it took my breath away, but then some part of my mind knew this was "not real," but instead I was housed in a small, cozy room somewhere.

THE REAL LIFE UFO TRANSFORMATION OF DIANE TESSMAN

TURN ON THE LIGHT SWITCH

I was indeed in this room but when I thought about a cool, dark night with oodles of bright stars overhead, I was "there!" This was because, someone had taught me, "Diane, if you think of this cozy, safe room "just like turning on the light switch, you will be back in that room."

Someone had continued, "If you "hit the other button" (in your mind), you will be under these gorgeous stars again. YOU have control."

The room was the real place (I think?); at least I was told that. In this instance, the wonderful nighttime under the stars was virtual reality. I remember the elation of having great mental power to alter my whole environment with the ease of mentally turning a light switch.

I should note here that as a child, I loved the dark. I would play outside in utter darkness if allowed by my mother, for hours. If I was at a nighttime event with lights, like a football game, I would head off for some darkness to enjoy the night. I realize this would be dangerous in today's world, but this was in the 1950s in a village.

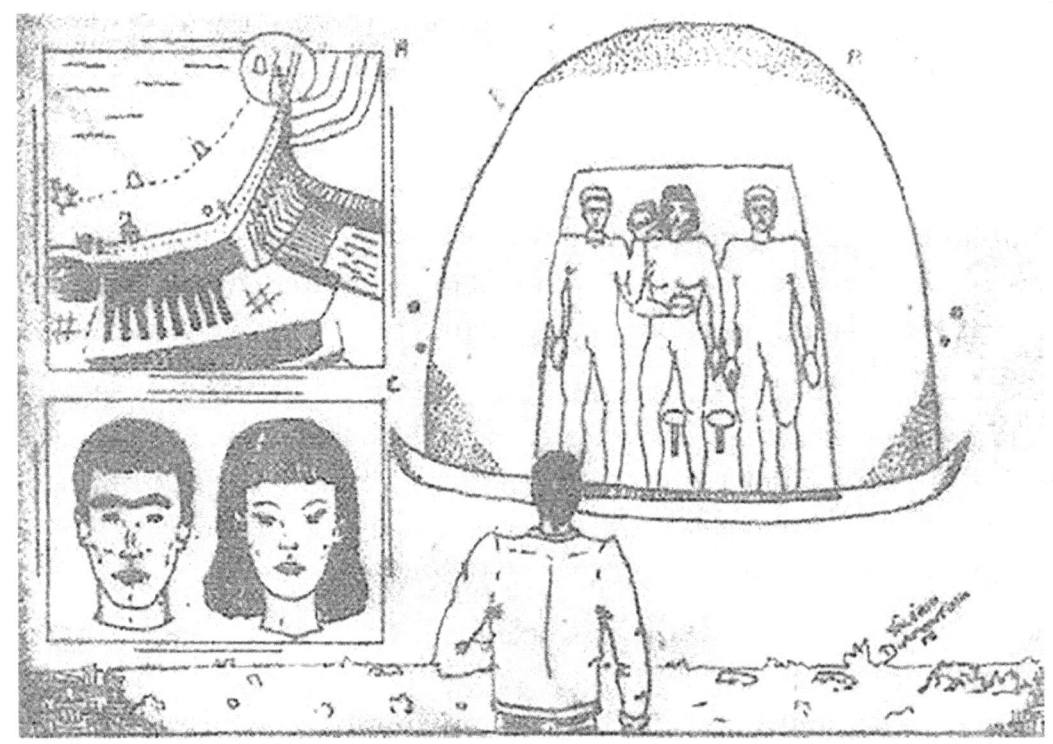

This is a sketch done for the Jesus Antunes Moreira encounter in Brazil, 1978, but the type of UFO occupants on-board, resonate with me regarding my second encounter.

THE REAL LIFE UFO TRANSFORMATION OF DIANE TESSMAN

TIBUS, SECOND ENCOUNTER

Instantly I realized that Tibus was that "someone" giving me that "light switch" instruction about the stars and the cozy room, so I set out to figure out how this new memory fit into my encounters. I have always stated there were at least two of them. The first encounter is the one Dr. Sprinkle helped me remember, detailed in *"The Transformation."*

The second encounter was on the shore of Eagle Lake, Ontario, Canada. I have known this for years but always came to an abrupt wall as I tried to remember more about it. I am not sure which encounter came first but I think it was the one remembered with Dr. Sprinkle.

The Ontario lakes are famous for UFOs, UAPs, orbs, unidentified submerged objects, and more. Reputable UFO researchers believe there are extraterrestrial and/or future human bases under several of these lakes. Books and websites have been devoted to this area and its UFO activity.

Here is my conscious memory of the Eagle Lake encounter, and then I will add the new memories which have finally come to the surfaces, as well as the "keying in" memory of Tibus explaining to me how to control virtual reality with my mind as we sat in a cozy, safe room, there are more new revelations.

EAGLE LAKE VACATION

In 1952, my family drove from our home in North Iowa to Eagle Lake, Ontario, for a two day vacation. My family consisted of my parents and brother who was ten years older than me. We stayed in a very primitive fishing cabin by Eagle Lake.

We were to meet with mom's brother's family at the lake. The adults didn't get along very well, not sure why we even attempted this vacation. My brother was at a difficult adolescent stage, and as usual, I was a lone entity. My cousins, two boys, were always busy trying to kill each other. Uncle Bill and Aunt Marge had a separate cabin with their sons.

That morning, my parents left our cabin for a while, my brother was fishing, and that left me in the cabin alone. It was unlike my mother to leave me, she was a hovering "helicopter mother," so that was a bit odd in itself.

I had brought some of my books along in a box of family stuff. My favorite was from the Little Golden book series, *"Toys in the Attic,"* which was about not fearing the unknown. The book listed items commonly seen in attics, as I remember, a rooster statue, a Native head-dress, an old music box, and other supposedly frightening stuff.

VISITOR FROM BEYOND

I have always had the memory that suddenly, when I was alone in the cabin, this man from my first encounter walked in the door rather quickly, almost like someone was chasing him.

Rather than the "casual" uniform he wore in my first encounter, he now had dark glasses, a red checkered shirt, and jeans. Obviously, he was trying to fit in with the fishermen. He somehow seemed not at all like those fishermen at the lake shore!

He then put the dark glasses up on his head, like people do. His eyes were as I remembered, not hazel but amber, very distinctive and different from any other eyes I had ever seen. Were his eyes sensitive to the sun?

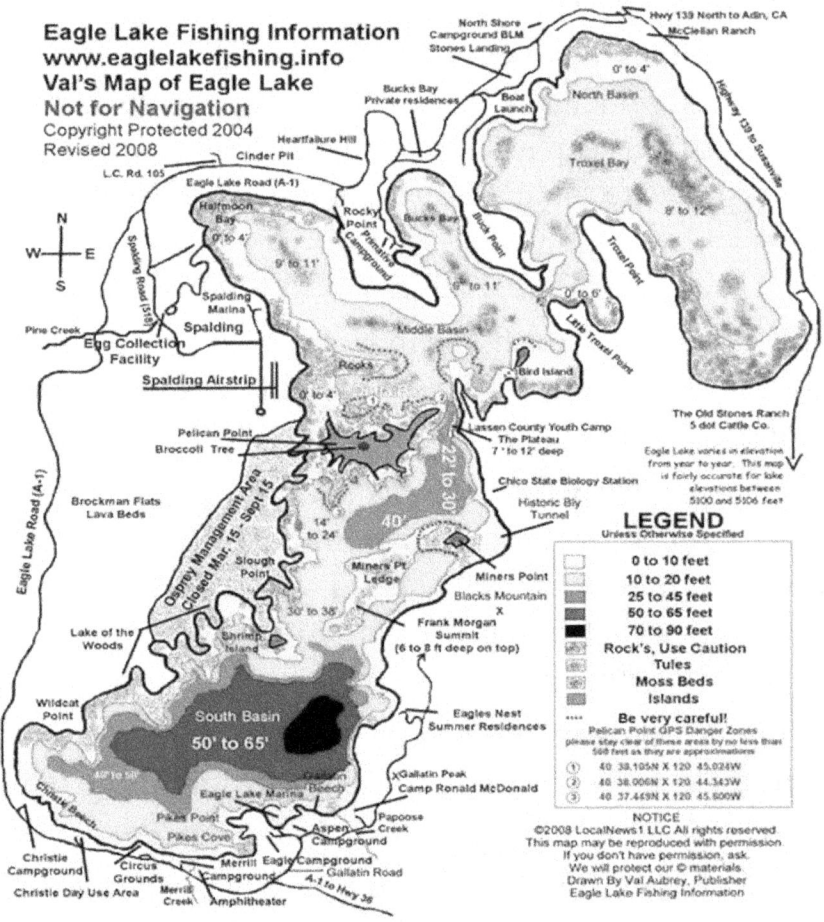

Here is a detailed map of this mysterious Canadian Lake which has a tradition of strange lights in the skies.

I consciously remember he asked two questions, "Do you remember me?" ("Yes," said I). "Diane, are you frightened?" ("No," said I).

I can see myself through his eyes: I was holding my Little Golden book, long red braids, a little girl standing before me (Tibus) about 5 feet away. In other words, our two identities briefly switched for a nano-second, similar to the virtual reality stars and the cozy room, which I had just remembered.

As with my first encounter, was this conversation telepathic? I am not sure.

I remembered him from "before." I was strangely never afraid on either encounter. I felt close to home, I was always a stranger in my Earth family, but I was home when he was around, because he was from my home too. I knew that, but I was very young and so did not manifest it into a complete conscious thought.

I felt no fear. He held out his hand.

At this point I want to state that these days, we would think that maybe he was going to molest me. It was nothing like that. I have no psychological signs or memories of having been molested. Dr. Sprinkle and others gave me psychological tests, partially wondering this. This being was extremely "proper," (decent). I admit that he had an agenda, apparently, and taking a child without parental consent is against our laws, but there was nothing sexual or aggressive about it. It was as I report it.

As well, he and I had a natural harmony; we were somehow kindred and recognized each other. Was it self-recognition?

I remembered nothing else about this encounter until the past several weeks, prompted by my daughter mentioning virtual reality.

ALIEN SUBSTANCE

To complete what I have remembered consciously for years:

I remember showing my mother the "lard" that got on my book; it was my favorite book about the unknown, the one I had been holding when he came in the door. Mom called the substance "lard," but we had no lard in our family box of snack foods. Mom was a health food believer even in the 1950s. She detested lard, partly because her in-laws always used it.

Was there lard in the cabin? It was a primitive cabin with a big hole for a toilet (I feared I would fall in), no food provided, not even sure there was a stove. I would not put my book on a stove anyway. I had this book (and others), until I was 22 years old when we moved to the Virgin Islands and lost stuff in the move.

It was very unusual lard, it saturated every page equally, same design each page (covering about half the page), not dissipating in amount through the book, including the heavy cardboard back and front covers. The "design" of the substance was the same on every page and cover; it had not seeped but appeared to have been stamped into the book all at once.

Was it a byproduct of "beaming up" or an "angel hair" substance which is related to some UFO sightings, especially in the 1950s? Or was it simply Tibus' reminder that he had been there? The "just lard" explanation makes no sense and I am sure there was not lard on the book when he first came in the cabin door. It was my most cherished book, I knew it well.

SIMULTANEOUS OTHER

When I think of the encounters, I often find myself looking at "little Diane" from his perspective. "Feet dangling off bench" is one of them, because my feet did not reach the floor. In this 2nd encounter, I plainly see Little Diane holding her Little Golden book. I realize, this is HIS perception and memory.

TWO UFOS SPOTTED OVERHEAD

On that family vacation, my family met at Eagle Lake with my Uncle Bill and his wife Marge and their two sons. As the years passed after the Ontario vacation, Bill and Marge got divorced and Marge did not keep contact with my family since Bill was our blood relative.

However, one Christmas over thirty years later, Marge sent a brief hello to my mother in the mail and then they exchanged one phone call as a "catch up" over all the years that had passed. When Marge asked "How is Diane?" my mother said, "Ah, she's interested in UFOs." I was teaching school in Florida at the time and I was active in MUFON and APRO.

Marge then exclaimed, "You know when Bill and I were out in the boat on Eagle Lake that time, we saw two UFOs."

THE REAL LIFE UFO TRANSFORMATION OF DIANE TESSMAN

This is a photo of Eagle Lake, showing fishing cabins on the shore.

When my mother told me about this, chills ran down my spine, because I had partially remembered that encounter on that Eagle Lake vacation but had never mentioned my suspicions to anyone. Our families only stayed one full day at Eagle Lake and so this must

have been on the same day as my encounter in the cabin. Bill and Marge almost saw "my alien," and two of his ships.

Here are the new memories, which join my just-recovered memory of turning the switch on to experience the stars or to remain in the cozy room. These surfaced only two weeks ago!

1) After Tibus held out his hand to me, I took it and next I knew, I was in this "cozy room," and I could see out the open door (not a hinged door) that this was the same huge place (ship) I had seen before. There were people walking by the door now and then, going somewhere with purpose, not just ambling by. I saw several who were not human, but they were humanoid; all of them were short. The others were normal-size humans, but I could not see their features plainly. It seemed important that I knew the door was open and that I was "free" (not that I even thought of getting up).

THE REAL LIFE UFO TRANSFORMATION OF DIANE TESSMAN

There was a davenport in the room (in those days we in Iowa called "sofa" by the name "davenport"), but it was smaller than my family's davenport and did not have a wood framework. There was also a nice chair, not just a wooden kitchen chair, and he sat on that.

2) He sat down across from me, sunglasses still on top of his head, and told me about the virtual reality "light switch," showing me the dark night and the stars, then having me switch back to the "cozy room." I put "cozy room" in quotation marks because this must be what he called it.

There is an intended analogy here on different levels of perception; we might say, there is an acknowledgement that our consciousness can travel to this dimension or that dimension. I believe he also implanted the quest in me at that moment, to try to help humankind evolve to a higher level of consciousness. The "light switch" is the "Change Point."

3) As with the first encounter, I do not remember something medical that was done, but I know it happened.

4) At some point I said, "My mother will looking for me. I don't want her to worry." He said, "She won't even know you are gone, Diane. Don't worry about that."

I do believe that my parents and brother were "kept away" and did not realize I was gone and that possibly only a few moments passed for them. I feel I was gone for several hours, at least from my point of view. This "family stasis field" is something other abductees have experienced too. Betty Andreasson's entire family was held unmoving – frozen in place – during her first abduction.

5) Tibus then said, "Do you worry a lot? I think you do. Try not to worry so much, Diane." He seemed to know about my family's personal situation.

I answered, "Yes, I do worry. My dad needs to act better."

He smiled and said, "Here is a little rhyme I always say when I get worried, 'Stick to the river, river to the sea, carry my troubles away from me' If you can, say it as you toss a little twig into the creek by your house."

Note: I was indeed a worrier; I was more adult than either of my parents, which is not a good thing for a child. My mother confided in me all the time about my dad's drinking; a parent should never do this to a child. Dad was a nice person and I loved him. This contradiction and conflict should not have been in my young life constantly, but it was. I was only a happy child when I was out in nature by myself with my animals.

Later I did toss a twig into Turtle Creek, saying those magic words. I did it many times. It helped.

Back to that moment with Tibus: I exclaimed, "That rhyme is in one of my books! Did you see it in my book?" He said, "No, I saw it in one of my books when I was a boy."

This was obviously an intentional mind twister. I have wondered recently if he was (or is) artificial intelligence and so didn't have a human childhood, but from the sounds of it, he was young human boy with books. Do they have books made of paper in the future? Is he, me in a future life?

6. He then said, "You will write books one day."

7. I hated to leave, just as with the first encounter, but he left me with a chant. He chanted it softly at least twice, **"The past creates the future and the future creates the past."**

I had explored the retro-causality concept in physics before remembering recently that he said this. I would have no problem accepting it if he had said, "The past *influences* the future and the future *influences*" the past," but creates?

Before he left me with that "chant," there was something about moments in time being like playing cards and these moments can be shuffled, "Each card has a snapshot-picture on it which is that moment of "Now." I was only four years old but I remember the visualization of playing cards with snapshots of my family's life on it, including a card with my cats and me. I think there were other snapshots of an older woman (me?). I did manage to get the idea that "time" is not what we think it is.

I also have the impression that he was knocking himself out to present and implant concepts a smart four year old child could assimilate. I can only imagine how much he had to simplify his own thoughts, in order to try to reach my mind. However, he did succeed!

Next I knew, I was back in the Eagle Lake cabin, holding my Little Golden book. I do not remember holding it that whole time, I don't think I did. So where was it? But then it returned with me and I was still holding it.

THE REAL LIFE UFO TRANSFORMATION OF DIANE TESSMAN

I am hoping to remember more, now that I have this cosmic egg cracked open! I am sharing these new memories for the first time anywhere. There are many intriguing metaphors and mysteries in these new memories.

Some hard-nosed skeptic might say, "Maybe the whole thing was virtual reality, not just the dark night and the stars." In that case, it would still involve technology far beyond 1952, and Tibus could still be a future human, as he has stated. Or, I suppose he could then be some total alien life-form with advanced technology, a shape-shifter via virtual reality or the use of holograms.

However, as far as I am concerned, it has been proven beyond any shadow of a doubt, that he is a time traveling human or post-human.

I am hoping that my sharing these memories will help jog other star people's hidden memories, whether your memories are about extraterrestrial contact or advanced human contact through time travel. We are sure you have memories waiting to be uncovered which are spiritually inspiring as well as real.

These are insane days; memories which have been locked behind a dam will come bursting through into the light of reality. This is our Disclosure. Let the academics and scientists disclose the advanced vehicles of time ships and star ships, we will remember and disclose to the world, our contact with the incredible but real occupants of those ships!

Chapter Eleven
Unconditional Love, Thy Name is Cats and Dogs!

What would my life have been without my many cats and dogs? Without their empowering, unconditional love, I would have been lost as a child and perhaps as an adult as well. I would not have been one with nature, I would not have known myself, and I would not have been as good a survivor as I have been. Animal friends taught me responsibility as well.

Many readers may understand and even share the truth that childhood was difficult and that our animal friends saved the day. My family was composed of my parents and my half-brother who was ten years older than me. We had no extended family to offer support and friendship. We lived in our own stew, so to speak, because my mother who was college educated, was bipolar. My father, who was college educated, was an alcoholic. They argued incessantly with each other.

They were older parents and they both loved me, but I knew they stayed together because of me. The whole "parental thing" became a burden as I got older. My mother's love was conditional, based on if I sided with her or my dad in the latest argument.

Both my parents had many good qualities and I suspect would have been more successful financially and emotionally, if not married to each other.

My half-brother (now deceased), completed our little family. He resented me from the get-go as the new baby his mother had with his stepfather (my dad), and he was one confused teenager. He was sadistic, mostly in emotional ways but occasionally in physical ways. When I was six years old, he killed six of my beloved kittens with his shotgun, knowing how I loved and needed them. Some people say, "Get over it." No, I never will. No bond could be formed with him as a loving sibling.

THE REAL LIFE UFO TRANSFORMATION OF DIANE TESSMAN

I was the only child of my two parents and it seemed the world did indeed revolve around me, but only in a hurtful, negative manner which proclaimed, "It must be all your fault, Diane, so feel guilty about the family state of affairs." I love the way cats do not succumb to guilt jobs!

MY FIRST CAT, MAMA MARIAH, AND HER KITTENS

When I was three years old, one of my snap-shot memories is that there was a mama cat whom I named Mariah, as in "They Call the Wind Mariah," and her four kittens who lived in a cardboard box upstairs at Grandpa Tessman's farm implement shop. When we moved from a house in the Iowa village, to a small farm, I insisted that Mariah and all four kittens move with us.

Thank goodness for Mariah and her kittens, because a lonely little girl with an upsetting life, was saved! I discovered the magic of nature; I suddenly had unconditionally loving friends with whom to explore nature; I had my cats!

HERE COME THE DOGS!

Soon enough, Jenny, a lovely black Labrador, joined us. My brother, who was an avid hunter, bought Jenny as a hunting dog, but Jenny was too wise and decent; she refused to hunt. Jenny did have puppies and soon Pat, the yellow Lab-mix joined us along with Mama Jenny. Incidentally, I was playing with Pat when I was abducted one evening in November 1952 by UFO occupants.

I wish I had childhood photos but they were lost along the way in my many moves. I would like to feature photos I do have of a few of my animal friends over the years.

SINSEE, THE ANGEL DOG

My daughter Gianna arrived in Ireland with me then spread her time between Ireland and California, over the five years I remained in Ireland. She was a young woman but like me, she missed the animals she had always had in her childhood. Our animals were in Irish quarantine for six months, including Gianna's Saint Bernard, Diva.

So, at Gianna's urging, I searched classified want ads for "Puppies." We found a breeder offering the puppies whose parents were international champions. The breeder just wanted the puppies to have great homes, not necessarily compete for trophies. Soon we met Elizabeth and Liza, adorable yellow Lab puppies.

Which to choose? Gianna made the decision when Liza gave a big pull on Gianna's jacket string, proving to be extremely mischievous and creative.

Our puppy Liza was re-named by my daughter as "Sinsee." And thus, the Great Sinsee joined our family. She explored Ireland with us in my old Volvo, standing on her hind legs to stick her head out the sunroof. She had a fetish for retrieving and carrying around rocks, something we never understood. Our sofa once had 62 rocks, dropped by Sinsee into the springs.

Sinsee was an angel and the smartest dog I've ever known – that's saying a lot! The breeder had related to us that Sinsee was born dead along with two others in her litter. The other two came to life after a few seconds on their own but Sinsee remained dead. The breeder then gave the tiny puppy mouth to mouth resuscitation and after three minutes, the little puppy Sinsee-Liza sprang to life! Perhaps the angels sent her back down, to help us through life.

Diane and Sinsee, so much love!

THE REAL LIFE UFO TRANSFORMATION OF DIANE TESSMAN

Diane and Sinsee smile for the camera.

As an adult, Sinsee always led the way on our adventures, as if humans needed leading (perhaps we did). She delighted in understanding our language to an incredible degree. Best of all, Sinsee was caring and unconditionally loving as a unique individual of great intelligence and gentle goodness.

Before I left Ireland in 1995, I found good homes for a few of the cats I had rescued but could not abandon others. I still had four of the cats I had originally brought with me from California as well. And so, I arrived at JFK Airport, New York, on a flight from Ireland with fifteen cats in five kennels, plus our St. Bernard and dear Sinsee. This was before 9/11 and so Customs at the airport as well as the baggage handlers, just laughed us right through. Welcome back to the U.S.!

I am grateful to Tim Beckley and Gianna, who waited for me outside JFK with the U-Haul truck I'd asked them to rent. I said a quick hello and thanks to Tim, then Gianna, me, fifteen cats, and two large dogs, left New York and headed for Joshua Tree, California, where my friend Della van Hise gave us shelter until I could rent a house. "I get by with a little help from my friends!"

Sinsee "rode shotgun" in the U-Haul cab, usually stretched across both of us. She found the desert too hot but was thrilled when I moved to Iowa after two years in Joshua Tree. She guided me through the fields and woods in the cool Iowa weather until she passed on at age fifteen. I still miss her today. I have loved several dogs since and have three great dogs currently, but I still miss Sinsee as the magnificent individual she was – my Angel Dog!

HANNAH, THE WOUNDED PUPPY

Hannah poses with her most-favorite cat friends, Mustaf and Saoirse.

I stopped by the North Iowa Humane Society and just then, a bloody puppy was brought in. I was not allowed in the room with her due to her severe strep infection from the wounds all over her body, but our eyes met. In that second, I knew she was Sinsee, reincarnated. Sinsee had died in December 2004, and this was January, 2005.

Right before she passed on, Sinsee had said to me telepathically, "I will come back to you, but as a hardship case." At the time, I was puzzled by her use of "hardship case," certainly a phrase she had never heard. Her life as Sinsee had been almost ideal; she was perfectly suited to Gianna and me, she loved adventure and did not need a secure situation to be secure within herself.

Right then, I knew I had to adopt this badly wounded puppy, but the Humane Society said they would have to keep her until she healed, and there was a chance she would die. I donated money for her medical care for three months. During much of that time, Hannah could not move but only wag her tail. A wonderful foster mother took her to her home and cared for her daily. At one point, they thought Hannah's leg would have to be amputated and at another point, they thought she would die.

She lived! Would her foster mother, who loved her a lot, decide to keep her? Stacy wanted to keep her, but received a message from Hannah telepathically saying, "I love you, Stacy, but I am not your dog." Stacy called me, asking if I still wanted Hannah. Did I ever want her!

I let Hannah be Hannah but she preferred to answer to the name "Sinsee." Once when Hannah got too close to the road, I called her name sternly, telling her to come back. She ignored me. In desperation I called "Sinsee!" She came right away as if trying to demonstrate to me who she really was.

Another time, Hannah showed excitement as I was telling a friend about a neighbor I had known in Ireland named Mary Francis. Sinsee had really liked Mary Francis, and when I said her name quietly in conversation, Hannah suddenly jumped up and became excited, expecting Mary Francis to come in our door as she had in Ireland. No doubt about it, Hannah was part-Sinsee or, simply, the reincarnation of Sinsee.

No doubt about it, animals have taught me the greatest spiritual messages of my life. There is much about them we don't understand because we have not evolved far enough in the spiritual sense.

Hannah always had huge bite marks (scars) on her skin which did not grow hair, and strep run-off scars were all over her. The Humane Society told me that people had brought the poor puppy in days after the tragedy happened, so the strep infection had gotten a real foothold.

Hannah had been used as bait in a dog fighting ring. The Humane Society was certain of this. They use puppies as bait to stimulate the fighting dogs to intense action. In my opinion, people like this should be locked up for murder, or put another way, dog fighting should be punished severely.

However, Hannah was a happy soul. Her spirit was mighty indeed, and she never looked back as far as I could tell. She loved life! Her upper right leg was stapled together but she joyfully ran like mad and was a wonderful, super-intelligent, funny companion. Hannah and I did promotions locally against dog fighting, and I hope we made awareness grow about this horrific practice. Hannah also lived an ideal life once she got back to me and I take great joy in that.

EXTRAORDINARY TALES OF TWO EXTRAORDINAY DOGS

Ripley, The Wookie

When I visited the Hillsborough County, Florida, animal shelter in 1978, intending to get "just a cat," I not only ended up with Gunther, the abandoned Persian cat who felt he was a highking, but also a tiny puppy who was a mess. He had tangled long hair (or fur) and obviously had come from a deprived background. As soon as I got him home, he became very ill; standards at shelters in those days were not as good as today.

My young daughter Gianna named him Ripley, and for nearly a week, we didn't know if Puppy Ripley would live or die at the vet's. He finally pulled through because this little pup had a ferocious, great spirit. The vet told me that Ripley had a variety of worms and goodness knows what else, but the medicines and antibiotics had worked!

Ripley loved to ride in the car and people in other cars would laugh because he "talked" as we drove. He yakked and yakked but if you couldn't hear him, it looked like intense conversation. To boot, he looked like the **Star Wars** Wookie!

When our publisher Tim Beckley came to visit us in San Diego, Ripley felt he was the man of the house, not Tim. He tried to pull Tim out the door, taking hold of Tim's jacket cuff.

Ripley lived a long and happy life, he passed on in Ireland. Of course, he went with us to Ireland; he was a cherished member of the family.

ZIGGY, THE FABULOUS DOG, LONE SURVIVOR OF HER LITTER

When we returned from Ireland, Gianna and I lived in Joshua Tree, California. The Mojave is such mystical place and Giant Rock, where George van Tassel gathered thousands of people to welcome the UFO occupants, was nearby.

Gianna and I went to a garage sale in Joshua Tree to find some "new" clothes, because when I brought all my animals from Ireland (two huge dogs and 15 cats), I brought no suitcases back for myself. The "extra baggage charge" was just too much.

THE REAL LIFE UFO TRANSFORMATION OF DIANE TESSMAN

Diane bestows a little kiss on Ziggy's nose.

Ziggy kisses too, as Cisco gets a hug.

THE REAL LIFE UFO TRANSFORMATION OF DIANE TESSMAN

Instead of clothes, the garage sale family had a litter of puppies that they were trying to sell while their mother was chained in the backyard. Five weeks old is too young to take a puppy from its mother, but this was a dire situation and we were determined to save one of these poor puppies. Of course, we wanted to save them all and their mother.

Gianna picked out one of them whom she immediately named Ziggy. The shivering puppy clung to Gianna as we drove back to our house. Ziggy blossomed right away, she was soon healthy and growing quickly. She had a delightful, loving, hilarious personality. Sinsee loved her right away and Diva thought she was okay too.

What sends chills though Gianna and me to this day, is that we saw one of the teenage children from that garage sale house in the supermarket a few months later. She told us that all Ziggy's entire litter died a few days after we took little Ziggy. Their mother had a virus in her milk, but the mother lived while the puppies did not.

Gianna with Sinsee, Ziggy, and Cisco, running to join the fun.

THE REAL LIFE UFO TRANSFORMATION OF DIANE TESSMAN

Diane and her current dog family, Darcy, Elsa, and Danny.

Sinsee, Diva the St. Bernard, and Diane overlooking an Irish lake.

Ripley, the Wookie and Diane at San Diego home, 1982.

Elsa was a rather large puppy.

Elsa tells Diane, "We want to play, stop writing!"

Sweet Danny as a puppy with his favorite stuffed sheep.

THE REAL LIFE UFO TRANSFORMATION OF DIANE TESSMAN

We saved Ziggy just by a day or two! Did she call us telepathically to that garage sale, or maybe Tibus guided us there? Perhaps.

Ziggy lived to be fifteen years old and was a lovingly affectionate, important (just ask her), member of the family.

Since we always have more than one dog, I can tell you about more wonderful dogs, like Cisco and his sister Maya who were found out in the blistering hot desert, all alone, or Cocoa, the chocolate Lab, who was about to be shot by the "city council" of a small Iowa village in Iowa, because she loved to greet people but managed to knock them down on the ice. These dogs and more became part of our family, as did others. We loved them all!

Currently, I have Danny, the Golden Retriever, Elsa, the German Shepherd, and Darcy who is a black Lab mix. They keep me active, laughing, and loving, and are great companions in these difficult times for us all. So many good people know that animals are truly life savers.

CATS GALORE, ONE OF THE GREAT JOYS OF MY LIFE

My Cat Section will be shorter than my Dog Section, not because cats are any "less," not because their love is conditional, and not because they are my second favorites. They are my soul. I cannot even attach human words and tags to them like "favorite," or "more," or "less."Cats are indeed creatures of pure spirit, indefinable and yet, an endless source of unconditional love, joy, laughter, and wisdom.

BIG BAD POOKA

Mary Frances, the teenage daughter of my neighbors in Ireland, had several cats. For three weeks, she mentioned a tiny kitten she was trying to keep alive. I tried not to get involved because I already had four cats from my neighbors, plus the cats I brought from California; I was adopting their overflow because I didn't want anything to happen to the ones who were just "too many." (Note: My cats are always spayed/neutered, though I hate it on the day of surgery).

I stopped at my neighbors' house one afternoon on the way home to ask about Mary Francis' cat, Boo-Boo. He had suffered a serious injury to his tail but their country cure of applying maggots was working. The maggots were eating away the infection and dead skin. I was horrified at first, but Boo-Boo's tail did heal, although it was shorter.

THE REAL LIFE UFO TRANSFORMATION OF DIANE TESSMAN

At a distance, I saw the kitten that Mary Francis had been nursing since he was three weeks old, but I got in the car and drove home. However, I began thinking about how to diplomatically bring him to my house.

I took the perishable groceries into my cottage. About five minutes later, I went out to get the rest of the groceries, and lo and behold, there sat the tiny kitten! It was indeed the kitten I'd seen at the neighbors' house. But how did such a tiny kitten walk over a mile in five or ten minutes? On top of that, the little guy had a cold and had been weak and struggling for weeks.

He was sitting right by the car and I realized, he had ridden from their house underneath my car. Why did he climb onto that underneath framework? How had he managed to stay on the framework as the car bumped over the country road?

A word about this car: It qualified as a jalopy! In Ireland, 1991, the middle and lower class people had stick shifts and only the wealthy had automatic shifts; this was opposite to the U.S. wherein expensive sports cars had stick shifts and the rest of us had automatic gear shifts. I only drove "automatics" and didn't think it feasible to learn a "stick" while also carefully driving on the left side of narrow, bumpy roads. I was far from wealthy and so when the old Volvo gave up the ghost (we had explored County Meath in it), the only automatic gear which could be found was this car I called "Buck." It was more like a go-cart than a car, but Buck was at least an automatic. It had an open frame underneath.

So, the only answer as to how the tiny sick kitten got to my house was – balancing under the car. No traffic had gone by in those ten minutes I'd been home.

My theory is that the kitten sized me up, when he saw me at the neighbors' house and decided I might be able to help him. I had cat antibiotics on hand, for instance. Could a kitten have known this? Perhaps he simply got the feeling, "Go to this human woman."

I named him The Pooka after an Irish legend of a mysterious, huge, dog-like creature who roams the land. I felt this aggressive name would give him a fighting spirit. I put him in a large cake mixing bowl, padded with soft material. I even laid a cloth over the top so he could be warm and feel cuddled and safe. He was about five weeks old and could eat food, so I would take him out of his bowl at least four times a day, give him food and water, hold him, talk to him, then put him back in his bowl. I also gave him antibiotics. He was too weak and sick to want to leave the bowl until about two weeks later. One morning I hurried in to feed him and The Pooka not only wanted out of the bowl, he wanted to play a little bit. I cried in relief and joy!

THE REAL LIFE UFO TRANSFORMATION OF DIANE TESSMAN

Pooka and Diane at their new place in Joshua Tree, California.

Just before Pooka arrived under my car, my beloved cat Sakima, whom I had brought with me from California, had died. The two cats were almost identical in the color and markings. As Pooka became healthy, he had small habits and traits which were exactly like Sakima's. I do believe that Sakima's spirit entered Pooka, helping him live; another way of looking at it, Pooka was the reincarnation of beloved Sakima.

Pooka flew with me from Ireland to JFK Airport, New York, along with fourteen fellow cats and two large dogs. We then drove across the country and Pooka lived with us, his family, in Joshua Tree, California, for two years. Then we all moved to Iowa; Pooka adored the cool Iowa fields and woods.

Pooka knew how much I loved him, and he mischievously delighted in getting away from me far enough that I would begin to worry. I'd go trudging through the countryside searching for him, and then carry him back to the house, wondering why I was tired. He was a big fat cat by then. Once I found him squared off with a wild tom cat but before I could pick him up, he pounced on the tom and scared him away. What a big, bad cat he was!

THE REAL LIFE UFO TRANSFORMATION OF DIANE TESSMAN

Pooka died at age 15 of a tumor which formed on the side of his upper throat. He could not purr for months because of it. Strangely, on the morning he passed as I held him, he purred loudly for me. How could he have physically done that? My Pooka was always an amazing cat, a mischievous and incredible spirit.

PAVAROTTI SINGS

I moved back to my native Iowa in 1997 from Joshua Tree. I was not a desert person. Iowa looked gorgeous to me and I had just bought an old farmhouse with a big barn on ten acres. Gianna was with me when we drove into the yard. I had not seen the place before I bought it, nor had I seen Iowa since I was ten years old. The house was primitive in some ways and still is, but it is home not just to me but to so many animal friends. The big barn also houses our cats; they love the hay loft especially.

Pavarotti, with frost-bitten ears, was our much-loved "tuxedo tom."

It is a shame Iowa's natural land is enslaved and harnessed, being used only for GMO crops and saturated yearly with chemicals. Corn and soybean fields owned by corporations, now stretch for miles where family farms used to be. The family farmers would have barn cats to keep the rodent population under control, and perhaps the cats were given fresh cow's milk. However, these days, even the hedge groves are cut to make more room for the crops; it is all about money. In winter, there is no prey for feral cats to eat and there is no family farmer to give them a warm barn and milk.

I immediately saw a huge need here for a shelter for feral and stray cats. This acreage (once a family farm), came with two mama cats mistreated by the previous owners, but who managed to have six kittens each, twice a year in spring and fall. Also, adult feral cats began to arrive, desperate for food; they seemed to know instinctively that I offered help. Although the winters are becoming warmer due to global warming, some winters do get down to 40 below zero and the cats have no warm shelters. Most of the cats I take in have frost bitten ears. If they are not strong, they freeze to death.

In the spring of 2007, a handsome, young black and white "tuxedo tom" arrived. I tried to touch that stubborn boy for over a year! He would let me come close and then move away an inch. I discovered that if I meowed at him, he meowed back. We had long conversations as I sat there on the often-cold ground, begging to be his friend. He had obviously been born feral and simply did not trust a human. Because of his talking and singing, I named him Pavarotti, "Pavy" for short.

Finally, he let me touch him, next I stroked him, and he was all mine. Alas, I then had to shove him into a big kennel and take him to the vet. No doubt Pavy hated me at that point. At the vets, he got loose and trashed the entire exam room, running up and down the window blinds and around and around like a mad man. The poor vet had to send someone to get "the net," but Pavy wouldn't let her come in the door with the net. He wasn't vicious, but he was still running wild, and we feared he'd escape into the outer office.

Pavy was twelve years old when he died in 2019. He should have lived longer but he had cancer under his tongue which was hard for the vet to diagnose quickly. Pavarotti was very special to me, and his story is similar to many formerly feral cats I have made a part of my **Star Network Cat Sanctuary** family.

BRODY, THE BIG, SOFT ORANGE AND WHITE FUNNY BOY

At one point, about 120 cats made their way to me. I also adopted several from the town veterinarian. Once in a while she has a cat who just won't fit into a normal home. I told her not to euthanize any of them, I would take the rejects. Those "rejects" have in every case, turned out to be normal, loving cats; they were simply traumatized.

Currently I have "only" fifty-one cats at the **Star Network Sanctuary.** Twenty-three years have passed since our **Sanctuary** began and so the many kittens that were here at first, have had good cat lifetimes and passed on due to old age. Cats live an average of 12 to 15 years. I do have several at present who are 20 years old.

THE REAL LIFE UFO TRANSFORMATION OF DIANE TESSMAN

Big, soft Brody, looking wise.

One cat who arrived several years ago is the soft, silly orange and white boy named Brody. He was feral but looked like a pet cat with short legs, short tail, and he was plump for a stray. Probably someone dumped him here, which has happened many times.

I had to live-trap Brody because he simply would not make friends; he was terrified of humans. I took him straight to the vet; usually, a feral cat will be friendly the minute they are brought home from the vet. However, Brody ran into a far corner of the small upstairs bedroom which I couldn't reach comfortably.

And there stubborn, scared Brody stayed for the next ten months. I tried to stroke him, to work my charms, and he remained rigid and unfriendly, always wedged in his corner. I would have surrendered and let him out the window, but we were on the second floor, too high to jump down.

Finally, one morning, another cat named Callisto followed me in to feed Brody. Suddenly, Brody emerged from his hidey-hole and rubbed Callisto. Then timidly, Brody came to me and I had a chance to really stroke and love him. He broke into a mighty purr, and he has been my best friend ever since. He sleeps pressed up against me; he is ultra-friendly, and loving. He has a unique language of trills and grunts which he uses constantly, commenting to me or to himself, or about things around the house. Everyone loves Brody, all the other cats the dogs, and especially, me.

THE REAL LIFE UFO TRANSFORMATION OF DIANE TESSMAN

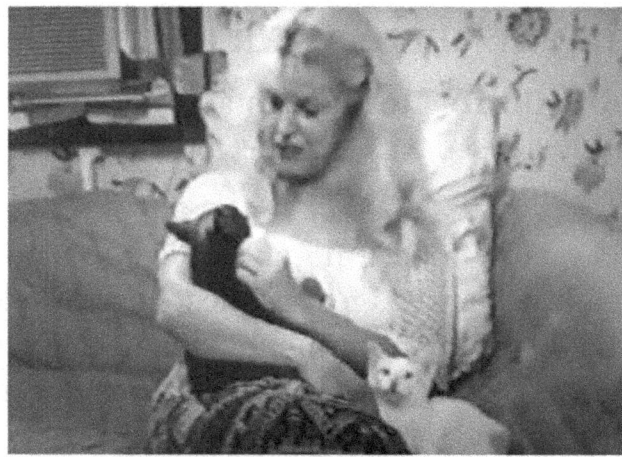

Odin and Sesame enjoy a loving time on the sofa with Diane.

One of our current wonderful cats named Moe, licking his chops.

Diane and Nutmeg, a lovely calico from Ireland.

Callisto, the cat who persuaded Brody to come out of his hidey-hole.

Phobos, our resident Manx, came running down the ice-covered road in a snowstorm when Diane called out, asking him to join the family.

THE REAL LIFE UFO TRANSFORMATION OF DIANE TESSMAN

OUR STAR NETWORK SANCTUARY NEEDS YOUR HELP!

The Star Network Cat Sanctuary and Wildlife Refuge, established twenty-four years ago, gives feral, stray, and formerly abused cats, a great forever home. It exists through the donations of good-hearted humans like you.

Vet fees keep going up, as does good quality food. I do not draw a salary as Director of the **Star Sanctuary** nor do we have overhead fees as most charities do. We do not send out tons of advertising which costs 85% of money-donated. Every penny goes to our cats, the wildlife, and the upkeep on this ten acres (I consider my three dogs to be my personal financial responsibility).

Many of our love offerings come from the wonderful readers of my publications, **The Star Network Heartline** and **The Change Times Quarterly.** If you subscribe, these profits go to the animals also. Many of my readers become my good friends; some have been with me since 1983 and we exchange messages often.

We welcome one-time donations or your ongoing patronage. Please feel free to write to me with questions about the **Star Network Sanctuary** or to simply share your experiences with your own dear animals.

Our cats would appreciate your donation; we really need it! This rural county has no animal shelter. The Humane Societies in neighboring towns refuse to take animals from outside their immediate areas. We are literally saving lives here, and these seemingly feral cats become amazingly loving cats with huge personalities. They just need love and care in order to blossom! My work with them is fulltime every day, no holidays, no profit, but I never tire of it. That's how transformative they are!

Thank you so much for considering a donation.

Diane Tessman, Star Network Cat Sanctuary

P.O. Box 352

St. Ansgar, Iowa, 50472

U.S. checks or money orders, only. **YES!** We do take donations through Paypal.

THE REAL LIFE UFO TRANSFORMATION OF DIANE TESSMAN

Do you want to subscribe to **THE STAR NETWORK HEARTLINE**, which has been cherished by star seeds, experiencers, abductees, and enlightened humans, for 39 years? Tibus always has a timely and inspiring message!

ONLINE SUBSCRIPTION: $15.00 FOR ONE YEAR, 6 ISSUES

POSTAL SUBSCRIPTION: $25.00 FOR ONE YEAR, 6 ISSUES

Do you wish to subscribe to **THE CHANGE TIMES QUARTERLY,** with astounding warnings and predictions, powerful healing meditations, and channelings from a variety of space/time friends in ships above Earth.

ONLINE SUBSCRIPTION: $20.00 FOR 4 ISSUES

POSTAL SUBSCRIPTION: $60.00 FOR 4 ISSUES

If you would like a free, current issue of either publication, just let me know!

My website: www.earthchangepredictions.com

dianetessman0@gmail.com

THE REAL LIFE UFO TRANSFORMATION OF DIANE TESSMAN

Diane's Galactic Goddess Gems

The Goddess is Mother Earth, who with Father Sun, has created the most exquisite crystals and gemstones! Do other star systems create gems and crystals also? They do! Some arrive on the wings of a comet or shooting star composed of stone and crystal. My gems and crystals are energized by me. They possess positive energies of creation, goodness, peace, and love.

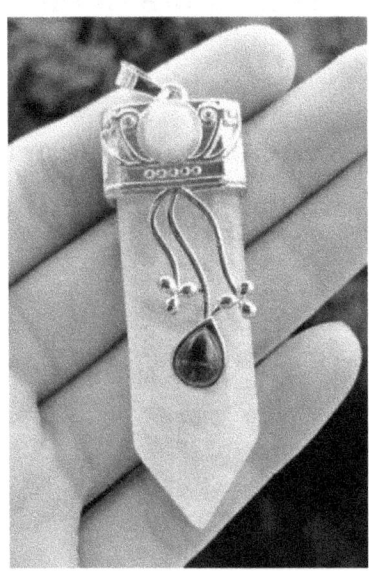

This is not the usual big, commercial crystal and gemstone company, this is ME, Diane Tessman, carefully choosing the crystals and gemstones I feel are worthy to offer my readers. I will help you choose which one that is right for you if you just ask. Remember, too, you are helping our Star Network Animal Sanctuary!

Which crystal will help you most *right now*? 2020 is NOT the best of years! There is so much to worry about, from the pandemic to climate chaos to political unrest. People are being honest to say, *"I am afraid. There I have said it. I am afraid."*

THE REAL LIFE UFO TRANSFORMATION OF DIANE TESSMAN

Alas, constant FEAR is our biggest enemy! It is paralyzing, it is stressful and hurts the physical body, it gets us nowhere. Fear works against our health and welfare. I speak of mindless fear, the fear which keeps you up at night, FEAR- you can do nothing about. There are times when reasonable fear is needed to protect yourself, we are not speaking of these moments.

Tibus and I have discovered one gemstone which is amazing in alleviating and calming FEAR! Carry it in your pocket, take a deep breath, hold it in your hand. Focus on its beauty and power! It is not magic nor a medical cure, but this gemstone takes the burden off you, it facilitates YOU conquering the fear within YOU, especially in the middle of the night when dark fears seem to multiply; KNOW this beautiful creation of Earth will help you overcome being afraid.

Polished Shaman's Stones from British Isles: Look at Gaia's artwork on the stones! Messages therein! Colors: sky blue, mixed with electric deep blue, some with electric purple, orange, gold. Dive in, feel calm, serenity, confidence returns, your serenity, even happiness, returns! These help YOU reach within YOU.

"QUELL YOUR FEAR" GEMSTONE, which I chose precisely for these crazy, insane times! $20.00 each, no shipping charge!

Photos of our QUELL THE FEAR gemstones.

THE REAL LIFE UFO TRANSFORMATION OF DIANE TESSMAN

I am also stocking vibrant, gorgeous channeling and healing crystals and more; DIANE'S GALACTIC GODDESS GEMS is just getting started. Stay in touch and see what else we offer soon; it is a quest for me to discover special crystals from all over the world and offer them to you.

COUNSELING AND/OR CHANNELING

Whatever type of reading you wish or need, I offer! I have 39 years of counseling experience with experiencers, UFO abductees, star seeds and "simply humans." I have experienced it too, not only alien contact, but also LIFE itself! I offer empathy, no judgment, but we will give clear advice.

A personal, private reading is $60.00 but my website www.earthchangepredictions.com "Empowering Readings" page, has other possibilities for you. I do a very few video readings, this would have to be discussed. Feel free to contact me with any questions.

Tibus and I are not mind-readers, we would not want to be! Give us your specific topics, no detail necessary (but you can if you wish). Input will flood to you from him, or I will call on my life time of knowledge to help you. Specify if you wish counseling, space-time channeling (Tibus), or a combination. Past life (parallel aspect) readings are available. Do you want your reading sent online or thru the post? Specify.

I accept ONLY PayPal online or check/money order thru the post, made out to Diane Tessman. My email is dianetessman0@gmail.com. When you contact me, ask for a free current sample of my Star Network newsletter with warnings, predictions, meditations, and mind-boggling channelings! Specify if you want online or paper/postal. And, thank you for enjoying my book!

Diane's mailing address is:

Diane Tessman

P.O. Box 352

St. Ansgar, IA 50472

IT IS SAID THEIR MAGICK TURNED MEN INTO GODS!
EXPERIENCE FIRST HAND THE SUPERNATURAL WONDERS OF THE MAYANS, THE AZTECS AND THE SPIRITUALITY OF OLD MESOAMERICA

Two types of individuals exist in our world— those who hang on daily hoping things will get better, and those who seem to streak through life, successful at nearly everything they do. We believe our specially created "Super Sensory Mesoamerican Power Pack"—consisting of a beautiful "good luck" medallion, workbook/studyguide and transformational audio CD—could redirect your life, sending it in a more positive direction.

Gem settings and color may vary. Silver plated.

We have just obtained a small shipment of a powerful Mayan charm suitable for wearing (includes simple chain) or carrying in your pocket for immediate results.

Researcher Jeremy Coltman says about Mesoamerican occultism (*does not constitute an endrosement*): "It should be remembered that ancient Mesoamericans were first and foremost human beings and there were both good and bad among them... Witchcraft and sorcery was powerful business in ancient Mexico. It was feared, respected, and often sought after by everyone from kings to common folk. In many ways, one person's sorcery was another's cure. Such things operated at the state level of Aztec-Mexican society. One colonial account describes Moctezuma II sending his various sorcerers and magicians to unleash a barrage of magic and witchcraft upon the Spaniards at Cempoala. This was to be done in the form of terrifying dreams, dangerous insects, and illness, all common weapons in the modern day sorcerer's arsenal."

☐ BONUS: NOW INCLUDES A SHAMAN'S EXCLUSIVE SPELLS, BLESSINGS CANDLE AND SPIRITUAL OIL — SPECIAL PRICE — Entire Kit Just $79.00 + $7.00 S/H

INCLUDES 210 PAGE, LARGE FORMAT, DOSSIER:
"THE MAGICK AND MYSTERIES OF MEXICO: ARCANE SECRETS AND OCCULT LORE OF ANCIENT MEXICANS AND THE MAYA

This study guide is the first and only effort to include in one volume all that is known regarding the arcane knowledge and occult lore of the ancient Mesoamerican peoples. Compiled by James L. Spence, it is the product of more than 35 years of research into "Pure Magick," as practiced south of the border. Says Dragonstar: "The author is an expert on ancient civilizations and their impact on the modern world. It is amazing how beliefs in ghosts, witches, the old gods and other magical practices are still alive and relevent today." Adds occultist Zetehyan: "This wonderful book takes the student on a merry romp through the cultures of ancient Mexico with tons of information about gods, magic and witchcraft, shamanism, negualism, the ancient Aztec and Maya."

Exclusively From:
TIMOTHY G. BECKLEY, 11 EAST 30TH STREET, 4R, NY, NY 10016
mrufo8@hotmail.com — Paypal and credit cards accepted 646 331-6777
Leave message with all ordering information.

COME ON BOARD THE MOTHER SHIP
THE ASHTAR COMMAND WANTS YOU

NOW YOU CAN OWN THE COMPLETE LIBRARY OF TUELLA, THE PRIMARY CHANNEL FOR THE FEDERATION OF PLANETS

All Titles Available Directly From The Publisher Tim Beckley, 11 East 30th Street (4R), NY, NY, 10016 – Or Through Amazon.com

Paypal Preferred – mrufo8@hotmail.com – Credit cards: 646 331-6777

  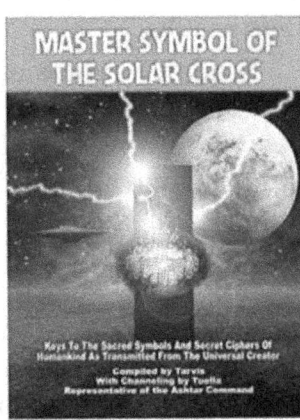 

( ) – A New Book of Revelations - A Harvesting Of Souls At Earth's Final Moment

For serious students of cosmic awareness and the laws of creation. We are told that, "All beings, worlds, planes and dimensions are in an eternal process toward Absolute Perfection. This process develops within the Divine Plan so as to give everyone, without exception, the opportunities of multiple periods of existence that the long journey throughout the entire Universe requires to finally ascend or evolve upon the dimension of Conscious Awareness and Services of Life. In the Integral Universe everything evolves from the simplest forms to those levels of existence which are more complicated and advanced. In all worlds, planes and Dimensions of Nature, this Great Awaken is being fulfilled AS IT IS ABOVE, SO IT IS BELOW!" REVEALED FOR THE FIRST TIME – THESE GALACTIC TRUTHS SHALL SET YOU FREE THE SOLAR CROSS symbolizes the developing relationship of our awareness to reality, which is All Creation. THE SOLAR TONGUE is the language of our thoughts converting the colors, sounds, and symbols of meaning. THE UNIVERSAL SCIENCE is the system of basic laws governing every phase of our Awareness, as a complete unit of being. THE UNIVERSAL LAWS are the principles by which we can progress to the level where we are co-creative spirits of Gods. **Large Format – $19.95**

( ) – Master Symbol Of The Solar Cross

HERE ARE THE SECRET MASTER KEYS TO THE GREAT AWAKENING FOR THE FIRST TIME THE SPIRITUAL HIERARCHY EXPOSES THE UNIVERSAL LAWS OF . . LIFE – MAGNETIC RESONANCE –

ACTION AND REACTION – LIGHT -- VIBRATION – MIND – HARMONY – DIMENSIONS – LOVE – POLARITY – ATTRACTION – MANIFESTATION The primary channel for the Ashtar Command reveals the hidden Sacred Symbols and Secret Ciphers of humankind as transmitted from the Universal Creator at this imperative time in the history of our planet. . . . The Solar Cross symbolizes the developing relationship of our awareness to reality, which is all encompassing . . .In ancient history, sacred symbols were used in teaching all the basic principles of nature. Everything was taught in the simplest, most comprehensive language of symbols. . **Large Format – $29.00**

( ) – Ashtar: Revealing the Secret Identity of the Forces of Light and Their Spiritual Program for Earth: Channeled Messages From The Ashtar Command The Space Brotherhood

WHO IS ASHTAR? Man or Myth? Name or Title? Space Commander or Archangel? Intergalactic Spiritual Leader? The name Ashtar has become widely known in UFO Channeling circles for several decades. It is said that his messages are being beamed from a colossal Starship -- or Space Station -- beyond our atmosphere. According to his primary channel, Tuella (author of Project World Evacuation and On Earth Assignment), Ashtar is directly under the sponsorship of Lord Michael and the Great Central Sun Government of our galaxy, and is second only to the Beloved Jesus-Sananda in responsibility for the airborne division of the Brotherhood of Light. A great deal of Ashtar's popularity is due to his philosophical approach to our global problems and his efforts to raise our planetary vibrations. His work is aligned to that of the Federation of Free Worlds that comprises the totality of the Space Commands throughout the entire Omniverse. This volume contains the most recent information channeled by the Ashtar Command and consists of vital data on coming world events; the ongoing war against evil; and personal messages for world leaders and world conspirators; as well as those serving the Light regardless of their status on Earth at the present moment. **Large Format – $19.95**

( ) – On Earth Assignment: The Cosmic Awakening of Light Workers, Walk-Ins & All Star: Updated

The planet earth at this time is heavily populated with Ambassadors from far flung vistas of our Universe, a vast corps of volunteers. These dedicated ones are here on heavenly assignments to aid the coming of Light and Understanding to mankind, enduring the limitations of fleshly existence to fulfill that ideal. Are you one of them? They are the "seed souls" through whom great ideals are transferable, incorporated within creative personalities through whom the past and future become integrated.

Light workers unite – the time has almost arrived. According to the Ashtar Command you have been born upon this planet at this specific time in order to help in humankind's spiritual development. Some of you have arrived from a far distant star systems. Others may be reincarnated from Atlantis, Mu or Pan to assist in a cosmic plan that is long in the making. Many do not realize yet what their assignment is, while others are just starting to see the veil lifted as their consciousness starts to expand in a more cosmic direction. Do you feel you are an "outsider?"That something is adrift in your life, that there has to be more meaning to "all of this? Do you love nature? Animals? All of Gods creations equally? Do you see through the sinister plot by certain greedy elements of society to keep us enslaved as a species so that we can be kept under the master's thumb? This book is not meant for everyone – far from it! It is meant for those who feel they have been "chosen" for a mind altering opportunity that will help to lead those who are worthy to a new place among the stars. Your time is here Starchild – REJOICE! – **Large Format – $19.95**

( ) – Cosmic Telepathy: A How-To Guide To Mental Telepathy

A SIMPLE HOW TO PERSONAL EMPOWERMENT BOOK PRESENTED IN AN ORGANIZED BOMBARDMENT OF SPIRITUAL TRUTH. . . EXPERTS PROCLAIM: MIND TO MIND COMMUNICATION IS NOW POSSIBLE AROUND THE WORLD AND ACROSS THE GALAXY. Shrouded in secrecy since ancient times, now it is possible for all sincere individuals to tap into that 80 percent unused portion of the human brain that will eventually enable humankind to cross the barriers of space and time, link up with our "cosmic cousins" and break down the walls of false illusion that exist between many races and groups on Earth. This vital workbook and study guide to expanding your clairvoyant and telepathic powers has been compiled by two of the foremost authorities on altered states of human awareness. TUELLA is widely recognized as the primary channel for the ASHTAR COMMAND, a galactic spiritual force that for decades has rendered valuable assistance in providing "shortcuts" guaranteed to bring about the removal of the wraps of secrecy and unnecessary ritual that have kept clairvoyant abilities out of the hands of the average person Written with T. Lobsang Rampa. **Large Format – $25.00**

( ) – Project World Evacuation: UFOs to Assist in the "Great Exodus" of Human Souls Off This Planet

THIS IS THE ONLY OFFICIAL EDITION OF THIS BOOK BY THE ASHTAR COMMAND -- AS TRANSFERED TO THE PUBLISHER BY TUELLA SHORTLY BEFORE HER PASSING. The primary channel for the Ashtar Command, Tuella's calling as a Messenger of Light began in the early seventies with her channeling worked commissioned personally on behalf of the Intergalactic Space Confederation. Says the channel: "Just as many are called and few are chosen, likewise many who read this book will neither understand nor receive the information. But those special souls for whom it is intended will rejoice in its guidance and accept its timely and imperative revelations."This information is not not entertainment. It is comparable to sealed orders given to dedicated volunteers on a strategic mission. It is dispersed to them, compiled for them and will be cherished by them. It is neither defended nor justified. It is data recorded as given and passed to those for whom it is intended."Here are details of the three evacuations: Understanding the three phrases of the Evacuation schedule. * Who will qualify? * Summary of what to expect. * The planned departure of the children. * What does the "Boarding Pass" consist of? * Total evacuation in 15 minutes. * Where will the rescued be taken? * The cause and effects of planetary acceleration. * Three months the earth will stand still...AND MUCH MORE! –

Large Format – $19.95

( ) – Cosmic Revelations Until The End Of Time: Channeled Prophecies From The Galactic Guardians

In a series of telepathic "broadcasts," from a highly intelligent being who identified himself as Ashtar, Commander of a huge spaceship orbiting Earth, we are given prophetic revelations on a variety of relevant subjects, including: * The folly of our political systems * The TOP-SECRET mission of the Space Brothers * Spiritual development of humankind * The selection of the "Chosen Ones" to be removed from the planetary in event of a global disaster * The inside of our planet is really inhabited * Physical changes to be undergone by the planet in years to come o Meditation key to lifting our vibrations * Educational craft orbiting Earth * Negative beings have infiltrated the military and government o More assassination attempts to be made on world leaders * The coming of open relations between Earth and other worlds *Teleportation soon to be commonplace * True meaning of "the beast" whose number is said to be 666. * Earth is a living entity * Life in other dimensions. **BONUS TWO BOOKS IN ONE** – ALSO CONTAINS AMAZING "COSMIC PROPHECIES" CHANNELED THROUGH TUELLA, PRIMARY REPRESENTATIVE FOR THE FREE FEDERATION OF PLANETS – **Large Format – $19.95**

All Books As Listed Above – SPECIAL PRICE $129.95 + $10.00 S/H

ALSO OF INTEREST

( ) – Secrets Of Death Valley: Mysteries And Haunts Of The Mojave Desert (Includes Full Text of I Rode In A Flying Saucer)

"Wow!" What a road trip this book turned out to be. Every page reveals new and fascinating details of the bizarre and mysterious Mojave⋯a place that seems to attract flying saucers and paranormal phenomenon like no other place that I can think of." --Tim Swartz - UFO Review

Contains the first known transmissions from the Ashtar Command, early 1950s as received by George Van Tassel, as he went into a light trance under Giant Rock. This has to be one of the most magical looks at one of the most mystical places in North America. So many strange things have happened here that the Mojave has gotten a reputation for the place to go should an individual wish an authentic UFO or spiritual experience. . . .As early as the late 1940s disc shaped craft were being seen by credible witnesses, some with telescopes or binoculars at the ready. Photos were taken. There were those who claim they met the space people. And some like George Van Tassel professed to have been go for a ride onboard a flying saucer⋯In fact, Van Tassel's messages from alien beings are included in a part of the book, making this even a more important collector's edition. - **Large Format – $19.95**

All Items Available from Timothy Green Beckley
11 East 30th Street, (4R)
NY, NY 10016

Email: mrufo8@hotmail.com

www.ingramcontent.com/pod-product-compliance
Lightning Source LLC
Chambersburg PA
CBHW080358170426
43193CB00016B/2748